THE BOOK OF
JOHN MANDEVILLE

MIDDLE ENGLISH TEXTS SERIES

GENERAL EDITOR
Russell A. Peck
University of Rochester

ASSOCIATE EDITOR
Alan Lupack
University of Rochester

ASSISTANT EDITOR
Michael Livingston
University of Rochester

ADVISORY BOARD
Rita Copeland
University of Pennsylvania

Thomas G. Hahn
University of Rochester

Lisa Kiser
Ohio State University

R. A. Shoaf
University of Florida

Bonnie Wheeler
Southern Methodist University

The Middle English Texts Series is designed for classroom use. Its goal is to make available to teachers and students texts that occupy an important place in the literary and cultural canon but have not been readily available in student editions. The series does not include those authors, such as Chaucer, Langland, or Malory, whose English works are normally in print in good student editions. The focus is, instead, upon Middle English literature adjacent to those authors that teachers need in compiling the syllabuses they wish to teach. The editions maintain the linguistic integrity of the original work but within the parameters of modern reading conventions. The texts are printed in the modern alphabet and follow the practices of modern capitalization, word formation, and punctuation. Manuscript abbreviations are silently expanded, and *u/v* and *j/i* spellings are regularized according to modern orthography. Yogh (3) is transcribed as *g*, *gh*, *y*, or *s*, according to the sound in Modern English spelling to which it corresponds; thorn (þ) and eth (ð) are transcribed as *th*. Distinction between the second person pronoun and the definite article is made by spelling the one *thee* and the other *the*, and final *-e* that receives full syllabic value is accented (e.g., *charité*). Hard words, difficult phrases, and unusual idioms are glossed on the page, either in the right margin or at the foot of the page. Explanatory and textual notes appear at the end of the text, often along with a glossary. The editions include short introductions on the history of the work, its merits and points of topical interest, and brief working bibliographies.

THE BOOK OF
JOHN MANDEVILLE

Edited by
Tamarah Kohanski and
C. David Benson

Published for TEAMS
(The Consortium for the Teaching of the Middle Ages)
in Association with the University of Rochester

by

MEDIEVAL INSTITUTE PUBLICATIONS
Kalamazoo, Michigan
2007

Library of Congress Cataloging-in-Publication Data

Mandeville, John, Sir.
   [Itinerarium. English]
   The book of John Mandeville / edited by Tamarah Kohanski and C.
David Benson.
      p. cm. -- (Middle English texts series)
   "Published for TEAMS (The Consortium for the Teaching of the
Middle Ages) in association with the University of Rochester."
   Includes bibliographical references and index.
   ISBN 978-1-58044-113-1 (paperbound : alk. paper)
   1. Mandeville, John, Sir. Itinerarium. 2. Mandeville, John,
Sir--Travel. 3. Palestine--Description and travel. 4.
Orient--Description and travel. 5. Geography, Medieval. 6. Travel,
Medieval. I. Kohanski, Tamarah. II. Benson, C. David. III. Western
Michigan University. Medieval Institute Publications. IV. Consortium
for the Teaching of the Middle Ages. V. Title.
G370.M2M3613 2007
910.4092--dc22
[B]

2007001647

ISBN 978-1-58044-113-1

 # CONTENTS

ACKNOWLEDGMENTS

We wish to thank Benjamin Kohanski and Katherine O'Sullivan for their careful reading of drafts of this edition. We are grateful for support provided by the Research Foundation of the University of Connecticut and by Dean Ross MacKinnon of the College of Liberal Arts and Sciences, and to the National Endowment for the Humanities for its continued and generous support of the series. At the University of Rochester, the intelligence, learning, and eagle eyes of Emily Rebekah Huber, Michael Livingston, and John H. Chandler have improved our work throughout, as they formatted the volume, read the text against the manuscript, caught numerous errors, and made suggestions along the way. Finally, we thank Russell Peck for his invitation to edit Mandeville and for his generous advice and assistance. Patricia Hollahan gave the manuscript its final copy editing once the volume went to press.

🌿 INTRODUCTION

The Book of John Mandeville has tended to be neglected by modern teachers and scholars, yet this intriguing and copious work has much to offer the student of medieval literature, history, and culture.[1] *The Book of John Mandeville* was a contemporary bestseller, providing readers with exotic information about locales from Constantinople to China and about the social and religious practices of peoples such as the Greeks, Muslims, and Brahmins. The *Book* first appeared in the middle of the fourteenth century and by the next century could be found in an extraordinary range of European languages: not only Latin, French, German, English, and Italian, but also Czech, Danish, and Irish. Its wide readership is also attested by the two hundred and fifty to three hundred medieval manuscripts that still survive today. One scholar even insists that "few literate men in the fourteenth and fifteenth centuries could have avoided coming across the *Travels* at some time."[2] Among others, Chaucer borrowed from it, as did the *Gawain*-poet in the Middle English *Cleanness*, and its popularity continued long after the Middle Ages; there were early printed editions in various Continental languages, often, as in many manuscripts, with illustrations. Christopher Columbus apparently consulted the work, as did Sir Walter Ralegh; there were English editions in the seventeenth and eighteenth centuries, and in his great *Dictionary*, Samuel Johnson praised the work for its "force of thought and beauty of expression."[3]

The author of the *Book* identifies himself as Sir John Mandeville, an English knight from St. Albans, and declares that he will present the many amazing sights, creatures, and customs he observed during his more than thirty years of travel. Although *The Book of John Mandeville* was suspected by some early readers of containing the exaggerations and inventions often associated with travelers,[4] the reputations of both the work and its creator were relatively secure until the discovery in the nineteenth century that much of its material was not only unreliable but had been lifted wholesale from others. Add to this the mounting evidence that the *Book* had been originally composed in French rather than English, and soon

---

[1] Throughout the volume, we use the title under which the work was usually known in the Middle Ages — *The Book of John Mandeville* — as opposed to the later *Mandeville's Travels*.

[2] Moseley, "Availability of *Mandeville's Travels* in England," p. 126. Seymour makes a similar point about the text's popularity in fifteenth-century England: "There can scarcely have been anyone in the realm who had not heard of the wonderful adventures of the English knight, and most who had the means and the opportunity would have read or heard his story, in hall or refectory. The number and variety of the manuscripts make so much certain" ("English Manuscripts," p. 175).

[3] Preface to Johnson's *Dictionary*, cited by Seymour, *Sir John Mandeville*, p. 1. Seymour's volume gives the fullest account of the printing history of Mandeville's *Book*.

[4] Sir Thomas Browne considered Mandeville a liar; see Letts, *Sir John Mandeville*, p. 36.

instead of being celebrated as the first great English traveler or as the father of English prose, the *Mandeville*-author was being roundly denounced as a plagiarist and impostor. In his magisterial 1889 edition of the work, George Warner notes Henry Yule's very public denunciation in the *Encyclopedia Britannica* (in an entry titled "Mandeville, Jehan de" expressly to draw attention to the French character of the supposed author). Warner credits Yule with having "disposed once for all of Mandeville's pretensions to be regarded, at least to any extent, as an authentic and veracious traveller," and goes on to say that he himself has "endeavoured to complete and press home the indictment by . . . tracing every passage, so far as possible, to its actual source in some earlier writer."[5] As Warner's indignation mounts, his usually judicious tone at times becomes increasingly prosecutorial: he charges the author with "fraud and mendacity" and with possessing a "blunted moral sense which saw nothing reprehensible in an elaborate literary imposture."[6] Since Warner, some have tried to rehabilitate Mandeville in various ways (by noting the different ideas of authenticity in the Middle Ages, for example, or by regarding him as a writer of fiction rather than history), and others continue to believe that he may not have lied about his national origin. Nevertheless, the general scholarly consensus today is that "Sir John Mandeville, knight of St. Albans" was probably not a knight, not named Mandeville, not English, and perhaps never traveled much at all, except among the volumes of a well-stocked library — though any of these claims might yet prove to be true. The general stigma of falsehood and imposture that has since surrounded the book, compounded by a generic complexity that makes it difficult to define or categorize (it is not genuine history or anthropology, of course, but not really literature or theology in the usual sense) has led to its absence from the central canons of medieval writing.

AUTHOR, DATE OF COMPOSITION, AND ORIGINAL LANGUAGE

Before we can understand why *The Book of John Mandeville* is important for the study of the Middle Ages, we have to know something about its creation. Unfortunately, there has been little agreement about this over the centuries. The original language of the work has been the subject of much debate. Given that its reputed author claimed to come from St. Albans, English was long assumed, though one version in that language, the Cotton Version, insists that the work was first written in Latin, then translated into French, and only after that translated into English.[7] It is now generally agreed that the *Book* was first written in French, but whether Continental or Norman has been debated.[8] Its date of composition is also uncertain, and, in the absence of any definite evidence, the statement found at the end of most of the French texts that it was written in 1357 has been accepted as roughly accurate, given that the earliest datable manuscript (itself derived from a poor exemplar) was copied in 1371.[9] Nevertheless, the English texts do not generally agree on a date of 1357 (the manuscript edited here gives 1366) and the actual date remains far from certain.

---

[5] *Buke of John Maundeuill*, ed. Warner, pp. xiv–xv.

[6] *Buke of John Maundeuill*, ed. Warner, p. xxix.

[7] *Mandeville's Travels*, ed. Seymour (1967), pp. 3.36–4.2.

[8] *Book of John Mandeville*, ed. Kohanski, pp. xxi–xxii.

[9] Higgins, *Writing East*, p. 6.

Debate about the identity of the author also continues. Some popular English opinion still holds out for Sir John Mandeville — there is a plaque in his honor in St. Albans Cathedral and a Fleet Street veteran has recently taken up his cause — but scholars have also suggested other candidates, including Jean d'Outremeuse, a notary of Liège, and Brother Jean de Long of the Benedictine Abbey Church of St. Bertin.[10] It seems unlikely that we shall ever be certain about the authorship of the *Book*. Indeed, applying the term *author* to this work is imprecise and somewhat misleading. Obviously someone first assembled the materials we know as *The Book of John Mandeville*, but, as has been noted, he borrowed rather than created most of those contents. Rather than a wholly original author, Mandeville is best considered a compiler, one who collects and rearranges the writings of others into a new form.[11]

The narrative voice of *The Book of John Mandeville* constantly makes claims for the truth of what is being related. Sir John (which is what we shall call this first-person voice) often adopts a pedagogical tone, emphasizing points by directly addressing readers with phrases such as "you shall understand" and presenting his testimony as first-person observation. Sir John varies his usual objective reporting with occasional moments that are more private, such as describing his closeness to the Sultan or the beneficial effects of his drinking from a fountain of youth. He even tries to enhance his credibility by mentioning sites that he was *not* able to visit such as Noah's Ark on Mount Ararat (lines 1434–48) and the Earthly Paradise (lines 2705–06). Many English versions include a passage near the end in which he claims to have submitted his book to the pope at Rome, who declared that everything in it was true (lines 2838–48). The elusiveness of the author of the *Book*, however, is shown by the plasticity of this first-person voice. Many of Sir John's most "personal" moments are borrowed from other writers, such as the passage in our manuscript in which he dares to question the opinions of old wise men about the circumference of the earth (lines 1755–58): a passage that appears to characterize Sir John as a daring freethinker but is in fact taken directly from Brunetto Latini. Events such as Odoric of Pordenone's account of his passing through the infernal valley in India are appropriated and then presented transformed as the experience of the knight, the original traveler's ideas, beliefs, and interpretations represented as his own (lines 2492–2523).

In addition, the phrases that insist that Sir John has witnessed what he reports and that it is true also vary widely from text to text of the *Book*. Later redactors, such as the one who produced the English Bodley Version, sometimes add additional first-person statements, such as "I, John Mandeville, say this is true," thus ventriloquizing the voice of Sir John. Cambridge University Library MS Gg. I. 34. iii, a text of the Defective Version, multiplies the text's pedagogical tone out of all proportion, adding phrases such as "you shall understand," "you shall well understand," "you shall know," and "you shall well know" on virtually every subject the *Book* covers. Thus in reading any particular text of the *Book*, one is dealing

---

[10] For Jean d'Outremeuse as author, see *Mandeville's Travels*, ed. Hamelius, pp. 8–13; for Jean de Long, see Seymour, *Sir John Mandeville*, pp. 23–24. For recent surveys of the theories about who might have first written the *Book*, and where, when, and how, see Seymour, *Sir John Mandeville*, pp. 5–24, and Higgins, *Writing East*, pp. 8–13. The Fleet Street veteran is Giles Milton, whose book is *The Riddle and the Knight*.

[11] Higgins, *Writing East*, p. 10. For the medieval conception of *compilatio*, see especially Parkes, "Influence of the Concepts of *Ordinatio* and *Compilatio*."

with a composite narrator whose persona includes not only that created by the original author/compiler of the *Book*, but also echoes of the narrators of his sources and additional qualities interpolated by later scribes and redactors.

SOURCES AND FORM

The sources that lie behind *The Book of John Mandeville* are so many and varied that a better alternative title for the work than *Mandeville's Travels* might have been *Mandeville's Library* (for an annotated bibliography of these sources, see the appendix at the end of this edition). The two most important works behind the *Book* were originally in Latin, though apparently known by the compiler in French translation, and were written in the 1330s by authentic clerical travelers. The primary source for the first part of the *Book* (travel to and around Jerusalem) is the *Liber de Quibusdam Ultramarinis Partibus* (a.k.a. the *Itinerarius*) by the German Dominican William of Boldensele, whereas that for the second part (travel farther east) is Friar Odoric of Pordenone's *Itinerarius*, which tells of the Franciscan's missionary experiences in China and India.[12] Portions of many other works, also apparently known to the *Mandeville*-author primarily in French translation, were also used to make up the *Book*: these include some of the most learned and influential reference works of the Middle Ages, such as Vincent de Beauvais' *Speculum Historiale* and *Speculum Naturale* and Brunetto Latini's *Li Livres dou Tresors*, as well as older authorities such as Macrobius and Isidore of Seville. Scholars have also identified material taken from other travel books and from writings as varied as saints' lives (Jacobus of Voragine's *Legenda Aurea*), historical romances (those about Alexander), and at least one scientific work (John of Sacrobosco's *De Sphaera*).[13] The author's skill as a compiler is revealed in the deftness with which he melds these various sources into a convincing whole, principally by means of the voice and personality of his narrator: the alert, energetic, and always eager to instruct Sir John Mandeville, who manages to function convincingly as the voice of the narrative in almost every extant text, despite his composite nature.

Just as whoever first put together the *Book* combined and rewrote previous texts, the work he produced proved equally malleable, for it was itself, in turn, adapted, abridged, and supplemented by later redactors in a variety of ways including but not limited to the kinds of alterations to the narrative voice we have already discussed. What we call the *Book* resists precise definition because it differs from version to version as well as from text to text within a particular version.[14] *The Book of John Mandeville* refers less to a single stable entity than to what Iain Higgins, in the most illuminating current study of the work, has called a "multi-text."[15] The original composition of the *Book* did not fix the work because it was so quickly and variously transformed by those who received it. In French three distinct versions survive, and there are four in German/Dutch. As the work was translated into other languages, it was often altered significantly, for, as M. C. Seymour notes, the "book was much given to

---

[12] Higgins, *Writing East*, p. 9. See the account of the *Mandeville*-author's sources in the Appendix.

[13] Christiane Deluz, *Livre de Jehan de Mandeville*, pp. 428–92. See also *Book of John Mandeville*, ed. Kohanski, p. xlvi n54. Again see the account of sources in the Appendix.

[14] For a brief description see pp. 11–12 below. For a full listing of manuscripts and their rescensions see *Defective Version*, ed. Seymour, pp. xvi–xxvi.

[15] See Higgins, *Writing East*, pp. 17–25.

interpolation."[16] Sometimes the changes are radical. The most popular Latin version, called the Vulgate, significantly modifies the voice of the narrator so that the "originally open-minded Sir John here becomes a fierce advocate of Catholic orthodoxy and a sharp critic of pagan blindness."[17] The lengthy passage found in our manuscript about the size and shape of the world (lines 1687–1778) is found in relatively few texts of the *Book* but becomes a clear focal point of those in which it does appear, greatly enhancing their geographical interest. Many previous commentators on Mandeville, especially literary critics, have made the mistake of assuming that the details or tone they find in the single edition they have before them are characteristic of the work as a whole. But the variance of the texts of the *Book* often makes such natural assumptions misleading. Instead of treating the *Book* as the product of a single creator with a single meaning, it is better to regard it as an organic work, continuously metamorphosing over the course of its transmission from manuscript to manuscript and coming over time to mean different things to different audiences.

WHAT IS *THE BOOK OF JOHN MANDEVILLE*?

Although the textual instability of *The Book of John Mandeville* should never be forgotten, there are central elements that are shared by most versions and provide a general sense of the original writer's ambitions and interests. The *Book* begins with a preface that seems to present the work as a guide for pilgrims to Jerusalem, a well-known medieval genre. After praising the Holy Land because it was the place chosen by Christ to live and die (being in the middle of the world), the narrator introduces himself as one who as the result of his extensive traveling is able to offer information for those intending to visit Jerusalem and the holy places nearby. Although this preface is more militantly sectarian than anything else in the *Book* (it urges Christians to retake the heritage of the Holy Land given them by God and now in the hands of unbelievers), it already contains hints that the work will be more than just a guide for religious pilgrims. Sir John announces that in addition to the Holy Land, he has journeyed to stranger, non-biblical lands, including Ethiopia and India. He also suggests that his ambitions are not merely pious when he notes the "greet solas, spoort, and comfort" (line 57) that men take in hearing about the Holy Land. Moreover, it is not pilgrimage sites but human curiosity that Sir John emphasizes in respect to the non-biblical lands: he promises to tell of "many diverse folk of maneris and diverse lawes and shappes" (line 66).

The *Book* proper opens with a description of Constantinople and the routes by which to go there. In addition to discussion of Jesus' Cross and Crown (lines 109–97), which characteristically emphasizes not the devotional but the material (the physical composition of each relic and where the authentic pieces are currently located), Sir John, as he will throughout, details the practices of the local religion, here Greek Orthodox, especially as it differs from, and is even critical of, Roman Catholicism (see especially lines 234–79). Dramatic contrasts in subject matter, such as the description of St. John the Evangelist's tomb at Ephesus (lines 288–98) followed by a story of a woman changed into a dragon who can return to human shape only with a knight's kiss (lines 304–41), enliven the *Book*.

---

[16] Seymour, *Sir John Mandeville*, p. 25; Seymour counts one hundred such interpolations in French, Latin, English, and Irish manuscripts of the Insular Version alone.

[17] Higgins, *Writing East*, p. 25.

Sir John then gives various routes to Jerusalem and outlines the sights along their ways. He describes different routes to reach particular destinations but never gives his own itinerary because, especially in the first part, he claims to have undertaken many journeys and also because, as we have seen, the work is a compendium of the travels of others. After a large section about Egypt, which is missing in the version here edited, the works tells about the Holy Land itself. Important surrounding sites are recorded, such as Bethlehem (lines 534–83), but it is Jerusalem that is described in most detail, especially those places associated with major Jewish figures such as David and with the life and death of Christ (see lines 611–79, 686–91, 692–96, 818–27, 833–41, 857–60, 865–85). At times, the account reads very much like a guide for travelers: we are told of the spatial relationship of one building to another and specific points of their individual architecture. Sir John emphasizes that Jerusalem is now controlled by Muslims (lines 699–701, 730–34), and he records a long conversation that he had with their Sultan, who details the many moral failings of contemporary Christians that have caused God to deprive them of the Holy Land (lines 1295–1318).[18]

Although Jerusalem may be at the center of the world and the ultimate aim of religious pilgrims, it cannot hold such an insatiable traveler as Sir John. He is soon away to more remote and exotic climes and cultures. After passing through Armenia (lines 1406–48), he continues further east through the land of Job (lines 1461–73), the country of the Amazons (lines 1476–93), and Ethiopia (lines 1496–1505), some of whose people have only one foot, which, in addition to propelling them quickly, serves to shade their bodies from the sun. Sir John eventually reaches the lands around India with their various and exotic religions — some worship snakes (lines 1586–87) and others allow themselves to be crushed under the wheels of a chariot bearing their idol (lines 1655–59). After a discussion of the roundness of the world (lines 1687–1778) and mention of additional marvels, such as men and women with heads like dogs (lines 1854–68) or others with both male and female genitals (lines 1892–95), Sir John arrives in China and describes the almost unimaginable wealth, luxury, and pomp at the court of the Great Khan with a full account of the realm's particular laws and customs (lines 1968–2017, 2100 ff.). As he continues on, Sir John encounters additional strange beings and practices, and, after a warning about the dangers that Jews will pose at the time of the Antichrist (lines 2366–82), he describes Prester John (an emperor and a priest), who though allied with the Khan is a Christian, but not a Catholic (lines 2392 ff.). Near the end of his *Book*, Sir John describes a kind of ideal society: that of the Brahmins and Synoplians, who even though they lack Christian revelation follow its essential precepts by natural law and whose faith, simple life, and love and charity toward one another make them beloved of God (lines 2573–2637). After observing gold-digging ants in Ceylon, passing by but not being able to visit the Earthly Paradise (lines 2681–2706), and describing the Tibetan practice by which a son honors his dead father by offering his body to birds and the flesh of his head to special friends (lines 2763–83), Sir John, having circumnavigated the earth, returns home to England to rest in his old age.

---

[18] While Mandeville's *Book* often "feels" like a guide for travelers, this is somewhat deceptive because much of its information, taken from older sources, is quite out of date.

WHY *THE BOOK OF JOHN MANDEVILLE* MATTERS

Although *The Book of John Mandeville* was for centuries read as a guide to the Holy Land and especially to the more mysterious lands and peoples farther east, obviously the work has no such use today. Names of places it mentions are often confused or simply unrecoverable, especially when distorted by transmission: historical locales, such as Jerusalem, are mixed with mythological ones, such as Gog and Magog, just as genuine names from biblical or secular history appear with the legendary Prester John. As is still true with many books of travel, the *Book* often tells us less about the foreign locales it purports to visit than about the compiler himself and the culture that produced him. Instead of a guide to Jerusalem and regions beyond, it is most reliable as a guide to contemporary literary, social, and religious concerns in the late-medieval West. That the work was so widely popular suggests that its interests, fears, and dreams were shared by many in Europe.

One of the first and perhaps most surprising elements of *The Book of John Mandeville*, which clearly appealed to early readers and still makes the work interesting today, is its generic variety. As we have just seen, though it begins as if it were a simple travel guide, it quickly becomes something more. The *Book* is a capacious and inclusive work that contains a wide spectrum of different kinds of writing: objective and detailed architectural descriptions of the holy sites in Jerusalem to be sure, but also a personal testimony to the health benefits of a fountain of youth (lines 1594–1600); a long conversation with the Sultan about the failures of Christians (lines 1295–1318), but also mention of fish in Java that voluntarily offer themselves to be eaten (lines 1820–29). Within a few pages near the end of his book we are told, among other things, how Alexander the Great gave over his plans to conquer the Brahmins once he saw their simple and peaceful life (lines 2590–2604), about a race of small men who need the scent of apples to live (lines 2638–42), how Prester John got his name (lines 2656–69), and the layout of the Earthly Paradise — though this last is admittedly secondhand (lines 2698–2736).

Failure to recognize the constant switching of genres in the *Book* threatens to sacrifice its richness to a more limited idea of coherence. Commentators searching for structural order, thematic consistency, or unity of tone in the *Book* are bound to be frustrated and, as a result, may label it disjointed and incoherent, missing its real accomplishment.[19] Seymour notes that Mandeville had "no intense preoccupation with the form of the book," and Higgins finds the most striking literary quality of the work to be "its discursive and generic variety."[20] What Higgins calls Mandeville's "accumulative style" produces "a fascinating geographical grab-bag of objects, events, and persons": the effect of this diverse and contrasting material is not, however, a hopeless jumble, but the creation of "a textual space within which fundamentally distinct views of the world could be articulated."[21] The sense of "helter-skelter" in the *Book* as well as the "disjunctive" perspectives noted by Donald Howard, are not signs of its failure but rather indicate its open-ended, dialogic achievement.[22] Although

---

[19] For an example of one who does seek to discover a "formal principle" in the work, see Butturff, "Satire in *Mandeville's Travels*."

[20] *Mandeville's Travels*, ed. Seymour (1967), p. xvii; Higgins, *Writing East*, p. 11; compare Kohanski, "'What Is a "Travel Book," Anyway?'" esp. p. 125.

[21] Higgins, *Writing East*, pp. 66, 264.

[22] Howard, "World of Mandeville's Travels," p. 9; also in his *Writers and Pilgrims*, p. 71.

the variety of genres, voices, tones, and judgments has bothered some modern commentators, it seems to have been accepted with pleasure by most of the work's early readers.[23] With its mixture of genres and discourses, the *Book* deserves to take a place with the English poetic masterpieces that were soon to follow in the fourteenth century, especially *The Canterbury Tales* and *Piers Plowman*, and it anticipates such later idiosyncratic English compilations as Richard Burton's *Anatomy of Melancholy*.

One reason for the popularity of *The Book of John Mandeville* is that it presented new and formerly restricted material and ideas to a wide, general, and not necessarily highly educated audience. Higgins associates the author of the *Book* with those, such as Brunetto Latini, John Trevisa, and Christine de Pizan, "who sought to enlarge the domain of the vernacular by adapting into it the concerns of Latin learning."[24] More of a reader than a traveler, the original compiler drew on a range of erudite authorities, most of whom he appears to have known in translation, and thus succeeded in bringing this sophisticated and sometimes esoteric material to a large public.[25]

A travel book is the ideal vehicle for such an entertaining and commodious creation.[26] As a traveler, Sir John presents himself as always on the go in search of new places. The result is a text that Stephen Greenblatt calls a "hymn to mobility."[27] Its numerous accounts of people, places, and things are not merely the record of any one man's experiences, but rather "a *summa* of travel lore."[28] But just as movement provides a succession of different experiences, it also prevents the development of a single, unified story. The work contains whatever it is that Sir John happens to encounter. The only logical link between, for example, the statue of Justinian the Emperor in front of the Church of Saint Sophia in Constantinople (lines 98–108) and the crocodiles of India (lines 2555–58) is that Sir John saw them both. Sir John is a listener as well as an observer, and thus he also reports a great range of opinions he hears expressed by others, often without direct comment, such as Greek Orthodox attacks on the pope (lines 243–49) or the Tartar belief that the worst human sin is pissing in one's own house (line 2201). Many unrelated and even clashing views are reported without their truth or validity being assessed. No voice is necessarily definitive in the *Book*, not even Sir John's, for even he does not usually attempt to adjudicate among them.

The character created by first-person voice has often been considered to be one of the most distinctive elements of *The Book of John Mandeville*. Ralph Hanna refers to the "definable personality" of Sir John, and Josephine Bennett insists that he is "a personality who gives inner coherence and life to the book," to such an extent that, if this narrator is fic-

---

[23] Higgins refers to the "composite world" of the *Travels* in which "charity, prejudice, hatred, piety, and tolerance — no less than entertainment, instruction, self-criticism, and propaganda —are perfectly compatible with each other" (*Writing East*, p. 81).

[24] Higgins, *Writing East*, pp. 9–10.

[25] This is not to say that there might not be dangers in some of the ideas presented in the *Book*. Carlo Ginsburg recounts the case of a miller who was executed for the heresy of believing in the salvation of non-Christians, an idea that he testified in court he had learned from reading Mandeville's *Book* (Ginzburg, *Cheese and the Worms*, pp. 41 ff.)

[26] See Kohanski, "'What Is a "Travel Book," Anyway?'"

[27] Greenblatt, *Marvelous Possessions*, p. 38.

[28] Howard, "World of Mandeville's Travels," p. 2; Howard, *Writers and Pilgrims*, p. 58.

tional, its "author deserves to be ranked with the foremost creators of characters in litera-ture."[29] But the more closely we examine him, the more elusive the figure of Sir John becomes, and the less stable and consistent he seems as a character. Often described by commentators as tolerant, genial, and sophisticated, the narrative "I" is also capable of harsh judgments about peoples he does not like, such as the Bedouin and Tartars. More-over, his tolerance toward Saracens and pagans coexists with a fierce bigotry toward the Jews. For all his apparent chattiness, he is remarkably reticent about anything truly inti-mate: most of the personal information he supplies occurs in two short passages at the beginning and end of the work (lines 1–9 and 2832–37), and Howard notes that he "gives no circumstantial details of his day-to-day activities in travel."[30] Sir John says nothing about family, lovers, or individual friends, for example, and only rarely expresses any emotional reactions to what he sees. An important reason for many readers' sense of the narrator's per-sonality comes from his periodic first-person statements about what he has observed and his desire to impress the reader with the truth of his information. But as we have already noted, these observations are not only biographically suspect (they are often taken directly from a source), but also may not even be authorial. It is ironic indeed that as scribes add first-person phrases and assertions of pedagogical authority to the text, their versions may come to be perceived as ever more "personal" to the narrator whose original characterization they alter.

Ultimately the observer is less important in *The Book of John Mandeville* than what is observed. The world of the book is overwhelmingly public and material. It consists of persons, places, and things that can be listed, described, even counted and measured: rivers, mountains, palaces, walls, churches, flora and fauna, strangely shaped humans, and foreign customs. The unique and exotic excite the narrator, yet what is reported is almost always the outer rather than the inner reality — what is apparent to the eye or heard by the ear rather than what is experienced within. The *Book* is full of physical, public details rather than those of private or personal life. This is perhaps most striking in the section on Jerusalem, which we might usefully compare with the account of another Holy Land traveler, Margery Kempe. In contrast to Kempe's record of her pilgrimage, we hear nothing about Sir John's spiritual reaction to the Holy Land (or about anyone else's) but instead are given the number of miles from Jerusalem to the different cities that surround it, the exact measurements of the Temple of the Lord (lines 735–38), and the number of steps (forty-two) from the altar on Mount Calvary down to the place where St. Helena found the True Cross. Kempe's account of Jerusalem offers insight into one late-medieval person's understanding of Jesus' life and death and her own devotional response to them, whereas Sir John's provides information more relevant to constructing a scale model of the city.

In addition to its emphasis on the physical, the *Book* also sometimes reads like a work of cultural anthropology because of its interest in pagan practices such as cannibalism and in different styles of government, from the great imperial Khanate to the communal society of the Brahmins. But if so, it is an old-fashioned kind of anthropology in which Sir John indulges in the most sweeping generalizations, assuring us that the peoples of a particular

---

[29] Hanna, "Mandeville," p. 121; Bennett, *Rediscovery of Sir John Mandeville*, p. 5. Moseley claims that the "attractive *persona*" of Sir John makes the material of the *Book* memorable ("Metamorphoses," p. 5.)

[30] Howard, "World of Mandeville's Travels," p. 4; Howard, *Writers and Pilgrims*, p. 63.

place do this or that or believe this or that, as though each member of the group described were absolutely alike. We are told about many different societies but given almost no sense that there might be tensions and contradictions within any one.

The Book of John Mandeville does, however, contain a sense that things may change over time. It reports on what the traveler sees, but also on what could have been seen in the past. Sir John is alert to surviving physical traces, such as the still-visible footprint made by Jesus during His Ascension (lines 865–66, 1030–31), but also to the extended history of particular locales. Sites in the Holy Land are described as geographical palimpsests with events written on them over the centuries. Old and New Testament events are yoked together not because (like the sacrifice of Isaac and the crucifixion of Christ) they have an important allegorical relationship to one another or any other interpretive significance, but simply because they happen to have taken place on the same physical spot. The rock at the Temple of the Lord is the location of an amazing miscellany of events from the Old and New Testaments, including those involving the Ark with the Tablet of Moses, Jacob's wrestling with an angel, Christ's forgiving the woman taken in adultery, and a prayer by David for mercy. Other versions of the *Book* also locate pseudo-biblical events on this rock, including Mary's learning her psalter and Christ's circumcision. As Stephen Greenblatt puts it: "The Holy Land for Mandeville is the place of sacred metonymy: one biblical story or holy legend is propped tightly against another, and it seems as if the major events of Jesus's life, along with the careers of the patriarchs and prophets, transpired in a confused rush within a space of some ten square meters."[31]

Sir John presents himself as a Roman Catholic addressing a Roman Catholic audience (whose devotions he often says are those "we" practice), but the historical development described in the *Book* is anything but positive for Christianity in general or for the Roman Church in particular. The preface urges Christians to retake their heritage in the Holy Land, and Muslims are said to believe that this will eventually occur, but the present state of the faith is repeatedly shown to be one of decay and decline. As is appropriate in a work that pays so much attention to geography, this sad state is frequently represented by accounts of ground having been lost. Sir John constantly visits places that were formerly Christian but that are now pagan. It is not only Jerusalem that is in the hands of unbelievers but also other locales associated with the faith. The city of Tyre, once "a fair cité of Cristen men," is reported as lost to the Saracens and largely destroyed by them (lines 379–81).

In addition to loss of territory, Western Christianity is also constantly blamed in the *Book* for its tepid religious devotion and current sinfulness. The account of the virtues of the non-orthodox Christian Prester John, for example, reveals "a nostalgia for the better days of Christendom."[32] Although there is no direct account of the West in the book, its degraded spiritual state, and especially the faults of its leaders, secular and religious, are a constant topic. The preface to the *Book* attacks Christian lords for weakening the hold of the faith on the Holy Land because of their pride, covetousness, and envy, and the Greeks have sharp things to say about the Roman pope. Christian clergy are excoriated by the Sultan of Jerusalem because of their neglect of God's service ("For they sholde geve ensaumple to men to do well, and they gyve wickid ensaumple" [line 1301]), and the Sultan goes on to note the disastrous effect of such clerical laxity on the laity, who instead of attending church

---

[31] Greenblatt, *Marvelous Possessions*, p. 41.

[32] Higgins, "Imagining Christendom," p. 102.

indulge in gluttony, deceive one another, and prostitute their children, sisters, and wives for money.

More surprising, perhaps, than this criticism of the current state of Christianity in the *Book* is the sympathetic view of most other religions. The one exception is the Jews, who are treated with "a paradoxically matter-of-fact hostility that borders on paranoia."[33] Muslims, in contrast, are generally treated with respect, and Sir John has many good things to say about their behavior. While the *Book* clearly regards Islam as a false religion, practiced by "misbelievers" who will one day lose their power over the Holy Land, Sir John also frequently praises the Muslims for their devotion. He expresses respect for the constancy of their faith, calling them "trywe, for they kepe truly the comaundementz of her *Ackaron* [Koran]" (1329–30).

Especially as it moves further east, the *Book* finds other religious practices to admire and suggests that there may be different ways of worshiping God. The Brahmins and their followers are given special praise: "Although hit be so that they have noght alle the articles of our feith, yit Y trowe that God love hem neverthelasse for her good purpoos, and that they take her the same degré as He dide of Jope [Job] that was a paynem, the which He helde hym for His triwe servaunt, and many other" (lines 2621–24). Soon after, Sir John interprets a vision of St. Peter to mean that "men sholde have no man in dispite for hire diverse lyvenge, for we wyteth noght wham God loveth most, and wham he hateth most" (lines 2636–37). Although the idea of righteous heathens earning salvation outside the Church by their own merits was not unknown in the Middle Ages (parallels can be found in advanced theological circles as well as in Alexander romances), it is striking to find it expressed so directly in such a widely accessible text. The Brahmins are shown to exist in an almost Edenic state of grace, going naked and following natural law: "And though they be noght Cristen, yit of lawe of kynde they beth full of good vertues" (lines 2574–75). We are told that they have achieved Christ's two great commandments (to love God and to love one's neighbor) without the help of either the Catholic Church or Christian revelation and that they are pleasing to God.

THE TEXT

As has already been suggested, *The Book of John Mandeville* was a thoroughly unstable work, existing in many languages as well as in many versions within a single language and in many individual texts within a single version. Higgins has forcefully argued that "there is no necessarily 'authoritative' text" of the *Book*.[34] Warning us against taking any one example of the "mandevillian multi-text" as definitive, he instead offers the work as "a model for reading medieval writing in its various forms of multiplicity."[35] Whatever its actual origins, the work was quickly taken up by writers, translators, and copyists throughout Europe and transformed in ways great and small. The lack of a single creator of its many forms forces us to think about the work as "an unstable, open-ended, collective production."[36] The original compiler of the *Book* is believed to have written it in French, yet three distinct

---

[33] Higgins, *Writing East*, p. 81; compare Greenblatt, *Marvelous Possessions*, p. 50.

[34] Higgins, *Writing East*, p. 17.

[35] Higgins, *Writing East*, p. viii.

[36] Greenblatt, *Marvelous Possessions*, p. 35.

versions survive in that language: the Continental (over thirty manuscripts are extant), thought to be the closest to the compiler's own copy, the Liège (seven manuscripts), which adds several additional passages about the Carolingian hero Ogier the Dane, and the Insular (over twenty manuscripts), thought to have been produced in England and the basis for all later translations into English.[37] Four German/Dutch translations were also made. The two most popular were written in the late fourteenth century by Michel Velser (40 manuscripts are extant) and Otto von Diemeringen (45 manuscripts). The former adapts his primary source (Continental) by adding personal testimony to certain episodes to enhance their credibility; the latter adapts his (Liège) by postponing the central account of the Saracens as well as passages about other religions until the end.[38] Five translations were made into Latin, the most popular, the Vulgate (41 manuscripts are extant), is much more religiously orthodox and anti-pagan than its source (Liège). Translations also survive in Czech, Danish, Irish, Italian, and Spanish, as well as one version, apparently Czech, that has only illustrations and no text.

The Middle English *Book*, which survives in approximately forty manuscripts, is no less diverse. Modern scholarly writing on the *Book* has often cited a single text (usually Egerton or Cotton because they have previously been the most accessible in modern editions) as if it fully represented the work as a whole. But the *Book* exists in five distinct Middle English versions — four in prose (Bodley, Cotton, Defective, and Egerton) and one in verse (Metrical) — not to mention shorter extracts and epitomes.[39] Even though most English versions descend directly or indirectly from a single French textual tradition (Insular), they nevertheless differ, sometimes radically, from one another. For instance, Cotton and Egerton, each extant in a single manuscript (British Library MS Cotton Titus C.xvi, and British Library MS Egerton 1982), are generally full versions apparently based on some form of the Defective Version with additional material supplied from elsewhere.[40] They are similar in organization and incident, but each is nevertheless unique. Cotton is divided into thirty-six chapters, but Egerton has none. Cotton contains passages not in Egerton, such as Lot sleeping with his daughters, just as Egerton has some not in Cotton, such as an interpolation about Thule and St. Thomas of Canterbury.[41]

Other English versions are more radically individual. The much shorter Bodley Version (Bodleian Library MS eMusaeo 116 and MS Rawlinson D.99) changes the sequence of events and concentrates on marvels.[42] The 3,000-line Metrical Version is in verse; it reduces and rearranges the material found in other versions, adds a long section describing Rome, and

---

[37] See Seymour, *Sir John Mandeville*, especially pp. 3–5, and Higgins, *Writing East*, p. 22 and *passim*.

[38] Higgins, *Writing East*, pp. 24–25.

[39] See Seymour's "Early English Editions of *Mandeville's Travels*," his "English Manuscripts," and his *Sir John Mandeville*. See, most recently, Higgins, "Mandeville." But see also Hanna, "Mandeville," who divides the manuscripts into six versions, two of which (Coventry Corp. Records Office and Bodleian 3692) are in verse.

[40] Seymour, *Sir John Mandeville*, p. 45; *Book of John Mandeville*, ed. Kohanski, pp. xxii–xxiii. See also Seymour, "Origin of the Egerton Version."

[41] For discussion of differences between the two texts, see Bennett, *Rediscovery of Sir John Mandeville*, pp. 85–86, and Higgins, *Writing East*, pp. 24, 44, 57, 101–02.

[42] See *Bodley Version of Mandeville's Travels*, ed. Seymour, and his "Medieval Redactor at Work."

changes the narrative voice from the first to the third person.[43] A stanzaic fragment (Bodleian Library MS eMusaeo 160), prose epitome (British Library MS Additional 37049), and extracts found in Bodleian Library MS Ashmole 751, and Bodleian Library MS Digby 88, all in their own ways emphasize theological and devotional elements.[44]

The most popular English version of *The Book of John Mandeville* was the Defective Version, so called because of the omission of a large section early in the narrative known as the "Egypt Gap," apparently the result of a missing quire in the French Insular copy-text (for a summary of the omitted text, see the explanatory note to line 457). The Defective survives in approximately thirty-five manuscripts (as opposed to one each for Cotton and Egerton) and was the basis for the first printed text of the *Book* in English by Richard Pynson (1496).[45] Ralph Hanna has insisted that the Defective Version is the only one that "has any real claims to be the English *Mandeville*."[46] And yet this version has only rarely been cited in critical discussions of the *Book* and then, perhaps in part because of its unfortunate name, generally regarded as an inferior and uninteresting form of the work. Indeed, until very recently there was no critical edition of any form of Defective. That has been remedied in the new century by Kohanski's edition of Pynson's print (2001), Seymour's critical edition for the Early English Text Society (2002), and the volume you have in your hand.

The original translation of the Defective Version from an Insular French manuscript has been tentatively dated by Seymour (he admits it is only a guess), to "after 1377, perhaps c. 1385."[47] The various manuscripts of the Defective Version share the general textual instability found in other versions of *The Book of John Mandeville*, and so no single Defective text can reasonably stand for the version as a whole.[48] In his recent critical edition, Seymour

---

[43] See *Metrical Version of Mandeville's Travels*, ed. Seymour; Moseley, "Metamorphoses," pp. 14–15; Higgins, *Writing East*, esp. pp. 61–62, 127. Indicative of the plasticity of the narrative voice in the *Book*, which has already been noted, is that whereas the "I" disappears entirely from the Metrical Version because it is narrated in the third person, other English versions give more emphasis to Sir John's voice. Although the Bodley Version generally abbreviates, it repeatedly adds and expands first-person statements, such as this unique address to the reader by Sir John just before the Sultan's speech: "Trowith this wel, for this have I bothe herd and sen with mynne eyne and mynne eryn and myne felawys that were with me that weryn of dyuers regionys, for wete ye wel that al be it wondyr to youre heryng, I am not set to lye yow lesyngis" (*Bodley Version of Mandeville's Travels*, ed. Seymour, p. 75.28–31).

[44] See Seymour's "English Epitome"; his "Mandeville and Marco Polo"; his "Secundum Iohannem Maundvyle"; and Horner, "*Mandeville's Travels*: A New Manuscript Extract." Kohanski has argued that the Metrical Version and even more the Stanzaic should not be treated as genuine versions of the *Book*, but rather as texts that use material from the *Book* to produce something new (*Book of John Mandeville*, pp. xiii–xiv).

[45] Kohanski puts the number of surviving manuscripts at thirty-five, while noting problems with determining the exact number (*Book of John Mandeville*, appendix 1 and p. xiii n9), Higgins gave the number as roughly thirty-eight (*Writing East*, p. 22) and, most recently, as thirty-eight of which thirty-three are complete ("Mandeville," 105), and Seymour lists thirty-three manuscripts and six fragments in his edition (*Defective Version*, p. xii). Pynson's edition was the basis of three editions by Wynkyn de Worde between 1499 and 1510. Higgins notes that it appeared in print "at least fifteen times between 1612 and 1722 " ("Mandeville," p. 107).

[46] Hanna, "Mandeville," p. 123.

[47] *Defective Version*, ed. Seymour, p. xiii.

[48] See *Book of John Mandeville*, ed. Kohanski, pp. xxxi–xli.

defines five manuscript subgroups of Defective (subgroups 1–5), of which the manuscripts
of groups 1 and 2 are generally considered the most complete and authoritative.[49] The base
text of Seymour's edition, Queen's College, Oxford MS 383, is a manuscript of subgroup
1, though the characteristic omissions of subgroup 1 are supplied (mainly) from a manuscript of subgroup 2, British Library MS Arundel 140.[50] The Pynson Version (edited by
Kohanski in 2001) derives from subgroup 2.

The manuscript that has been edited here, British Library MS Royal 17 C. xxxviii, is
described by Seymour as "associated with" his subgroup 2, though he notes that it was
derived independently from the lost archetype of the Defective Version, "from a place in the
scribal tradition immediately superior to the common ancestor of the five manuscripts of
subgroup 2," and that it contains one feature of subgroup 1, the lengthy passage on the
roundness of the world (lines 1687–1778 in this edition).[51] Thus Royal 17 C. xxxviii is a
natural choice for the next available edition of a Defective text, combining the best traits of
both subgroups 1 and 2 with its own highly individualistic treatment of the *Book*'s material.

Despite what may seem to modern readers a large number of errors and confusions
(true to some extent for all medieval English versions of the *Book*), the Royal 17 C manuscript was evidently produced with some care. That care is attested by its physical features:
ornamental capitals, division of the work into twenty-two numbered and headed chapters,
brief marginal notes that repeat key words from the text and thus allow the reader quickly
to find subjects of interest, and more than one hundred colored drawings of scenes from the
text, mainly at the bottoms of folios, with a particular attention to buildings (see figure 1,
p. 20). The material itself reflects this care as well. The manuscript includes a long listing
of contents, apparently imported from a second copy-text, as well as a unique introductory
paragraph.[52] It is also a very thorough and inclusive text of the *Book*, offering the
opportunity for the reader to witness virtually all of the critical "cruxes" of the *Book*, such
as the roundness of the world passage (lines 1687–1778), the papal interpolation (lines
2838–48), the Egypt Gap (line 457), and the narrator's ongoing effort to create a realistic
character for himself. It showcases many of the qualities generally thought of as "textbook
Mandeville," like the clear and traceable use of sources interspersed with what may be firsthand experience; the sympathetic treatment of foreign cultural and religious practices

---

[49] See *Defective Version*, ed. Seymour, pp. xvi–xxvi. Seymour's 1966 classification of the Defective
manuscripts divides them into subgroups A–E, on very basic grounds: "sub-group A (ch. xx) includes
an account of the rotundity of the world, otherwise found only in the exceptional MS. Royal 17C.
xxxviii; sub-group B (ch. xxxii) gives a duplicate account of Alexander's discomfiture by the virtuous
islanders; sub-group C (ch. xii) omits the Hebrew alphabet; sub-group D corrupts the phrase *roys ils*
(which marks a major lacuna in ch. vi) to *yles* and *valeyes*; and sub-group D [sic] (ch. xxxii) interpolates
a Latin translation of part of Dindimus [sic] correspondence" ("English Manuscripts," p. 169). His
more recent classification is essentially similar, renaming subgroups A–E as subgroups 1–5, but explains the manuscript groupings largely in terms of omissions rather than inclusions.

[50] The appendix to Seymour's EETS edition of the Defective Version also includes a long but by
no means exhaustive list of unique additions and lacunae in individual witnesses. For other examples
of variation within Defective, see Kohanski, "Two Manuscripts of *Mandeville's Travels*."

[51] *Defective Version*, ed. Seymour, p. xxi; see also *Book of John Mandeville*, ed. Kohanski, pp. xl–xli

[52] The separate derivation of the table of contents, evident in the difficulty of lining it up with the
actual contents of the manuscript's text, has led us to omit this portion of the manuscript from our
edition.

interspersed with Catholic dogmatism and ethnocentrism (e.g., the Saracens secretly want to be Christians, some eastern customs are wicked and disgusting); and the narrator's very human obsession with opulence, wealth, power, and sex.[53]

At the same time, however, Royal 17C is a somewhat compressed text of the *Book.* Seymour describes it as "robustly edited."[54] All Defective texts appear to be abridged from the original Insular Version to some degree, and this manuscript is uniquely so. In the passage wherein Seth is given the four grains that later produce the four woods of the Cross, for example, the Pynson edition explains:

> And Seth went but the aungell wolde nat late hym come in at the dore. but sayde unto hym that he myght nat have of the oyle of mercy. but he toke to hym foure braunches of the same tree that hys fader etee the apple/ and bad hym as sone as his fader was dede that he shulde put these graynes under his tonge/ and grave hym/ and he dyd so. and of these foure braunches sprange a tre as the aungell sayde that shulde bere a frute thoroughe whyche frute adam shulde be saved.
>
> And whan Seth came ageyne he fonde hys fader nere dede/ and he dyd wyth the graynes as the aungell badde hym. of the whyche came foure trees. of whyche a crosse was made that bare goode frute. That is to say oure saveoure Iesu cryst. Thoroughe whome adam and all that came of hym were saved and delyvered from dethe Withouten ende/ but if it be their owne defaute. This holy crosse the iewes hydde . . .[55]

Royal 17C conveys the same information, but in rather more concise terms, omitting the repetition of Seth's compliance with the angel's mandate:

> And Seth wente theder, but the angel wold nought lete hym in, but seyde to hym that he myght nought have the oyle of mercy. But tho he toke hym foure graynes of the same tre that Adam eet of the apple and bad hym als so sone as his fader were deed, he sholde put tho graynes under his tonge and grave hym so. And he dide so. And of these foure graynes spronge foure trees, as the angel seyd, which sholde bere a fruyt, thorgh which fruyt Adam sholde be saved. Of which trees was maad the Cros that bare God Jhesu Crist, that sweet fruyt thorgh which Adam and alle that come of hym were saved and deliverid fram eyndelys deth, but hit be here owen defaute. This Holy Cros hadde the Jewes i-hudde . . . (lines 140–49)

Similarly, at Mount Zion, the Pynson text tells us:

> And there is the stone that the aungel bare to oure lady fro mounte Synay. and it is of that colour that the roche of saynt katheryn is of/ and there besyde is the gate where oure lady whan she was wyth chylde wente to Betheleem. Also at the entre of mount Syon is a chapell and in that chapell is that stone great and large wyth whiche the sepulcre Was covered whan cryst was layde therin. the whyche stone thre Iewes sawe turned upwarde whan they cam to the sepulcre and there they fonde an aungell that sayde to theym that cryste was rysen fro deth to lyfe. And there is a lytell pece of the pyller / to the whyche oure lorde was scourged.[56]

---

[53] Seymour concludes that MS Royal 17 C. xxxviii is thus likely to be a "commissioned" work, "most carefully edited by its scribe" ("English Manuscripts," p. 173).

[54] *Defective Version,* ed. Seymour, p. xiv.

[55] *Book of John Mandeville,* ed. Kohanski, pp 5–6.

[56] *Book of John Mandeville,* ed. Kohanski, p. 27.

Royal 17C gives an abbreviated version:

> And ther is the stone that the angel bare to Our Lady fro the Mount Synay, and hit is of that
> colour of that roch of Seynt Katerin.
>   Also at the entré of the Mount Syon is a chapel, and at that chapel is that greet ston, and
> hit is large, which that covereth the sepulcre when Crist was leyd therynne. And ther is a litle
> pece of the pilour to which Our Lord was bounde when he was scorged. (lines 815–21)

Royal 17C also tends to use abbreviated catalogues of minor wonders. Where the Pynson
text has a lengthy list of odd and dangerous women, consisting of women with stones in
their eyes who kill men with a look, women with snakes in their bodies that sting men in the
penis, and women who sorrow when their children are born but rejoice when they die,[57]
Royal 17C has only two, omitting the women who joy and sorrow at inappropriate times
(lines 2530–45). Thus, as commonly, the essential motif is maintained — in this case that
of "unnatural women in the East" — but the text elaborates upon it less. This occurs often
in briefer catalogues within the text as well. In the case of Mancy, for example, the more
usual catalogue of three minor wonders (wool-bearing hens, women who wear crowns as a
sign of marital status, and birds trained to catch fish)[58] is reduced to only two in the Royal
MS: "In this contré beth white hennes, but they have no fetheris but woll, as sheep in our
lond. And wymmen that beth y-wedded bereth crounes uppon her hede to be knowe fro
other" (lines 1915–17). While very little is actually "left out" of the Royal 17C text, its
tendency to use fewer examples, less repetition, and less rambling sentence structures gives
it a somewhat sharper, more focused quality than many of its cousins.
     Whatever the editor/scribe's other motives for his various abridgements, one is to avoid
corrupt phrases, just as he at times seeks to correct what he regards as mistakes in his
exemplar.[59] The classic example of this kind of micro-editing of the manuscript occurs at
the Egypt Gap. The site of the gap in the Pynson text merges two passages separated in the
more complete Cotton Version by nearly three chapters of information about Egypt and
environs, and reads like this:

> and the kyngdom of arab was to one of the thre kynges that made offerynge to oure lorde
> when he was borne. and many other londes he holdethe in his hande/ and also he holdeth
> Calaphes that is a greate thynge to the Soudan/ that is to say amonge theym Roys Ile [GAP]
> and this vale is full colde. and than men goo up on the mount of saynte Katheryn/ and that
> is moche hygher than the mounte Moyses.[60]

The two passages in Cotton are, for obvious reasons, quite distinct. The first is about the
Sultan of Babylon: "And many other lands he holdeth in his hand. And therewithal he
holdith caliphs, that is a full great thing in their language and it is as much to say as king."[61]
The second is about the burial place of St. Catherine: "And in that valley is a church of forty

---

[57] *Book of John Mandeville*, ed. Kohanski, pp. 82–83.

[58] *Book of John Mandeville*, ed. Kohanski, p. 60.

[59] *Defective Version*, ed. Seymour, pp. xiv–xv, xxi.

[60] *Book of John Mandeville*, ed. Kohanski, p.15.

[61] *Mandeville's Travels*, ed. Seymour (1968), p. 25.

martyrs, and there sing the monks of the abbeys often time, and that valley is right cold. And after men go up the mountain of St. Catherine that is more high than the Mount of Moses."[62]

The Royal 17C manuscript makes a smooth transition through the gap, recognizing that the two joined parts are innately separate: ". . . and that was oon of the thre kynges that bar offryng to Our Lord. And many other londes he holdeth on his hond. And the mount of Seynt Katerine is moch heyr than the Mount Moyses" (lines 456–58). Whereas most Defective texts leave the junction as Pynson does, somewhat raggedly patched together, Royal 17C, by the simple expedient of breaking the joined material into two discrete sentences, makes it no more jarring than many of the other sudden shifts of subject to be found in the *Book*.

The Royal 17C manuscript is thus of great interest, not merely as a genealogical curiosity among the English Defective texts but as a particularly readable, carefully edited, and highly inclusive manuscript of that version of *The Book of John Mandeville*. As the *Book* becomes available to modern readers in more of its forms, we will at last be in a position to appreciate more fully the beauty of its diversity, which arises so naturally from the manuscript tradition of the Middle Ages.

LANGUAGE AND ORTHOGRAPHY

British Library MS Royal 17 C. xxxviii consists of sixty-one folios written in two columns in a clear hand, and contains only the *Book*. It is bound in $3+1$–7^8, 8^4, and is missing the first and fourth folios of the eighth quire; these missing portions have been supplied in our edition from Pynson's first print.

Marginal glosses have been provided for words whose meanings, for whatever reason, may not be immediately clear. Two glossaries have also been provided at the end of the text: one of common words, the other of proper names. Proper names have been glossed in the text only where doing so seemed likely to create instant recognition.

Dialect

Seymour dates Royal 17 C. xxxviii to "1400–25, early" and assigns its dialect to Hampshire or West Sussex.[63] For a linguistic profile of the word formations of the Hampshire and Sussex dialects, see McIntosh, Samuels, and Benskin, *Linguistic Atlas*, 3.154–61 and 3.501–508. For readers familiar with the language of Geoffrey Chaucer and John Gower, the language of the *Book* should not present many significant differences.

Spelling

Y is commonly used in Middle English where we might use *i*. Thus *syghtes* ("sights"), *bynethe* ("beneath"), *heyghte* ("height"), *worthi* ("worthy"), and *payns* ("pains"). The scribe regularly uses *-i* rather than *-e* in terminal inflections. Thus *touchid* ("touched"), *callid* ("called"), or *contreis* ("countries").

---

[62] *Mandeville's Travels*, ed. Seymour (1968), p. 47.

[63] *Defective Version*, ed. Seymour, p. 189.

Verb formation

Weak verbs generally follow the pattern illustrated here by the verb "helen": "to heal."

I hele   we, ye, thei/hy helen
thou helest
he, she, (h)it heleth   thei/hy heleth

I helde/heled   we, ye, thei/hy held(en)/heled(en)
thou heldest/heledest
he, she, (h)it held(e)/heled(e)

Strong verbs generally follow the pattern illustrated here by the verb "helpen": "to help."

I helpe   we, ye, thei/hy helpen
thou helpest
he, she, (h)it helpeth

I halp(e)   we, ye, thei/hy hulp(en)
thou hulp(e)
he, she, (h)it halp(e)   they/hy helpeth

Participle formation

The y-/i- prefix (interchangeable in this text) commonly forms the past participle; thus "y-chose" (chosen), "i-bore" (born), "y-ete" (eaten). These forms have been hyphenated in the text to help readers identify the root verb. The past participle is also formed by the -ed/-id suffix, as in "nayled" (nailed) and "makid" (made).

The present participle/gerund is formed as in Modern English (i.e., with the -ing ending), here often spelled -*yng(e)*.

Pronouns

A basic outline of the nominative, objective, and possessive pronouns found in the text is as follows. Readers should keep in mind that the 3rd person genitive ending "-is" often appears, as in "Christis vicar" (Christ's vicar).

Nominative	Objective	Genitive
I	me	my/myn
thou/thow	thee	thy/thyn
ye/you	you/yow	your(e)
he	him	his
she/heo	her/hir(e)	her/hir(e)
hit/it	hit/it	his
we	us	our(e)
ye/you/yow	you/yow	your(e)
thei/hy	hem/them, theym	hir(e)/her(e)/their

EDITORIAL CONVENTIONS FOR THIS EDITION

The chapter headings in the text are those in the Royal MS. There are many Roman numerals in the manuscript that are transcribed here as Arabic. Tironian notes (7) are transcribed as *and*, and abbreviation signs for plural endings are expanded as *-es* rather than *-is*. Other expansions are made silently. Initial double *ff*s are transcribed as *f*, and crossed final double *l*s are expanded only when required by the sense. We have followed the EETS practice of using a vertical line to indicate divisions of foliation.

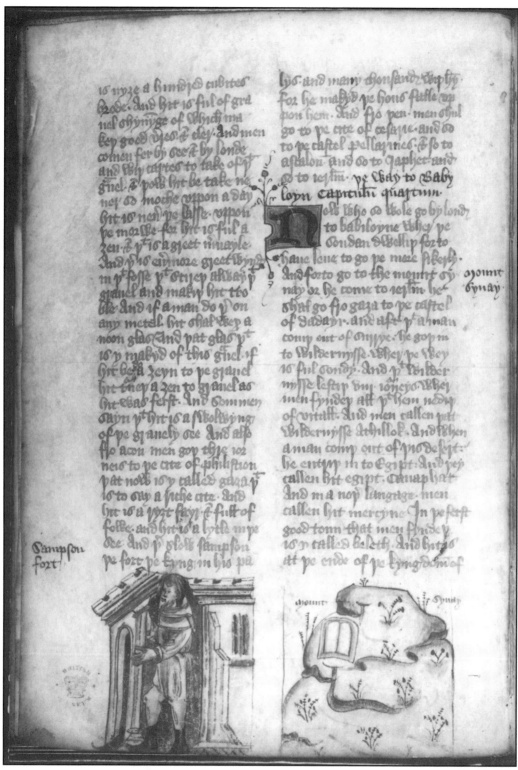

Figure 1. British Library MS Royal 17 C.xxxviii, fol. 15v. End of chapter 3 and beginning of chapter 4, showing chapter rubric, marginal annotations, and illustrations — Sampson the strong (left) and Mount Sinai (right). By permission of the British Library.

[PREFACE]

Here bygynneth *The Book of John Maundevile*, knyght of Ingelond, that was y-bore in the toun of Seynt Albons and travelide aboute in the worlde in many diverse contreis to se mervailes and customes of contreis and diversiteis of folkys and diverse shap of men and of beistis. And all the mervailles that he say he wrot and tellith in this book, the which book conteyneth 22 chapiteris. And this knyght wente of Ingelond and passid the see the yer of Our Lord 1332 and passid thorgh many londes, contreis, and iles, and compiled this book and let write hit the yer of Our Lord 1366, at 34 yer after that he wente out of his contré, for 34 yer he was in travelyng.

5

HIC INCIPIT PROLOGUS ISTIUS LIBRI.   [Here begins the Prologue of this book.]

10   For as moche as the lond over the see, that is to say the Holy Lond that men calleth the lond of Bethtony, amonge alle londes hit is most worthi and sovereyn of all other londes, and is y-blessed and y-halwed and sacred of the precious blode of Oure Lord Jhesu Crist. In the which londe hit liked Hym to take flessh and blood of the Virgyn Marie and to honoure that lond with His blessed foot. And

15   ther He wolde do many miracles and preche and teche the feyth and the lawe of us Cristyn men as to His dere children. And ther He wolde suffre many repreves and skornes for us. And He that was kyng of Heven and of eorthe, of eyr and see, and of thynges that beth y-conteyned on hem, He wolde only be callid kyng of that lond whan He seith thus: *Rex sum Judeorum.* That is to say: "I am kyng of Jewes."

fol. 7r   For that tyme was | that londe of Jewes.

21   And that londe He had y-chose bifore all other londes as the most vertuous and most worthi of the world. And therfore seith the philosofre thus: *virtus rerum in medio consistit.* That is to say: "vertu of thynges is in the myddel." And in that londe He wolde lede His liff and suffre passion and deth of Jewes for to bigge us and de-

25   livere us fro paynes of Hell and deth withouten eynde, which was ordeyned to us

1 **Ingelond**, England. 1–2 **y-bore**, born. 2 **Seynt Albons**, the monastery town of Saint Albans, near London; **aboute**, around. 3 **se mervailes**, see marvels; **diversiteis**, different kinds. 4 **diverse**, different; **beistis**, beasts; **say**, saw. 6 **of**, from; **passid**, crossed. 7 **iles**, islands; **hit**, it. 11 **Bethtony**, Bethany in Judea; **hit**, it. 12 **y-halwed**, hallowed; **of**, by. 13 **liked**, pleased. 15 **wolde**, wished to (i.e., chose to). 16 **Cristyn**, Christian; **suffre**, endure; **repreves**, insults. 18 **beth y-conteyned on hem**, are contained in them. 21 **y-chose**, chosen; **vertuous**, virtuous. 24 **wolde**, wished to; **suffre**, endure; **of**, by; **bigge**, buy (i.e., redeem). 25 **eynde**, end.

for synne of oure forme fader Adam and for oure owen synnes also. As for Hymself
nought, for He hadde noon yvel deserved, for He dide never yll. And He that was
kyng of joye, He myght best in that place suffre deth. For whoso wole do eny thyng
for the which he wole be knowe opynli, he wole do hit crie opynli in the myddel
30 place of a cité other of a toune, so that hit may be knowe to all parties of that cité
other of that toune. So dide He that was kyng of the worlde. He wolde suffre deth
at Jerusalem, that is in the middel of the worlde, so that hit myght be knowe to
men of all parties of the worlde how dire He bought man that He made to His licknys for the gret love that He hadde to us. For more worthy catel myght nought be
35 sette for us than His blessid body and His precious blood which He offred for us.

Lo, dere God, what love He hadde to His sogettes, when He that hadde don no
trespas, only for oure trespas suffred deth. Ryght wel ought men to love and drede
and worshippe soche a lord, and preise soch a lond so holy that brought forth soch
a fruyt, thorgh which every man is saved but hit be his owene defaute. This is the
40 lond that longeth to oure heritage. And in that lond He wolde deyghe and seysed
to leve hit to His children. For which every good Cristen man that hath wherof
sholde streynth hem for to conquere oure ryght heritage and chace away the
fol. 7v myssetrewantes. For we beth called Cristen men of Crist | Oure Fader. And if we
be right children of Crist we aughte then to chalenge the righte heritage of Oure
45 Fader and put hit out of strange men hondes.

But now pryde, covetise, and envye hath enflammed the herte of lordes of the
worlde, that they bien more bisy forto deserte her neyghbores than to chalange
and conquere here ryght heritage biforeseyd. And comyn peple that wolde put
here body and catel to conquere oure heritage may nought do withoute lordes. For
50 asemblé of comyn peple withoute a chief lorde beth as a flock of sheep that hath
no shephurd, which they parteth asoundre and woot nought whyder to go. But
wolde God that wordli lordis were of good acoord and eche of hem other and also
comune peple that they wolde take this holy viage over the see. I trowe then
withynne a litel while oure right heritage forsayde sholde be reconsiled and y-putte
55 in handes of the right eyres of Jhesu Crist.

And for as moch as men desireth to hyre speke of the Holy Lond and they have
therof greet solas, spoort, and comfort, I shal telle somwhat that I have sey. John
Maundevyle knyght, thow Y be nought worthi, that was bore in Engelond in the
toun of Seynt Albones and passed the see in the yer of the Incarnacioun of Oure

---

26 for, because of the; **forme fader**, ancestor. **26–27 As for Hymself nought**, i.e., He did
not suffer death for Himself. **27 yvel**, evil; **yll**, evil. **28 wole**, will. **29 knowe opynli**, known
publicly; **crie**, be announced. **30 other**, or; **parties**, parts. **33 dire**, dearly; **bought**, bought
(i.e., redeemed). **33–34 licknys**, likeness. **34 catel**, treasure. **35 sette for**, given to. **36
sogettes**, subjects. **37 trespas**, sin; **Ryght**, Very. **38 soche**, such; **preise**, praise. **39 defaute**,
fault. **40 longeth**, belongs; **deyghe**, die; **seysed**, took possession. **41 wherof**, i.e., the capacity. **42 streynth hem**, exert themselves; **ryght**, true. **43 myssetrewantes**, misbelievers. **44
right**, true; **aughte**, ought; **chalenge**, claim. **45 strange**, foreign. **47 bien**, are; **bisy**, busy;
deserte her, disinherit (take from) their. **48 comyn**, common. **49 catel**, possessions. **50
asemblé**, a gathering; **beth**, are. **51 parteth asoundre**, divide asunder; **woot**, know;
whyder, where. **52–53 acoord . . . peple**, accord with one another and with the common
people. **53 viage**, voyage; **see**, sea; **trowe**, believe. **54 reconsiled**, recovered. **55 eyres**,
heirs. **56 hyre**, hear. **57 sey**, seen. **58 thow**, although; **bore**, born. **59 passed**, crossed.

60   Lord Jhesu Crist 1332 uppon Seynt Michelis day. And sithe hiderward have Y be
        long tyme over the see, and have Y seye and go thorgh many londes, and Y leygh
        in many provinces and kyngdomes. I have passed thorgh Turky and Surry,
        Hermony the Lasse and the More, Tartari, Perce, Arabie, Egipte the Heigh and
        the Lowe, Libie, Caldee, and a greet party of Ethiope, Amazayn, and a greet partye
65   of Inde the More and the Lasse, and thorgh many other iles that beth aboute Inde,
        wher that dwelleth many diverse folk of maneris and diverse lawes and shappes.
fol. 8r Of which londes and iles Y | shal speke more plenerly. And Y shal divise a parti of
        that Y have seye in the worlde as hit may come to my mynde herafter. And speciali
        of hem that wole and beth in purpos to visite the holy cité of Jerusalem, and the
70   holy places that beth thereaboute, and weyes which men shul holde thider, for Y
        have many tymes y-passid and ryden to Jerusalem in company of greet lordes and
        other good companye.

EXPLICIT PROLOGUS DE MAUNDEVYLE.   [Here ends Mandeville's Prologue.]

A WAY TO JERUSALEM.   [Chapter 1.]

        In the name of God Almyghty, whoso wole passe over the see, he may go by
        many waies after the contré that he cometh fro, and many of hem cometh to oon
75   eynde. But troweth nought that Y wole telle all the tounes, citees, and castelles that
        men shul go by, for then sholde Y make a long tale, but sum contreis and most
        principal stedes that men shul go thorgh to the ryghte way.
        Ferst, if a man come fro the west side of the worlde as Ingelonde, Walys, Skot-
        lond, Irlond, Norway, he may if he wole go thorgh Almayne and the kyngdome of
80   Hungré, that marcheth to the lond of Poyaline and to the lond of Panonye and
        Alfeigh.
        The kyng of Hungré is right a greet lorde and holdeth greet londes and fele,
        for he holdeth the lond of Hungré, Savoyze, Comayne, a greet party of Bulgarie
        that men calleth the lond of Bugers, and a greet party of the kyngdome of Rosse,
85   and hit lastith to the lond of Neflond, and hit marcheth to Pruysse. And in the
        lond of Hungrie, men goon thorgh a cité that men calleth Chipproun and thorgh
        the castel of Newbow, by the same toun that is toward the eynde of Hungrie. And
        thenne men passeth by the ryver of Danubye, that is a greet ryver and hit goth to
        Almayne under the hilles of Lombardy, and hit taketh into hym 40 other ryvers
90   and hit renneth thorgh Hungry, thorgh Grecis, thorgh Tarchie, and goth into the
fol. 8v | see so swiftly that the water is fressh 20 mile in the see.

---

60 sithe hiderward, ever since then. **61 seye**, seen; **leygh**, resided. **62 Turky**, Turkey;
Surry, Syria. **63 Hermony**, Armenia; **More**, Greater; **Tartari**, Tartary; **Perce**, Persia. **64**
Libie, Libya; **Caldee**, Chaldea; **party**, part; **Amazayn**, Amazonia. **65 Inde**, India; **iles**,
islands; **aboute**, nearby. **66 shappes**, shapes. **67 plenerly**, fully; **divise**, tell; **parti**, part.
68 seye, seen. **69 hem**, them; **wole**, wish; **beth in purpos**, intend. **70 weyes**, routes; **thider**,
thither. **74 waies after**, routes according to. **75 eynde**, destination; **troweth**, believe. **77**
stedes, places. **78 Ferst**, First; **Ingelonde**, England. **79 Almayne**, Germany. **80 marcheth**,
extends; **Poyaline**, Poland. **82 right**, truly; **holdeth**, controls; **fele**, many. **83 party**, part.
84 Rosse, Russia. **85 lastith**, extends. **88 Danubye**, Danube. **89 hym**, itself.

And then men goth to Belgrave and entre into the lond of Bruges and ther men passith a brugge of stoon that is over the rever of Marrok. And so passith thorgh the lond of Pynceras and cometh to Grece, to the cité of Sternes, and to the cité of Affynpayn, and so to the cité of Bradremple, and thenne to Constantynople, that was sumtyme called Bessamoran, and ther dwelleth comunely the emperour of Grece.

Ther is the beste cherch of the worlde and fairest, and hit is of Seynt Sophie. And byfore this cherch is an image of Justinian the emperour y-gilded uppon an hors y-crouned. And hit was woned to holde an apple rounde in his hond. And men seyn ther that hit is a tockne that the emperour hath i-loste a greet party of his lond, for the appill is fall out of the imageis hond for he lost gret party of his lordship. For he was woned to be emperour of Romayne and Grece and all Asie the Lasse, of Syrrie, and of the lond of Jude, in the which is Jerusalem, and of the lond of Egipt, of Percie, and Arabie; but hit was lost — all but Grece. And men many tymes wolde putte the apple into the imageis hond, but he wolde nought holde hit. And his other hond he holt upward to the west in tockne to manasse mysdowers. This image stondeth uppon a pilour of marbell.

At Constantynople ther is the sponge and the reed of the which the Jewes gaf Oure Lorde to drynke galle uppon the Croys. Som men lyveth that half of the Croys of Crist be in Cipre in an abbey of monkes, that men calleth the hille of the Holy Croys; but hit is nought so, for that crosse that is in Cipre is that crosse that uppon which Dismas, the good theef, was honged. But all men woot nought, and that is nought wel y-do, for they seyn for getyng of offryng | that hit is the Croys of Our Lord Crist. And ye shal understonde that the Croys of Our Lord was i-makyd of foure maner of trees, and hit is conteyned in this verse: *In cruce fit palma, cedrus, cipressus, oliva.* For that pece that went upright fro the erthe into the heed was of cipresse; and that pece overthwart into the which the hondes wer nayled was of palme; and the mortais of cedre; and the table above his heed that was a foot and half long, uppon the which the title was wryten in Ebru, Greu, and Latyn, was of olive: *Jhesu Nazarenus, rex Judeorum.* And the Jewes makid this Cros of these foure maner of trees for they wened that Oure Lord sholde have honged uppon that Cros als longe as that Cros myght have dured. And therfore they maked the foot of cedre, for cedre may nought rote in erthe, nother in water. And for they wente that the body of Crist sholde have stonke, therfore was maked a peece that went fro the erthe upward of cipres: for that tre is wel smellyng, so that the stench of His body shold nought have greved men that passid therby. And that overthwart

93 brugge, bridge. **94 Sternes**, i.e., Sophia. **96 Bessamoran**, i.e., Byzantium; **comunely**, ordinarily. **99 image**, statue. **100 hit**, i.e., the statue of Justinian; **woned**, accustomed. **101 tockne**, symbol; **party**, part. **102 gret party**, large part. **103 Romayne**, Romania. **104 Jude**, Judea. **105 Percie**, Persia. **107 in tockne**, as a sign; **manasse mysdowers**, threaten evildoers. **110 Croys**, i.e., at the Crucifixion; **lyveth**, believe. **111 Cipre**, Cyprus. **113 woot**, know [that]. **114 y-do**, done (i.e., the monks' false claim). **116 maner**, kinds of. **117 pece**, piece; **heed**, head. **118 overthwart**, crosswise. **119 mortais**, mortice; **table**, tablet. **120 title**, inscription; **Ebru**, Hebrew; **Greu**, Greek. **121 Jhesu . . . Judeorum**, Jesus of Nazareth, King of the Jews. **122 wened**, believed. **123 als**, as; **dured**, endured. **124 rote**, rot. **125 wente**, believed; **stonke**, stunk. **127 greved**, distressed; **overthwart**, crosswise.

peece was maked of palme, for in the Olde Testament was ordeyned that when any man hadde victorye he was crouned with palme. And the table of the title was
130 maked of olive, for that tree tokned pees, as the story of Noe witnessith hit, whan the culver brought the branch of olive that bitokneth pees y-maad bytwixt God and man. And so trowed the Jewes to have pees when Crist were deed, for they seide that Crist makid the bate among hem.

And ye shal understonde that Our Lord was nayled to the Cros liggyng, and
135 therfore He suffred the more payn. As Grekes and Cristin men that dwelleth over the see seyn, that the tre of the Cros that we callen cipresse was of the tree that
fol. 9r Adam eet of the apple, and so fynde | they writen. And they sayn that her scripture telleth that Adam was sike and bad his son Seth that he sholde go to Paradis and pray the angel that kepid Paradis that he wolde sende hym of the oyle of mercy to
140 anoynty therwith his membris that he myght have heel. And Seth wente theder, but the angel wold nought lete hym in, but seyde to hym that he myght nought have the oyle of mercy. But tho he toke hym foure graynes of the same tre that Adam eet of the apple and bad hym als so sone as his fader were deed, he sholde put tho graynes under his tonge and grave hym so. And he dide so. And of these foure
145 graynes spronge foure trees, as the angel seyd, which sholde bere a fruyt, thorgh which fruyt Adam sholde be saved. Of which trees was maad the Cros that bare God Jhesu Crist, that sweet fruyt thorgh which Adam and alle that come of hym were saved and deliverid fram eyndelys deth, but hit be here owen defaute. This Holy Cros hadde the Jewes i-hudde in the erthe under the roch of the mount of
150 Calvarie, and hit lay ther 200 yer and more into that tyme that Seynt Eline fond hit. The which Seynt Eline was moder of Constantyn, the emperour of Rome, and sheo was doughter of a kyng, the which was kyng of Ingelond that was that tyme called the Greet Brytayne, when the emperour toke her to wyve for here greet fairnesse when he was in that contré. And ye shal understonde that the Cros of
155 Oure Lord was of leyngthe of eyght cubitis, and that overthwart was of thre cubitis and an half.

A party of the croune of Our Lord, wherwith He was i-crouned, and oon of the nailes, and the speer-heed, and many other relikes beth in Fraunce in the kynges chapel. And the croune beth in a vessel of cristal wel y-dight and richely. For a
160 kyng of Fraunce somtyme boughte these relikis of the Jewes, to wham the em-
fol. 10r perour had i-leyd to wedde for a greet somme of goolde and silver. And though | hit be so that men sayn that hit beth thornes, ye shal understond that His was risshes of the see that beth white, wecle, and priketh as sharply as thornes. For I have sey many tymes that croune of Parys and also of Constantinople, for they beth but of
165 oon y-maked of risshes of the see. But they have departed hem in two parties,

---

129 table, tablet. **130 tokned**, symbolized; **Noe**, Noah. **131 culver**, dove. **132 trowed**, thought. **133 bate**, dispute. **137 her**, their. **138 sike**, sick; **bad**, ordered. **140 heel**, health; **theder**, thither. **142 tho**, then; **toke**, gave; **graynes**, seeds. **143 als so sone as**, as soon as; **tho**, those. **144 grave**, bury. **148 eyndelys**, endless; **here**, their; **defaute**, fault. **149 i-hudde**, hidden; **roch**, rock. **150 into**, until; **Seynt Eline**, Saint Helen. **152 sheo**, she. **155 overthwart**, crossbeam. **158 beth**, are. **159 y-dight**, adorned. **160 somtyme**, formerly; **wham**, whom. **161 i-leyd to wedde**, pledged. **162 hit**, i.e., the crown; **risshes**, rushes. **163 wecle**, harmful; **sey**, seen. **165 departed**, separated; **parties**, parts.

of which oon party is at Parys and that other party is at Constantynople. And Y have a poynt therof, and that semeth whit thorn, and that was y-give to me for gret love, for ther beth many broken and fallen in the vessel wher the croun is, as they breken when men stiren the vessel to shewe the croune to greet lordes that cometh
170 thider.

And ye shal understonde that Our Lord, that nyght that He was take, He was lad into a gardeyn and there He was examined sharply. And ther the Jewes skorned Hym and makyd hym a croune of the branche of the albespine that growed in the same gardeyn and sette hit uppon His heed so faste that the blood
175 ran adoun by many places of His visage, and His necke, and His shuldres. And therfor hath the albespyne many vertues. For he that berith a branch uppon hym, ne shal no thundre ne no tempest in no maner hym deer. Ne in the hous that hit is ynne may noon yvel spirit com, ne in place wheer hit is. And in the same gardeyn Seynt Petir deneyd Oure Lord God thries.
180 And afterward Oure Lord was y-lad byfore the bysshopis of the lawe in another gardeyn of Anne, and ther He was examined and also y-skorned and y-crouned with a whit thorn that men callen barbarines that groweden in the same gardeyn, and that hath als many vertues. And then was He y-lad into the gardeyn of Cay-phas, and ther He was y-crouned with englenter. And then He was y-lad into the
185 chambre of Pilat, and ther He was examined and also y-crouned. And tho the
fol. 10v Jewes sette Hym | on a chayre and clothid Hym in a mantel, and they makyd the croune of rysshes of the see and knelid to Hym and skorned Hym and sayde: *Ave, rex Judeorum*. That is to say: "Hayl, kyng of Jewes." And of this croune is oon halfen deel at Parys and that other deel at Constantinople. And this croune He hadde
190 uppon His heed when He was doon on the Cros, and therfore hit is most worthi. And the sper shaft hath the emperour of Almayne, but the heed is at Paris. Also at Constantynnople lyth Seynt Anne Our Lady Moder, for Seynt Eline brought hure ther fro Jerusalem. And ther lith also the body of John Crisostom, that was bysshop of Constantinople. And ther lith Seynt Luke the Evangelist, for his bonys were
195 brought fro Bethany wher he was grave. And many other relikes beth ther. And ther is the vestel of ston as hit were marble, which men callen *ydrions*, that ever more droppeth water and fillith hymself ech yer.

And ye shal understond that Constantinople is right a fair cité and a good, and ryght wel y-walled, and hit is thre cornerid. And ther an arme of the see that men
200 callen Hellesponte, and som callen hit Bouch of Constantynople, and som callen hit Brace de Seynt Gorge. And this water closeth two parties of the cité. And upwarde to the see upon the water was y-woned to be the greet cité of Troye in a ful fair playn, but that cité was destroyed with men of Grece. And ther beth many

---

167 semeth, seems to be. **169 breken**, break. **170 thider**, thither. **173 albespine**, haw-thorn. **174 heed**, head; **faste**, firmly. **175 visage**, face. **176 vertues**, powers. **177 deer**, injure. **178 yvel**, evil; **wheer**, where. **179 deneyd**, denied. **181 Anne**, Annas. **182 barbar-ines**, barberry. **183 als**, as. **183–84 Cayphas**, Caiaphas. **184 englenter**, briar rose. **185 tho**, then. **188–89 halfen deel**, half part. **191 Almayne**, Germany. **192 lyth**, lies; **hure**, i.e., St. Helen brought St. Anne's body. **195 grave**, buried. **196 vestel**, vessel. **198 right**, truly. **200 Bouch**, Mouth. **201 Brace**, Arm; **Seynt Gorge**, St. George; **closeth**, encloses. **202 was y-woned to be**, there used to be. **203 ful**, very; **playn**, plain.

205 iles that men callen thus: Calastre, Calcas, Cetige, Tesbiria, Arynona, Faxton, Molo, Carpate, and Lempne. And in this ile is the Mount Athos that passeth the cloudes. And ther beth many spechis and many contreis the which beth obesshant to the emperour, that is to saye Turcople, Pynornard, Coma, Comange, Trachise, and Macidone, of which Alisaundre was kynge, and many other.

fol. 11r 210 | In this contré was Aristotle y-bore and in a cité that men callen Strages, a litle fro the cité of Trachye. And at Strages was Aristotle y-grave, and ther is an auter uppon his tumbe. And ther they make a greet feste every yer als though he were a seynt. And uppon his auter they holden greet conseylis. And they troweth that thorgh inspiracioun of God and of hym they shal have the better consail. In that contré beth right hyghe hilles, and toward the eynde of Macedone is a greet hille

215 that men callen Olimpus, that departith Macedone and Trachie and is high up to the cloudes. And that other hille that men calleth Aches is so high that the shade of hym recheth to Olimpus that is neygh 77 myle bytwyne. And above that hille is the eyr so cleir that men may feile no wynd ther. And therfore may no beest lyve ther, for the eyr is so drigh. And men seyn in that contré that philosopheris som-

220 tyme wente uppon thilke hill and helde to here nose a sponge i-moisted with water to have the eyr. And above, in the poudre of the hill, they writen letteris with here fyngres, and at the yeris eynde they come ageyn and fyndeth the same lettres with-oute eny faute. And at Constantynople the emperouris paleis is right fair and wel y-dight. And therin is a fair paleis for justyng, and hit is uppon stages, that alle

225 men may see the justes, and under thilke stages beth stables vauted for the em-perouris hors, and alle the pilouris beth of marbel.

And withinne the cherche of Seynt Sophie a emperour wolde have i-graven his fader when he was deed. And they makid the grave and fond a body in the erthe, and theruppon lay a greet plate of fyn goold. And theruppon was i-writen in Ebru,

230 Gru, and Latyn thus: *Jhesu Cristus nascetur de Virgine Maria et ego credo in eum.* That is to say: "Jhesu Crist shal be bore of the Virgyn Mari and I belyve on Hym." And

fol. 11v the date of this, when hit was leyd in the erthe, was 2000 yer byfore that | Our Lord was y-bore. And yit is that plate in the tresorie of that cherche. And men seyn that hit was the body of Hermogenes the wise man. And though hit be so that men of

235 Grece beth Cristyn, yit they varieth fro youre feith. For they sey that the Holy Goost com nought of the Sone but fro the Fader, and they beth nought obesshent to the Cherche of Rome, nother to the pope. And they seyn that her patriarch hath als moche power over the see as the pope on this side. And therfore the Pope John the Twelfthe sende lettres to hem how Cristin feyth shold be all oon. And that thei

240 sholde be obesshant to the Cherch of Rome and to the pope, that is Cristis vicar on erthe, to wham God gaf playn power for to bynde and to assoyle, and therfor

---

205 Mount Athos, Mount Athanasi; **passeth**, surpasses. **206 spechis**, languages; **obesshant**, obedient. **210 auter**, altar. **211 tumbe**, tomb; **feste**, festival; **yer**, year. **212 conseylis**, councils; **troweth**, believe. **214 Macedone**, Macedonia. **215 departith**, separates; **Trachie**, Thrace. **216 Aches**, i.e., Athos; **shade**, shadow. **217 neygh**, nearly. **218 feile**, feel. **219 drigh**, dry. **219–20 somtyme**, formerly. **220 thilke**, this; **here**, their; **i-moisted**, moistened. **221 poudre**, dust. **223 faute**, fault. **224 y-dight**, adorned; **justyng**, jousting; **stages**, tiers. **225 thilke**, these; **vauted**, vaulted. **229 fyn**, excellent; **Ebru**, Hebrew. **230 Gru**, Greek. **233 yit**, still. **235 yit**, yet. **236 obesshent**, obedient. **241 playn**, complete.

they sholde be obedient to hym. And they sent agen to hym, the pope, divers let-
ters and anaswers, and among other thyng they seyde thus: *Potenciam tuam summam circa tuos subdiectos firmiter credimus. Superbiam tuam summam tollerare non possumus.*

245   *Avariciam tuam summam saciare non intendimus. Dominus tecum sit. Quia Dominus nobis-cum est. Vale.* This is to say: "We trowe well thi power is greet uppon thy sogettis. We mai nought suffre thi greet pride. We beth nought in purpos to stanche thi greet covetise. Our Lord be with thee, for He is with us. Farwell." And other ans-wers had they non of hem. Also they makith here sacrament of sour loof breed, for

250   Our Lord makid His of whete in tockinyng of the Maundé, and they drien hit by the sonne and kepen hit all the yer, and geven hit to sike instede of Godis body. And they maken but oon unctioun when they cristne children, and they anoynten noon sike man afor his deth. And they seyn that ther is noun Purgatory, and that soules shal have ne joye ne payne into the Day of Dome. And they tellen that sim-

fol. 12r   ple fornicacioun is no deedly | synne but a kyndely thyng, and that men and wym-
256   men shul be weddid but ons, and whoso wole be wedded more, her children beth but bastardes and i-gete in synne. And her prestis ben wedded as other ben. And they seyn that oker is noon synne dedly. And they sillen benefis of Holy Cherch, and so doth men in this contré, and that is a greet sclaundre. For now is simonie

260   crouned kyng in Holi Cherche. They seyn also that in Lente men sholde synge no masse but uppon the Saterday and uppon the Soneday. And they fasteth nought the Saterday no tyme in all the yer, but hit be Youle Eve other Pasche Eve. And they suffre no man that cometh fro this side of the see to synge at her auters. But and hit falle that ther do by any happe, they wassh her autres afterward with holy water.

265   And they seyn that ther sholde be said but oon masse at oon autre uppon the day. They seyn that Our Lord ne eet never mete, but He makid tocknyng of etyng. Also they seyn that we synne deedly in chavyng of oure beerdis, for the berd is knowyng a man fro a womman. Also they seyn that we synne in etyng of beestis that were de-fendid in the Oolde Lawe, als swyn, hares, and other beestis. And they seyn that we

270   synne in etyng of flessh in the Wennesday, als when we eete cheese other eyron on the Fryday. And they cursen all tho that etyn no flessh uppon the Saturday. Also the emperour of Constantynople maketh alle the patriarkys, archebyssshoppes, and byssshoppes, and geveth alle the digniteis and cherches, and he depriveth hem that ben worthi of the pryvacion.

275   Now thowe hit be so that thes thynges toucheth nought to my way, yyt hit likith to many men to hyre of the condicioun and lawes and maneris of diverse londes

fol. 12v   and contrees. And | this is the ferst contré that is discordant agen our feithe, ther -

---

246 **sogettis**, subjects. 247 **in purpos**, intending; **stanche**, satisfy. 249 **loof**, loaf. 250 **in tockinyng**, as a symbol; **Maundé**, Maundy Thursday. 251 **sike**, the sick. 252 **unctioun**, oil for anointing. 253 **afor**, before. 255 **kyndely**, natural. 256 **ons**, once. 257 **i-gete**, begotten; **her prestis**, their priests. 258 **oker**, usury; **sillen benefis**, sell benefices to ecclesiastical offices; **simonie**, usury. 262 **Youle Eve**, Christmas Eve; **Pasche Eve**, Easter Eve. 263 **auters**, altars; **and**, if. 264 **falle**, happens; **happe**, chance. 266 **tocknyng**, a sign. 267 **chavyng**, shaving. 268–69 **defendid**, forbidden. 269 **als**, such as. 270 **als**, as well as; **eyron**, eggs. 271**tho**, those. 273 **digniteis**, offices. 275 **thowe**, although; **yyt**, yet; **likith**, is pleasing. 276 **hyre**, hear.

fore I have setten here that ye may wite the diversité that is bytwixt our feith and heres, for many man hath desier to here speke of diverse thynges.

AGEYN TO THE WAY. CAPITULUM SECUNDUM. [Chapter 2.]

280 Now come I ageyn to know the way fro Constantynople. Whoso wole go thorgh Turkye, he goth thorgh the cité of Nyke and passeth thorgh the gate of Thoimtot that is ful hygh, and hit is a myle and an half fro Nyke. And whoso wole may go by the Brace of Seynt George, and by the greet see, ther Seynt Nicholas lith. And ferst men cometh to the ile of Cilo. In that ile groweth mastik uppon smale trees, as

285 plum trees other chery trees. And then men goth thorgh the ile of Pathmos, ther wroot Seynt John the Evaungelist the Apocalips. And when Our Lord deide, Seynt John was of eelde of 32 yer and he levede after the Passion of Crist 62 yer.

Fro Pathmos men goth to Ephesome, a fair cité and neygh to the see, and ther deide Seynt John and was grave byhiende the autre in a tumbe. And ther is a fair

290 cherche in that place that Cristen men were woned holde. But in the tumbe of Seynt John is nothyng elles but manna, for his body was translatid into Paradis. Turkes haldeth now that cité and all Asie the Lasse, and therfor hit is called Turkey. And ye shal understande that Seynt John leet make his grave by his lyve and laide hymself therinne al quyk.

295 And therfor som seyn that he deide nought but that he restith therynne onto the Day of Dome. And forsothe ther is a greet mervaile, for men may se apartly the erthe of the tumbe many tymes stire and meve, as ther were a quyk thyng ther under. And fro Ephesome men goth thorghe many iles in the see unto the cité of Pathan, wher Seynt Nicholas was bore, and so to Marcha wher he was chose to be

fol. 13r bysshop, and ther | groweth ryght good wyn and strong, that men callen wyn of
301 Marcha. And fro then men may se the iles of Grece, the which the emperour gaff somtyme to Jonays. And then men passen thurgh the iles of Cofos and Lango, of wham Ypocras was lord.

And som sayn that in the ile of Lango is Ypocrasis doughter in maner of a
305 dragon that is a hundred foot long, as men seyn, for I have hit nought seye. And men of the iles callen here ladi of the contrees. And sheo lith in an old castel and shewith her thre tymes a yer. And she doth no man harm but if any man do her harm, and thus she is changed fro a damysel to dragon thorgh a goddas that men callen Diana. And men seyn that she shal dwelle so into the tyme that a knyght
310 come that is so hardy that der go to hure and kysse here mouth. And then shal she turne agen into hure owen kynde and be womman, and therafter heo shal nought lyve longe. And hit is nought ferne ago that a knyght of Rodes, that was doughti and hardy, seyde that he wolde kysse her. And when he was uppon his hors and wente to the castel and entred into the cave, the dragon bygan to lift up his heed
315 agen hym. And when the knyght say the huge beest he fled away. And the dragon

---

278 **setten**, written down; **wite**, know. 279 **heres**, theirs; **desier**, desire. 282 **ful**, very. 283 **Brace**, Arm. 284 **mastik**, resin. 287 **eelde**, age. 289 **autre**, altar; **tumbe**, tomb. 290 **woned**, accustomed to. 291 **translatid**, transported. 292 **haldeth**, hold. 293 **by his lyve**, during his life. 294 **quyk**, alive. 295 **onto**, until. 296 **apartly**, plainly. 297 **meve**, move. 301 **then**, thence; **gaff**, gave. 306 **here**, her. 307 **shewith her**, shows herself; **but if**, unless. 310 **der**, dare; **hure**, her. 311 **heo**, she. 312 **ferne**, long; **doughti**, brave.

folwed and took hym and bare hym maugre his teeth uppon a roch and cast hym into the see and so was he lost.

    And also a yong man that wist nought of that dragon went out of a shippe and went thorgh the ile tille he com to that castel and come to that cave. And he went

320 so longe til he fond a chambre. And ther he saw a damisel and she kembid hure heed and lokyde on a myrrour, and sheo hadde moche trosour aboute hure. And he wente that sheo hadde be a comyn womman that dwellid ther to kepe men to

fol. 13v dele with here. He abood ther, and tho the damysel saw the shade | of hym in the meroure. She turned her and asked what he wolde, and he seyde he wolde be hure

325 paramour other hure lemman. And she askid hym wher he were a knyght, and he saide nay. And then she saide that she myght nought be his lemman, but she baad hym go ageyn to his felawes and make hym a knyght and come ageyn on the morghe, and she wolde com out of hure cave and baad hym thenne kysse hure on the mouth. And she baad hym that he sholde have no drede. "For Y shal do thee

330 noon harme, for thow thou thenke that Y am hidous," she sayde, "ghit drede thee nought, for hit is don to me by enchauntement. And if thou kysse my mouth, thou shalt se me as thou dost nough. And thou shalt have alle these tresours, and be my lord and lord of these iles." And he departid fro here and come to his felawes to the shippe and ther they makyde hym knyght. And come aghen upon the morghe

335 to kysse that damsel. And when he saw her come out of her cave in shap of a drag- on he hadde so greet drede that he fleyghe to the shippe ayen. And she folwyd hym, and when she saw that he turned nought agen, she bygan to crie as a thyng that hadde gret drede and greet sorwe, and she went agen to hure cave. And anoon this knyght deide. And sithen hiderward myght no knyght se hure but he deyde

340 anoon. But when a knyght cometh that is so hardy to kysse hure mouth, he shal turne that damysel to hure owen shappe, and be lord of the contré byforeseyd.

    And fro thenne men cometh to ile of Rodes, whiche that the Hospitalers holden. And that ile was somtyme take fro the Emperour and was woned somtyme be y-called Colles, and so callen the Turkes yit. And Seynt Poule in his pistle wrot

fol. 14r to the men of that ile. | This yle is fer 8 hundred myle fro Constantinople.

346   And fro this yle of Rodis men goth to Cipre, wher beth many vines that ferst beth reed and after oon yer they wexen all white. And the vines that beth most white beth most cleer and most smellyng.

    And men passith by this way by a place where was woned be a greet cité that

350 men callid Satalay. And al that contré was lost thorgh foly of a yong man, for he hadde a fair damysel that he lovede, and she dayde sodenly and was y-do in grave of marble. And for the greet love that he hadde to hure, he wente on the nyght to here grave and oppenyd hit, and lay by here and went his way. And at the 9 monthes ende, a voys come to hym and seyde, "Go to the tumbe of that womman

---

316 bare, carried; **maugre his teeth,** despite his efforts. **318 wist,** knew. **320–21 kembid hure heed,** combed her hair. **321 trosour,** treasure. **322 wente,** thought; **comyn womman,** prostitute. **323 dele with here,** have sex with her; **abood,** remained; **tho,** then; **shade,** reflection. **324 wolde,** wanted. **325 lemman,** lover; **wher,** whether. **326–27 baad hym,** told him to. **328 morghe,** morrow. **330 thow,** although; **ghit,** yet. **332 nough,** now. **336 fleyghe,** fled. **338 anoon,** immediately. **339 sithen hiderward,** ever since then; **se,** see. **342 thenne,** thence. **344 yit,** still; **pistle,** epistle. **345 fer,** far. **347 wexen,** grow. **351 y-do,** put.

355 and opene the tumbe and byhold what thow hast gyte on here. And if thow lette
for to goo, thee worth greet harm have." And he yede and opened the tumbe, and
ther fley an heed ryght parolous to se that fley even aboute the cité. And anoon the
cité sanke adoun. And therfore ther beth many parolous passages.

    And fro Rodes to Cipre is neyr five hundred myle. But men may go to Cipre,
360 and come nought at Rodes. Cipre is a good ile and a greet, and ther beth many
good citeis. And ther is an erchebysshop at Nichosie, and foure other bysshoppis
is in that lond. And at Famagost is oon of the best haven uppon the see that is in
the worlde. And ther aryveth Cristen men and Sarizynes and many other nacions.
And in Cipre is the hille of the Holy Cros and is an abbey of monokis, and ther is
365 the cros of Dismas the good theef, as I seide byfore. And som men weneth that ther
is the half of the Cros of Our Lord, but hit is noght so.

    In Cipre lith Genonon of wham men of that contré maketh greet solemnté. And
fol. 14v in the castel | of Amors lith the body of Seynt Hillari. And biside Famagost was Seynt
Bernard i-bore. In Cipre men hunteth with paupyons, and tho beth like to libardes,
370 and tho take wylde beestis ryght wel. And they ben sumdel more than lyons.

    In Cipre is a maner that lordes and alle other men usen. They opne the erthe,
for they maken diches deep in the erthe al aboute the halle to the knee. And they
do pave the grounde bynethe. And when they wole ete they go therynne, and sitten
ther and eten, for they wold be the more fressh, for that londe is more hatter than
375 here. And at greet festes and also for strange men they setten formes and bordes
as men don heer, but hem were levere sitte on the erthe.

A WEY BY THE SEE TO JERUSALEM. CAPITULUM TERCIUM.   [Chapter 3.]

    Fro Cipres men goon by londe to Jerusalem and by see also. And in a day and
in a nyght he that hath good wynde may come to the haven of Tire, that is now i-
called Sirre. And hit is at the entré of Syrrie, wher was somtyme a fair cité of
380 Cristen men, but Sarizens hath destried hit a gret party therof, and they kepe well
that haven for drede of Cristyn men. Men myght go more ryght to that havene and
come noght to Cipre, but men goon gladly to Cipre to reste hem in the londe
other els to bye hem thyng that hem nedeth. Uppon the seeside bossh many men
may fynde. And ther is the well that holy wryt spekith of thus: *Fons ortorum puteus*
385 *aquarum vivencium*. That is to say: "well of gardeyns and dike of wateris lyvyng." In
the cité of Tire seyde the womman to Our Lord: *Beatus venter qui te portavit et ubera*
que suxisti. That is to say: "I-blessid be the body that thee baar, and the pappes that
thow souke." And ther Our Lord forgaf the womman of Canane here synnes. And

---

355 **thow**, thou; **gyte**, begotten; **lette**, neglect. 356 **thee worth**, you will; **yede**, went. 357 **fley**,
flew; **parolous**, dangerous; **anoon**, immediately. 358 **passages**, routes. 362 **haven**, harbor.
364 **monokis**, monks. 365 **weneth**, believe. 367 **Genonon**, Sozomon; **solemnté**, solemnity.
368 **Seynt Hillari**, St. Hilarion. 369 **paupyons**, panthers; **libardes**, leopards. 370 **sumdel**
more, somewhat larger. 371 **maner**, custom. 374 **hatter**, hotter. 375 **strange**, foreign;
formes, tables. 376 **hem were levere**, they would rather. 378 **haven**, harbor. 379 **entré**, port
of entry; **somtyme**, formerly. 380 **destried**, destroyed. 381 **ryght**, directly. 383 **bye hem**,
purchase for themselves; **bossh many**, many a merchant ship 387 **thee baar**, bore you;
pappes, breasts. 388 **thow**, thou.

389   byfore Tire was woned to be the ston uppon which Our Lord saat to preche. And
fol. 15r of that ston was y- | -founded the cherch of Seynt Savouris.

         Uppon that see is the Saphen, Sarepte or Sydonis, ther was woned to dwelle
         Helias the prophete. And ther raysed Jonas the prophete the wydew sone. And 5
         mile fro Saphen is the cité of Cidone, on which cité was Dido dwellyng that was
         somtyme Enyas wiff after the destruxion of Troye. And she fundide the cité of
395   Cartage in Affrik that now is y-called Didon. And in Tire reyneth Achilles that was
         Didois fader. And 18 mile fro Didon is the cité of Brenche, and fro Brenche to
         Sardana is thre journeis, and fro Sardana is 5 mile to Damas.

         Whoso wole go lenger wey by see, and come neer to Jerusalem, he shall go fro
         Cypre by see to port Jaffe, for that is the next haven to Jerusalem, for fro that
400   haven is but a dayes jorney and an half to Jerusalem. That haven is y-called Jaffe,
         and the toun Affe, after oon of Noeis sones that men callen Japhet that makid hit.
         And ye shal understonde that hit is the yldest toun of the worlde, for hit was makyd
         byfore Noeis floode. And ther beth bones of gyauntes sides that ben fourty foot
         long. And whoso ryveth at the ferst haven of Tire other of Surrye, they may go by
405   londe to Jerusalem. Then shal they go to the cité of Acon, and hit standith in the
         see. And fro Venyse hit is to Acon by the see 200 and 80 mile of Lumbardy. And
         fro Calabre, other Cecile, is Acon 1300 myle of Lumbardy. And byside the cité of
         Acon toward the see 120 furlang on the right side, toward the south, is the hille of
         Carme, wher Elias the prophete dwellide. And ther was the order of frere Carmes
410   ferst funded. And at the foot of this hille was somtyme a cité of Cristen men that
         men called Cayphas, for Cayphas funded hit, but now hyt is y-wasted. And at the
         lift side of that hille is a toun that men callen Caffere, and that is y-sette uppon
         another hille. Ther was Seynt Jame and Seynt John ybore. And fro Acon men goon
         to a greet hille that is y-called Scale de Terreys, that is of an hundred furlang. And
fol. 15v therby is the Fosse Ynone all rounde, that | is nyghe a hundred cubites brode, and
416   hit is ful of gravel shynynge of which maketh good verres and cler. And men
         comen fer by see and by londe and with cartes to take of that gravel. And thow hit
         be take never so moche uppon a day, hit is never the lasse uppon the morwe, for
         hit is ful agen, and that is a greet mervayle. And ther is evermore greet wynd in
420   that fosse that stireth alway that gravel and makith hit troble. And if a man do
         theron any metal, hit shal wex anoon glas. And that glas that is ymakyd of this
         gravel, if hit be do ageyn to the gravel hit turneth agen to gravel as hit was ferst.
         And som men sayn that hit is a swolwyng of the Gravely See. And also fro Acon
         men goth thre jorneis to the cité of Philistion that now is y-called Gaza, that is to
425   say a riche cité. And hit is a ryght fayr and full of folke, and hit is a lytle in the see.
         And ther slow Sampson the fort the kyng in his palys, and many thousand with
         hym, for he makyd the hous falle uppon hem. And fro then, men shul go to the

---

390 Seynt Savouris, St. Savior. **392 Helias**, Elijah; **raysed**, raised from the dead. **394 somtyme Enyas**, formerly Aeneas'. **396 Brenche**, Beirut. **397 journeis**, days' journey. **402 yld-
est**, oldest. **404 ryveth**, arrives. **408 furlang**, furlongs. **409 Carme**, Mount Carmel; **Elias**, Elijah; **frere Carmes**, Carmelite friars. **410 funded**, founded. **411 y-wasted**, ruined. **412 lift**,
left. **414 Scale de Terreys**, the Ladder of Tyre. **415 Fosse Ynone**, Foss (Ditch) of Memnon;
nyghe, nearly; **brode**, broad. **416 verres**, glass. **417 fer**, far. **420 fosse**, ditch; **troble**, roil; **do**,
put. **421 wex**, become. **423 swolwyng**, gulf. **426 slow**, slew; **fort**, strong. **427 then**, thence.

cité of Cesarie, and so to the castel Pellarines, and so to Ascalon and so to
Japhet, and so to Jerusalem.

THE WAY TO BABYLOYN. CAPITULUM QUARTUM. [Chapter 4.]

430   Now whoso wole go by lond to Babiloyne wher the soudan dwellith, for to have
leve to go the more sikerly and for to go to the Mount Synay or he come to Jerusalem, he shal go fro Gaza to the castel of Dadayr. And after that a man comth out
of Surrye, he goth into wildernysse, wher the wey is ful sondy. And that wildernysse
lestith 8 journeys, wher men fyndeth all that hem nedith of vitalles. And men
435   callen that wildernysse Athillok. And when a man comth out of this desert, he
entrith into Egipt. And they callen hit Egipt Canaphat, and in another langage,
men callen hit Mercyne. And the ferst good toun that men fyndeth is ycalled
fol. 16r   Beleth, and hit is at the ende of the kyngdom of | Alape.
        And fro thenne men come to Babiloyne, and to Cayr. And in Babiloyn is a fair
440   cherche of Our Lady wher she dwellid 7 yer when she was out of the lond of Jude,
for drede of the kyng Herodes. And ther lith the body of Seynt Barbara the virgyn.
And ther dwellid Joseph when he was y-sold of his bretherin, and ther Nabugodonosor let put thre children into the fuyr for they were of ryght feith, the which
children ben called Anania, Azaria, and Misael. But Nabugodonosor callid hem
445   thus: Cidrac, Misac, and Abdenago. Ther dwellith the soudan, for ther is a fayr cité
and a strong castel wel y-sette uppon a rooch. In that castel is dwellyng allway, to
kepe hit and to serve the soudan, more then 8000 persones of folk, whoch taketh
alle the necessaries of the soudan. For this is y-knowe wel, for Y dwelled in his
courte, and was soudier, and in his werris a greet while agenst the Bedoyns. And
450   he wolde have y-weddid me to a greet princes doghter ful richely, if Y wolde have
forsake my byleve.
        And ye shal understonde that the soudan is lord of fyve kyngdomis the which
he hath conquerid and y-gete by streyngthe. Thes beth tho: Canapate, that is
Egipte; the kyngdom of Jerusalem, of the which David and Salomon were kyngs;
455   the kyngdom of Surry, of which the cité of Damas was chief; the kyngdom of
Anolpe; and the kyngdom of Arabie, and that was oon of the thre kynges that bar
offryng to Our Lord. And many other londes he holdeth on his hond. And the
mount of Seynt Katerine is moch heyr than the Mount Moyses. And ther that Seynt
Katerine was y-grave is no cherche ne chapel ne non other dwellyng place, but ther
460   is a hille of stones y-gadred togedres with angeles. But ther was woned to be a
fol. 16v   chaple but hit was destruyd, and yit lith the stones ther. And thow hit be so | that the
orison of Seynt Katerin maketh mencion that hit is on the place wher Our Lord gaf
the Lawe to Moyses, and ther Seynt Katerin was y-grave, ye shullith understonde
that hit is in oon contré other in oon stede that berith al oon name. For they beth
465   bothe called Synay, but hit is a greet way bytwyne hem and a greet valey.

430 soudan, sultan. **431 sikerly**, securely; **or**, before. **433 ful sondy**, very sandy. **434
vitalles**, food. **436 Egipt Canaphat**, Egypt. **443 fuyr**, fire. **445 soudan**, sultan. **446 rooch**,
rock. **447 taketh**, take care of. **449 soudier**, a soldier; **werris**, wars. **453 y-gete**, acquired.
457 he, i.e., the sultan. **458 heyr**, higher. **460 with**, by. **461 yit**, still. **462 orison**, prayer.
464 oon contré . . . stede, a country or a place; **al oon name**, all the same name.

A WEY TO JERUSALEM. CAPITULUM QUINTUM.   [Chapter 5.]

Now sithen a man hath y-visited this holy place of Seynt Katerin and he traveyle agen to Jerusalem, he shal take leve of the monkes and recommende hym into here prayers. The which monkes geveth gladly vitaylis to pylgrimes that passith thorgh that wildernisse to Surry, which lasteth ney 12 journeys. And in that desert

470 dwellith many Arabynes, and Bydoynes, and Ascopardes, which ben folk of alle maner yvel condiciouns. And they have noon houses but tentis, which they make of beistis skynnes, as of camels and of other beistis. And they that dwellith ther may have noon water but of the Reede See, for in that greet wildernisse is a greet defaute of water. And hit fallith ofte tyme wher a man fyndeth water oon tyme, he

475 fyndeth noon another tyme, and therfore they maketh ther none hous but tentis. Thes men tylieth no lond, for they eetith no breed, but hit be eny that dwellith toward any good toun. And they rosteth all here flessh uppon hote stones ageyn the sonne. And they beth strong men and wel fyghtyng, and they doth noght elles but chase wilde deer and beestis for hure sustinaunce. And they tellen noght by her

480 liff, and therfore they dreden noght the soudan, for they beth ofte at werre with hym. And at that same tyme that Y was dwellyng with hym, they bare noght but a shilde and a sper to defende hem with. And they have noon other armure but wyndeth her hedis and here neckis in greet lynnen cloth.

And when men ben passid this wildernisse toward Jerusalem, they comen to

485 Bersabe, that was somtyme a fair toun of Cristen men and yit ther beth some of
fol. 17r here cherchis. | And in that toun dwellid Abraham the patriarch, which toun funde-ede Urie, of whas wyf David engendrid Salomon the wyse, that was kyng of Jerusalem and of the 12 kingdomes of Israel, and he regned 40 yer.

And fram then men goth to the Vale of Ebron, that is neye fro thenne 12 myle.

490 And som callen hit the Vale of Mambre. Also hit is called the Vale of Teres, for as moche as Adam wept in that valey an 100 yer for the deth of his sone Abel, the which Caim slow. And Ebron was somtyme the principal cité of Philistiens, and ther dwellid gyauntes. Ther Josue, Calofe, and her company com ferst to aspie how thay myghte wynne the Londe of Promission. In Ebron, David regned ferst 7 yer

495 and an half, and in Jerusalem he regned 33 yer and an half.

And in Ebron beth all graves of patriarkes, David, Abraham, Jacob, and her wyves, Eve, Sarra, and Rebecca; and they beth in a hongynge of an hull. And under hem is a wel fayr cherche corneld as a castel, which the Sarasynnes kepeth wel and they worshippeth moch that place for the holy patriarkes that lygen ther. And they

500 suffre noon Cristyn man to come therynne, but they have special leve of the soudan,

466 **sithen**, after. 468 **vitaylis**, food. 469 **ney**, nearly. 470 **Arabynes**, Arabians; **Bydoynes**, Bedouins; **Ascopardes**, desert people. 471 **maner**, kinds of. 472 **beistis**, beasts'. 473 **Reede See**, Red Sea. 473–74 **defaute**, lack. 476 **tylieth**, cultivate; **eny**, i.e., any of them. 477 **flessh**, meat; **ageyn**, against. 479 **tellen noght by**, have no regard for. 480 **soudan**, sultan; **werre**, war. 481 **hym$_2$**, i.e., the sultan; **bare**, carried. 482 **hem**, themselves. 485 **Bersabe**, Beersheba; **somtyme**, formerly. 487 **Urie**, Uriah; **whas wyf**, whose wife (i.e., Bathsheba); **wyse**, wise man. 489 **Ebron**, Hebron; **neye**, nearly. 490 **Teres**, Tears. 490–91 **for as moche as**, because. 492 **Caim slow**, Cain slew; **somtyme**, formerly; **Philistiens**, Philistines. 493 **gyauntes**, giants; **Josue**, Joshua; **Calofe**, Caleb; **aspie**, discover. 494 **Londe of Promission**, Promised Land. 497 **hongynge**, overhang; **hull**, hill. 498 **corneld**, crenelated; **Sarasynnes**, Saracens. 499 **lygen**, rest.

for thei holden Cristen men and Jewes but houndes that ne sholde come in none holy place. And they callen that place *Spelunke* other double cave, for that on is on that other. And Sarasynnes hit callith in her langage *Cariatharba*, that is to say Habrahamis hous. And that was he that sat in his dore and saw thre persones and
505   worshipped oon, as Holy Writ sayth: *Tres vidit et unum adoravit.* That is to say: "He say thre and oon worsheped." And hym toke Abraham into his hous.

And ryght ney to that place is a cave wher Adam and Eve dwellid in a rooch when they were dryve out of Paradise, and ther gete they her children. And in that same place was Adam makid as som men sayn, for men called that place the felde
510   of Damas, for hit was the lordship of Damas. And fro thenne he was translatyd into
fol. 17v   Paradis and afterward | he was dryven out of Paradis and y-put ther agen; for the same day that he was put into Paradys, the same day he was dryven out of Paradis, anoon as he hadde synned.

Ther bygynneth the Vale of Ebron and lasteth ney to Jerusalem. And the angel
515   bad Adam that he sholde dwelle with his wiff and ther engendre Seth, of which kyn Jhesu Crist was y-bore. And in that felde is a place that men draweth a thyng that men callen *cambil*, and they eten that instede of spyces. And may no man make that place so deep and so wyde that hit is at the yeres ende full agen by the grace of God.

And two myle fro Ebron is a grave of Loth that is Abrahamis brother. And a litle
520   fro Ebron is the Mount Mambre, of which the vale took his name. And ther is a tree of ook that Sarysynis callen *dirpe*, that is of Abrahamis tyme, that men callen the drie tree. And they say that hit hath be fro the bygynnyng of the worlde, and hit was somtyme grene and bar leves into that tyme that Our Lord deyde. And so dide all the trees in the worlde, other els they fayled here hertes, and yit beth many
525   soch in the worlde.

And som prophecie seith that a prince, lord of the west syde of the worlde, shal come and wynne the Londe of Promission with the help of Cristen men. And he shal do synge a messe under the drie tre, and hit shal wexe grene and bere fruyt and leves. And by that miracle many Sarysynes and Jewes and other shal be turned
530   to Cristen feythe. And therfore they do greet worship therto and kepith hit ful well. And thow hit be drie, hit hath gret vertue, for certayn he that hath a litle therof on hym, hit helith hym of the fallyng yvel. And hit hath many other vertues, and therfore hit is y-holde ryght precious.

Fro Ebron men goth to Bethleem on half a day, for hit is but 5 myle bytwyne,
535   and hit is a perlous way and thorgh wodes ryght lykynge. But Bedlem is right a
fol. 18r   lykyng cité and lytle, | but hit is long and narwe and wel y-walled and enclosid with dych. And hit was woned to be called Effrata, as Holy Writ seith: *Ecce audivimus eum in Effrata.* That is to say: "Lo, we have herd hym in Effrata." Toward the ende of

---

502 **other**, or; **on is**, one is. 504 **Habrahamis**, i.e., Abraham's; **he**, i.e., Abraham. 506 **hym toke . . . hous**, i.e., Abraham took the angel into his house. 508 **gete**, begot. 510 **Damas**, Damascus; **translatyd**, transported. 514 **lasteth**, extends. 515 **bad**, ordered. 516 **draweth**, extract. 519 **Loth**, Lot. 522 **hit hath be**, it has existed. 524 **hertes**, heartwood. 527 **Londe of Promission**, Promised Land. 528 **messe**, liturgy of the Mass; **wexe**, grow. 529 **turned**, converted. 532 **the fallyng yvel**, epilepsy. 533 **y-holde**, considered. 534 **Bethleem**, Bethlehem. 535 **perlous**, dangerous; **wodes**, woods; **lykynge**, pleasant; **Bedlem**, Bethlehem.

540 that cité toward the est is a fair cherch and a gracious, and hit hath many toures and many pynacles and corneld ful strongly. And in that cherch beth 43 pylers of marble, greet and fayr.

And bytwyne this cherch and this cité is a feyld that is callid *Feyld Floridous*, that is to seye Feyld Floryshid. For as moche as a fayr mayde was y-blamed falsly that she hadde y-do fornicacioun, for which cause heo was demed to the deth and to be 545 brende in that place to the which she was y-lad. And as the wode bygan to brenne aboute her, she prayed to God: as she was noght gylty of that thing, that He helpe here that hit were y-knowe to alle men. And when she had thus y-sayd, anoon was that fire oute. And the branches that were brennyng bycome ride roses, and the branches that were noght brennyng bycome white rosers and ful of roses. And ther 550 were the ferste roses and rosers that ever were y-seyn afore. And thus was this mayde y-saved.

Also byside the queir of the cherche, at the ryght syde as men cometh dounward 17 gres, is a place where God was y-bore, that is now ful wel y-dyght with marble, and gold, and sylver, and asure, and y-peynted with other riche colouris. 555 And a lytle thenne at thre paas is the cribbe of the oxe and the asse. And bysyde is the place wher the sterre fell that ladde the thre kynges: Jaspar, Melchiser, and Balthasar. But men of Grece thes thre kynges thus callen Galgalath, Galgagat, and Saragi. Thes thre kynges offeride to Our Lord ensence, goold, and myrre. And they come togedre thorw Godes grace, for they mette sommen in a cité of Inde that 560 men callen Casak, that is foure journeys fro Bethlem, and they were in Bethlem the ferthe day after they hadde i-seye the sterre.

fol. 18v   Also under the cloistre of the cherch, | 8 gres at the ryght side, is the charnel of the Innocentis wher the bones lyggen. And byfore that place that Crist was y-bore is the tumbe of Seynt Jerom, that was a cardinall that translatid the Bible and the 565 sautre fro Ebru into Latyn. And byside that cherch is a cherche of Seynt Nicholas wher Our Lady rested here when she was delyveryd of childe. And for she hadde so moche mylke in here pappes that hit greved here, she mylkyd hit out uppon the reed stones of marble, so that yit men may see the traces, for they beth y-sene uppon the stones.

570   And ye shal understonde that alle that dwellith in Bethlem beth Cristen men. And ther beth fair vines aboute the cité and greet plenté of wyn. But here bokes of Macametis lawe forbedeth hem to drynke wyn, for in that book he acurseth all tho that drynketh wyn, for synne that he slow an heremyte that he loved well in his dronknes. But his malys torned to hymself, as Holy Wryt seyth: *Et in verticem ipsius*

---

539 toures, towers. **540 pynacles**, turrets; **corneld**, crenelated. **543 Floryshid**, Flowering. **544 heo**, she; **demed**, judged. **545 brende**, burnt; **wode**, wood. **547 that**, so that. **548 ride**, red. **549 rosers**, rose bushes. **550 y-seyn afore**, seen before. **552 queir**, choir. **553 gres**, steps; **y-dyght**, decorated. **555 thre paas**, three paces; **cribbe of the oxe and the asse**, i.e., the manger where Jesus was laid. **559 sommen**, together. **562 gres**, steps. **563 Innocentis**, the male children killed by Herod in an attempt to destroy the infant Jesus. **565 sautre**, psalter; **Ebru**, Hebrew. **566 here**, herself. **567 pappes**, breasts; **greved**, distressed. **568 reed**, red. **571 plenté**, abundance; **here**, their. **572 Macametis**, Mohammed's; **he acurseth**, he (Mohammed) curses; **tho**, those. **573 for**, because of the; **heremyte**, hermit. **573–74 in his dronknes**, when drunk. **574 malys**, malice.

575   *iniquitas eius descendet*. That is to say: "And his wyckednesse descendid into his owen
        heed."

        Also thes Sarazens bryngeth forth noon gryces, nother they eteth of none, ne
        of noon swynes flessh, for hit is brother to man and hit was forbode in the Olde
        Lawe. Also in the lond of Palastine, nother in the lond of Egipte, they eten litle veel
580   other beoff, but hit be so olde that hit ne may namore travayle ne worche. But
        noght as hit were forbode, but forto kepe hem for telyng of here londe.

        Of this cité of Bedlem was David Kyng y-bore, and he hadde 60 wyves and 300
        lemans. Fro Bedlem to Jerusalem is bote two myle. At the half myle fro Jerusalem
        is a cherche wher the angel seyde to the shephurd of the beryng of Cryst. In the
585   way is the tumbe of Rachel, that was Joseph moder the patriarch. And she deyde
        also sone as she hadde bore Benjamyn, and Jacob here hosebande sette 12 greet
        stones uppon here in tocknyng that she hadde y-bore 12 children. In this way to
fol. 19r Jerusalem beth many Cristen cher|ches by which men goth to Jerusalem.

JERUSALEM. CAPITULUM SEXTUM.   [Chapter 6.]

        For to speke of Jerusalem, ye shal understonde that hit stondith fayre among
590   hilles, and ther is no ryver but water that cometh by condiht fro Ebron. And men
        callid hit ferst Jebus and sythe was hit called Solomee into the tyme of Kyng David,
        and he sette these two names in samen and callid hit Jebusalem. And then come
        Salomon and callid hit Jerusalem, and so hit is yit y-called.

        And aboute Jerusalem is the kyngdom of Syrry, and ther ney is the lond of Pal-
595   astine and Ascalon, but Jerusalem is in the lond Jude. And hit is y-called Jude for
        Judas Machabeus was kyng of that lond. And hit marcheth estward upon the kyng-
        dom of Arabye, on the south syde upon the lond of Egypte, on the west syde upon
        the Gret See, on the north side upon the kyngdom of Syrry and the see of Cipre.

        In Jerusalem was somtyme a patriarch and an erchebysshop, and bisshopes
600   aboute in the contré. Aboute Jerusalem beth thees citeis: Ebron at 7 myle, Jerico at
        6 myle, Bersabe at 8 myle, Ascalon at 18 myle, Jaffe at 27 myle, Ramatha at 3 myle,
        Bethlem at 2 myle. And toward the south is a cherche of Mercaritot, that was abbot
        of Seynt Mercaritot, for wham they makyd moche sorwe when he sholde deye. And
        hit is y-peyntyd there how they makyd deol when he deyde.

605   This lond of Jerusalem hath y-be in hond of diverse nacions, as Jewes, Can-
        aneus, Assirienes, Perces, Medoynes, Massydoyns, Grecis, Romayns, Cristen men,
        Sarasyns, Barbaryns, and Turkes, and many other naciouns with hem. For Crist
        wole noght that hit be longe in hondes of traytouris, nother of synwers, be hit
        Cristen men other no. And mysbylive men haveth holde that lond in her hond 40
610   yer and more, but they shul noght holde hit to longe yif God wole.

---

577 bryngeth forth, rear; **gryces**, pigs. **578 brother**, a brother. **580 beoff**, beef; **travayle**,
labor. **581 telynge**, tilling. **582 Bedlem**, Bethlehem. **583 lemans**, concubines; **bote**, only.
584 beryng, i.e., birth. **585 Joseph moder**, the mother of Joseph. **587 in tocknyng**,
signifying. **590 condiht**, conduit. **591 Solomee**, Salem. **592 in samen**, together. **595
Jude**, of Judea. **596 marcheth**, extends. **598 the Gret See**, the Mediterranean; **Syrry**,
Syria; **Cipre**, Cyprus. **602–03 a cherche . . . deye**, a confused way of saying that the church
of Mercaritot was named for St. Mercaritot. **603 wham**, whom. **604 deol**, sorrow. **608
synwers**, sinners. **609 mysbylive**, unbelieving (i.e., non-Christians). **610 to**, too.

When men beth at Jerusalem, they goth the ferste pilgrimage to the cherche
fol. 19v   wher is the holy grave. And that is out of the cité on the north | syde, but hit is y-
closed yn with toun walles. And ther is a fayr cherche round up above and wel y-
helid with leed. And on the west syde is a fayr tour and strong for bellys. In the
615   myddel of the cherche is a tabernacle, as a lytle hous, y-makyd in the manere of an
half compas, wel rychely of goolde and asure and other colouris. And on the ryght
syde is the sepulcre of Our Lord, and that tabernacle is 8 foot long and 5 foot wyde
and 11 foot of hythe.

And hit is noght longe siththe the sepulcre was all opne, that men myghte kysse
620   hit and touche hit. But for men that come thyder forfyde hem to breke the stone
in pecys, therfore the soudan hath do makyd a wal aboute the sepulcre, that no
man may touche hit but on the lyft syde. On that tabernacle is no wyndow, but
therynne beth many laumpes lyght. And ther is a laumpe that hongeth afore the
sepulcre brennynge, and on the Fryday he goth out by hymself and lyghtith agen
625   by hymself at that oure that Our Lord aroos fram deth to lyff.

Also withynne that cherche on the ryght syde is the mount of Calvarie, wher
Crist was don on the Cros. And the Cros was y-sette in a morteyse in the rooch, that
is whyte of colour and a lytle reed y-medled therwith. And uppon that rooch
droppyd that blood of Cristes woondis when He was pyned on the Cros. And in
630   that mortais was Adamis hed y-fonde after Noeis flood in tocknyng of Adamis
synnes sholde be bought in that place. And above makyd Adam sacrifise to Our
Lord, and ther is an auter and byfore that auter lith Godfray the Boleyn, and
Baudewyn, and other that were Cristyn kynges of Jerusalem.

And ther that Our Lord was doon on Cros is y-wryte in Gru: *Otheos basilion*
635   *ysmon presomas ergaste sothias oys.* That is to say in Latyn thus: *Hic deus rex noster ante*
fol. 20r   *secula operatus est salutem in medio terre.* | That is to say thus: "God, our kyng byfore
the worlde, hath makyd hele in the myd of the erthe." Also uppon the roche wher
the Cros is pyght is y-wryte withynne the roche in Gru: *Gros giust rasis tou pestes toy*
tesmoysy. That is to say in Latyn thus: *Quod vides est fundamentum tocius mundi et huius*
640   *fidei.* That is to say thus: "That thou seist is ground of alle the worlde and of this
feith." And ye shal understonde that Our Lord when He deyde was of 32 yer old
and thre monthes. And the prophecie of David seyde that He sholde have 40 yer
when he seyd thus: *Quadraginta annis proximus fui generacioni huic.* That is to say:
"40 yer was Y neyghbore to this generacioun." And thus sholde hit seme that the
645   prophecie of David were noght trywe. But ye shal understonde that hit is trywe, for
in the olde tyme men maked the yer of 10 monthes, of which Mars was first and

---

612 holy grave, Christ's sepulcher. **612–13 y-closed**, enclosed. **613 cherche round**, round
church. **613–14 y-helid**, covered. **614 leed**, lead; **a fayr tour and strong for bellys**, a tower
for bells that is fair and strong. **618 hythe**, height. **619 siththe**, since. **620 forfyde hem**,
misbehaved themselves. **621 pecys**, pieces. **624 lyghtith**, illuminates. **625 oure**, hour.
627 morteyse, mortice. **628 reed y-medled**, red mixed. **629 pyned**, tortured. **630
mortais**, mortice; **Noeis**, Noah's; **in tocknyng of**, as a sign that. **631 bought**, redeemed.
632 auter, altar; **Godfray the Boleyn**, Godfrey of Bouillon. **633 Baudewyn**, Baldwin. **634
Gru**, Greek. **637 hele**, salvation; **myd**, middle. **638 pyght**, placed. **640 seist**, sees. **643
Quadraginta . . . huic**, apparently a corruption of Vulgate Psalm 94:10. **646 Mars**, March.

Decembre was last. But Gayus Cesar, that was emperour of Rome, let sette thes two monthes therto, Janyver and Feverer, and ordeyned the yer of 12 monthes, that is to say 360 and 5 dayes withoute lepe yer. And therfore by a good countes of that ten monthes to yer of Cristes dayes in the 40 yer, and after oure yeres of 12 monthes, He had 32 yer and thre monthis.

Also withynne the mounte of Calvarie at the ryght syde is an auter wher the pylour lith that Crist was bounde to when He was y-skorgid. And ther at 42 gres deep was the very Cros founde by a seynt that was cleped Seynt Elene under a roche wher the Jewes hadde hydde hit. And hit was asayed, for they fonde thre crosses: oon of Our Lord and two of the two theves. For Seynt Elene asayed hem on a deed body, which that aroos anoon as the veray Cros was leyd on hym.

And ther neygh is the place in a wal wher the thre nayles of Our Lord were y-hydde, and He hadde two nayles in His hondes and oon in His feet. And of oon of these nayles the emperour of Constantynople | let make a brydel to his hors when he rood into batayl, for by vertu therof he overcome his enymyes and wan all the londes of Asy, Turky, Damacyn the More and the Lesse, Sirrye, Jerusalem, Arabie, Perce, Mesopotayne, the kyngdom of Alappe, Egipte the Hyghe and the Lowe, and other kyngdomes many into Ethiope and into Ynde the Lasse, that tho was Cristen. But they ben now in hondes of paynems and Sarasyns. But when God wole, ryght as these londes ben lost by synne of Cristen men, they shal be wonnen agen thorgh help of Almyghty God.

And in the myddel of this cherche is a compas in which Joseph of Barmathia leyd the body of Our Lord when he hadde Hym take doun of the Cros. And that compas, men seyn, hit is in the myddel of the world. And in the cherche of the Sepulcre in the north syde is the place wher Our Lord was don into prison, for He was in prison in many places. And ther is som of the cheyne with the which He was y-bounde. And ther He aperyd first to Marie Maudeleyn after His Uprysynge. In that Cherche of the Sepulcre were y-woned to be chanouns of the ordre of Seynt Benet, and they hadde a priour, but the patriarke was her soverayn.

And withoute the cherche dores at the ryght syde, as men gon up 18 gres, seyd Crist to His moder: *Mulier ecce filius tuus.* That is to say: "Woman, byhold thy sone." *Deinde dicit discipulo, ecce mater tua.* That is to say: "Then seyde He to His disciple, byhold thy moder." And these wordes He seyde uppon the Cros.

And under these gres, prestes syngen her Masses, but noght as we don. And they maketh alwey the sacrament on the auter of bred, as we don, seynge the Pater Noster and other thyng also as they sey the wordes of sacrament. But they have noght the addiciouns of the orisons in privité of the Masse. And that is for they know noght the addiciouns that we have.

650

655

fol. 20v
661

665

670

675

680

---

647 Gayus Cesar, Julius Caesar. **649–50 by a good countes . . . the 40 yer**, i.e., according to the 10-month calendar, Christ's age was 40. **650 after**, according to. **653 pylour**, pillar; **y-skorgid**, scourged; **gres**, steps. **654 cleped**, called; **Seynt Elene**, St. Helen, mother of the emperor Constantine. **655 asayed**, tested. **658 neygh**, nearby. **661 wan**, won. **662 Asy**, Asia; **Sirrye**, Syria. **663 Perce**, Persia. **664 Ynde**, India. **665 paynems**, pagans. **668 compas**, circle; **Joseph of Barmathia**, Joseph of Arimathea. **673 aperyd**, appeared; **Uprysynge**, Resurrection. **674–75 chanouns**, canons; **Seynt Benet**, St. Benedict. **675 priour**, prior. **680 prestes**, priests. **681–82 Pater Noster**, Our Father. **683 orisons in privité**, private prayers.

fol. 21r   And ye shal understonde that byfore | this cherche is the cité feblist, for the gret
686   playn that is bytwyne the cité and the cherche uppon the est syde. Withoute the
walles of the cité is the Vale of Josaphat that comth to the walles. In that vale
without that cité is a cherche of Seynt Stevene, wher he was stened to the deth. And
therby is the Gilden Gate that may noght be opned. Thorgh that gate Crist entred
690   on Palme Sonday on an asse, and that gat opned ageyn Hym. And yyt ben the
stappes y-sene in foure places, which were ful of harde stones.

Byfore the Cherche of the Sepulcre 200 pace is a gret hospital of Seynt John,
of which Hospitalers hath her foundacioun. And for to go estward fro this hospital
is a fair cherch which men callen *Nostre Dame le Graunt*. And also ther is a cherche
695   that is called *Nostre Dame de Vatyns*. And ther Marie Cleophe and Marie Magdalene
to-drow her her when Crist dayde.

And toward the est at the 8 score pace fro the cherche of the Sepulcre is
Templum Domini, that is a faire hous. And hit is all rounde and ryght hye, and hit
is heelyd with bord and y-paved with whit marbel. But Sarizens wole suffre no
700   Cristen man ne Jew come therynne, for they say that so foul men ne sholde come
therynne in so holy place. But Y was therynne and in other places wher Y wolde,
for Y hadde letters of the soudan with his greet seel, and comonly other men
haveth but a synet. And whoso haveth his letter with his greet seel, he hit shal bere
afore hym uppon a greet sper hangynge. And men do gret worship therto and
705   knelyn doun agen hit, as we don agen Godis body. For to wham that hit is y-send
to, ferst he shal encline therto, and thenne take hit on her heed, and thenne they
kysse hit and redith hit enclynyng with greet worschip, and then they profre hem
to do al the wyll of the brynger. And in this Templum Domini were y-woned to be
canones religious, and they hadde an abbot to wham they were obedyent. And in
fol. 21v   this temple was Charlemayn when | the angell brought hym prepuys of Crist when
711   he was circumcised, and sithe Kyng Charles let bryng hit to Parys.

And ye shal understande that this is noght the Temple that Salomon makyde,
for that Temple lestid but a 1200 and 2 yer, for Titus, and Vaspasianus son, that
was emperour of Rome, that byseged Jerusalem to destroye Jewes, for they slow
715   Crist withoute leve of the emperour. When he had take that cité, he leyt brenne the
Temple and cast hit adoun, and took alle the Jewes and slew of hem 1,100,000.
And other he put in prison and solde of hem 30 for oo peny, for they seyde they
bought Crist for 30 pens.

And sithe Julius Apostata gaf leve to the Jewes to make the Temple of Jeru-
720   salem, for they hatid Cristen men, and yit they were Christen hemself, but they

---

685 feblist, most vulnerable. **687 Josaphat**, Jehosaphat. **688 Seynt Stevene**, St. Stephen;
stened, stoned. **689 Gilden**, Golden. **690 ageyn**, before; **yyt**, still. **691 stappes**, hoof
marks. **692 pace**, paces. **695 Marie Cleophe**, Mary Cleophas; **Marie Magdalene**, Mary
Magdalene. **696 to-drow her her**, tore their hair; **dayde**, died. **697 the 8 score pace**, 160
steps. **698 hye**, tall. **699 heelyd**, covered; **suffre**, allow. **702 seel**, seal. **703 synet**, signet.
706 encline, bow; **take . . . heed**, allow it to touch their head. **707 redith**, read; **profre**,
offer. **710 Charlemayn**, Charlemagne; **prepuys**, the foreskin. **713 lestid**, lasted; **Titus,
and Vaspasianus son**, Titus, who was Vespasian's son. **715 leyt brenne**, caused to burn.
717 oo, one. **718 pens**, pence. **719 Julius Apostata**, Julian the Apostate.

hadde forsake her feith. And whenne the Jewes had makyd the Temple, tho come an erthquake, as God wolde, and cast hit adoun.

And sith Adrian the emperour makyd Jerusalem agen and the Temple in the same maner that Salomon makyd hit. And he wolde that no Jewe sholde dwelle
725 ther but Cristen men, for he thoughte, thow they ne were Cristen men, they loved more Cristen men than eny other men, save men of his owen feith. And this Adrian let close and walle the cherche of the Holy Sepulcre withynne the cité — that byfore was withoute — and wolde have y-chaunged the name of Jerusalem and calle hit Animote holy: that name last noght longe.
730 Also the Sarizyns doth gret worship to that Temple, for they seyn that place is ryght holy. And when they gon thiderynne, they goon barefoot and knelith adoun many tymes. And when my felawes and Y come thiderin, we dide of oure shone and come barefoot, in tocknynge that we sholde do also moche worship, other more, as they that were in mysbyleve.
735 And this Temple is of hithe 120 and 5 cubites and of wydnesse 64 cubites and also moch of leynthe, and hit is withynne al aboute ful of pilouris of marbel. And
fol. 22r in the myddel of | this Temple is a stage of 24 grecis of heithe and good pylouris aboute hit. This place is y-called *Sancta Sanctorum*, that is to say: "Holy of Halwes." And in that place cometh noon other but the prelate which that maketh her sac-
740 rifise, and the peple stondeth all aboute in stages as they ben of degré.

And ther beth 4 ontrees to the Temple, and the dores ben of cipresse wel y-dight. And withynne the north dore is a poule of water, of which Holy Wryt spekith and seith thus: *Vidi aquam egredientem de templo*. That is to say: "I saw water comyng out of the Temple." And on that other syde is the huge roch that somtyme was
745 called Morarche, but afterward hit was y-called Beleth, other Arke of God, with relikes of Jewes. This Arke let Titus lede with the same relikes to Rome when he hadde destruyed the Jewes.

In that Arke were the 10 Commaundemens and som of Aarons yerd and of Moyses yerd, with the which he departyd the Rede See when the peple of Israel
750 passide thorghout foot-dry. And with that yerd he smot the roch, and water com out of hym, and with that yerd he dide many wondres. And ther was a vessel of goold ful of manna, and clothyng, and ornamentes, and the tabernacle of Aaron, and other many relikes. And ther was a table, squar, of goold with 12 precious stones, and a beest of jasper grene with foure figuris, and 8 names of Our Lord
755 withynne, and 7 candelstyckes of goold, and 12 pottes of goold, and 4 ensensures of goold, and an auter of goold, and 4 lyons of goold uppon which they hadde a cherubyn of goold 12 spanne long, and a tabernacle of goold, and 12 trumpes of sylver, and a table of sylver, and 8 holy loves, and other relikes that were byfore.

And uppon that roch that Moyses smote, ther sleep Jacob when he saw angelis
760 go up and doun by a scale, and seyde thus: *Vere locus iste sanctus est et ego nesciebam*.

---

723 **Adrian**, Hadrian. 727 **let close and walle**, caused to be enclosed and walled. 731 **thider-ynne**, therein. 732 **of**, off; **shone**, shoes. 735 **hithe**, height. 737 **stage**, tier; **grecis**, steps. 738 **Halwes**, Holies. 739 **prelate**, churchman of superior rank. 740 **in stages . . . degré**, on tiers according to their rank. 741 **ontrees**, entrances. 742 **poule**, pool. 745 **Beleth**, Bethel. 748 **Aarons yerd**, the rod of Aaron. 751 **hym**, it. 755 **pottes**, vessels; **ensensures**, censers. 757 **cherubyn**, cherubim; **trumpes**, trumpets. 758 **loves**, loaves. 760 **scale**, stairway.

fol. 22v   That is to say: "Forsothe this place is holy, and Y wist hit noght." | And Jacob heilde
            stylle ther an angel and chaunged his name and called hym Israel. And in that
            place saw David the angel that smot the peple with a swerd and put hit al blody on
            the shethe.

765   And in the roche He sette Hym when the Jewes wolde have y-stened Hym. And
            that roch cleff in two, and in that clyft He hydde Hym, and an angel come and gaf
            Hym lyght. And ther forgaf Our Lord the womman that was y-take in adulteri. And
            ther the angel denounced the nativité of Seynt John the Baptist. And ther preyde
            David to Our Lord and to the angel that He wolde have mercy on hym and of his
770   peple. And Our Lord herde hym and his prayer. And therfore he wolde have
            makyd a temple in that place, but Our Lord forbed hym by a angel, for he hadde
            y-do treson when he dyde sle Urye, a good knyght, forto have his wiff. And
            therfore though he hadde ordeyned to make that temple, he lete Salomon his sone
            to make hit. And he prayed Our Lord that alle thilke that prayed in that place
775   devoutly and with good herte, that He wolde here hyre prayere. And Our Lord
            graunted hym, and therfor hit was y-called Templum of Counsel and helpe of God.
            In that temple was Zacary i-slayn. And toward the south is the temple of Salamon,
            that is a greet place and a fair place. And in this place dwellen knyghtes that ben
            callid Templers, and that was the foundacion of hem, and her order is withoute the
780   cloystre of the temple.

                 Toward the north syde is a fayr cherche of Seynt Anne, Our Lady moder. Ther
            was Our Lady conceyved, and byfore the cherche is a greet tre that bygan to growe
            that same nyght. And ther neygh lay somtyme Seynt Anne, but Seynt Elene leet
            translate her to Constantynople. In that cherche is a walle in the maner of a cis-
fol. 23r   terne that is y-called *probatica piscina*, that hadde 5 entrees. And in that | was woned
786   an angel to descende and stere the water. And what man that ferst bathid hym
            therynne, after that steryng of that water, was y-makyd hool of alle sicknesse that
            he hadde. And ther was a man in the palasye y-helyd, which was syke 38 yer. And
            Crist seide thus: *Tolle grabatum tuum et ambula*. That is to say: "Take thy bed and
790   go."

                 And a lytel thenne was the hous of Kyng Herodes that let sle the Innocentes.
            This Herodes was ful wyckyd man and fel, for he leet ferst sle his owen wyff, that
            he loved wel. And for greet love that he hadde to here, when she was deed he by-
            held here and waxe out of his wytte, and so was he long. And sithen he come ageyn
795   to hymself, and thenne let he sle his cheldren that he gat by that wyff. And then he
            let sle that other wyff and a sone that he gat on her.

                 And when he saw that he sholde deye, he sente for his soster and alle the gret
            lordes of the contré, and let put all the gret lordes in a tour, and seyde to his soster
            he wyste well that men of that contré wold make no sorwe for hym when he wer
800   deed. And therfore he leet her swer that she sholde let smyte of the hedes of all the

---

761 wist, knew; **heilde**, beheld. **762 hym**, himself. **763 on**, in. **764 shethe**, sheath. **765 y-
stened**, stoned. **766 cleff**, cleaved. **768 denounced**, proclaimed. **772 dyde sle Urye**, he
had Uriah killed. **774 thilke**, those. **777 Zacary**, Zechariah. **779 Templers**, Knights Templar. **783–84 leet translate**, transported. **785 entrees**, entrances. **786 stere**, move. **788
in the palasye y-helyd**, with palsy healed. **791 let sle**, caused to be killed. **792 fel**, cruel.
794 waxe out of his wytte, went crazy; **long**, for a long time. **799 wyste**, knew. **800 of**, off.

lordes when he were deed, and then sholde al the contré make sorwe for his deth and elles noght. And thus makyd he his testament. But his sostre wolde noght ful-fille hit, for as sone as he was deed, she delyveryd alle the lordes, and bade hem go home to her owen places, and tolde hem what her brother wolde that she hadde
805   y-do with hem.

And ye shal understonde that ther were thre Herodes of greet name. This of wham Y spak now was y-called Ascolonyte. And he that lete smyte of the hede of Seynt John the Baptist was Herodes Antipa. And Herodes Agrippa lete sle Seynt Jame.

810   Forthermore in the cité is the Cherche of the Saveour and ther is an arme of Seynt John Crisostome. And ther is the most partye of Seynt Steveneis heed. And
fol. 23v   in the other syde toward the south, a man may go to the Mount of Syon; | ther is a fayr cherche of Seynt Jame, wher his hed was smyte of. Now go we to the Mount Syon, and ther is a fayr cherch of God and of Oure Lady, wher she deyde. And fro
815   that place, she was y-bore with the aposteles to the Vale Josaphat. And ther is the stone that the angel bare to Our Lady fro the Mount Synay, and hit is of that colour of that roch of Seynt Katerin.

Also at the entré of the Mount Syon is a chapel, and at that chapel is that greet ston, and hit is large, which that covereth the sepulcre when Crist was leyd ther-
820   ynne. And ther is a litle pece of the pilour to which Our Lord was bounde when He was scorged. And ther was a hous that was that tyme the bysshopes of the Lawe. And in that same place Peter forsoke Our Lord 3. And ther is a partye of the table on which God makyd His Maundy. And ther apeyred Crist ferst to His disciples after His Uprysyng, when the gates were shytte, and seyde: *Pax vobis*. That is to sey:
825   "Pees to yow." And on that mount apered Crist to Seynt Thomas and bad hym asay His woundes, and thenne leved he ferst, and seyde thus: *Dominus meus et deus meus*. That is to say: "My Lord, my God."

In that same place, byhynde the hyghe auter, were alle the apostoles on Wit Soneday, when the Holy Gost descended on hem in lickens of fire. And ther makyd
830   God Pasche with His disciples. And ther slept John the Evaungelist uppon Our Lordes kne and sey slepyng many prevy thynges of hevene.

This Mount Syon is withynne the cité. And the cité is strengre on that syde than in eny other, for at the foot of Mount Syon is a fair castel and strong. On the Mount Syon was Kyng David and Salomon y-beryed and many other also. And a
835   stones cast fro that castel is another chapel wher Our Lord was jugged, for that tyme was Cayphas hous.

---

803 delyveryd, freed. **807 Ascolonyte**, Herod the Great. **808–09 Seynt Jame**, St. James (brother of St. John). **811 most partye**, largest part. **815 with**, by. **818 entré**, beginning. **821 scorged**, scourged; **was . . . the bysshopes of the Lawe**, i.e., belonged to the spiritual leader of the Jews (other versions identify him as Annas). **822 3**, i.e., three times. **823 Maundy**, Maundy Thursday, i.e., Last Supper; **apeyred**, appeared. **824 Uprysyng**, Resur-rection; **shytte**, shut. **825 asay**, test. **826 leved he ferst**, he (Thomas) first believed. **828–29 Wit Soneday**, Whitsun (Pentecost). **829 licknes**, likeness. **830 Pasche**, Passover. **831 sey**, saw; **prevy**, secret. **832 strengre**, more fortified. **835 stones cast**, stone's throw; **jugged**, judged. **836 Cayphas**, Caiaphas'.

Under Mount Syon toward the Vale of Josaphat is a well that men callen *Nata-*
fol. 24r   *tori Silo*. Ther was Our Lord y-wassh when He was | y-baptised. And ther neygh is
the tre of which Judas honge hymself. And ther nye is the synagoge wher Judas
840   caste the 30 pens byfore the Jewes and Fariseis and seyde thus: *Peccavi tradens*
sanguinem justum. That is to say: "I have synwed, disseyved ryghtfull blood."

And on that other syde of Mount Syon, toward the south a stones cast, is that
feeld that was bought with tho 30 pens, which is y-called *Acheldemak*, that is to say
the "Feeld of Blood." In that feeld beth many tumbes of Cristen men, for ther beth
845   many pilgrymes biried. And also toward the west syde of Jerusalem is a fair cherche
wher the tre grew of which the Cros was maked. And ther neygh is a cherch wher
Our Lady mette with Elizabeth when they were bothe with chylde, and Seynt John
stired in his moder wombe and dide worship to Our Lord, his makere. And ther
was Seynt John y-bore. And ther neygh is the castel of Emaux.
850   And two myle fro Jerusalem is Mount Joye, and that is a fayre place and a
lykyng. And ther lyth Samuel the prophete in a fayr tumbe. And hit is called Mount
Joye, for that may pylgrimes ferst y-se that cometh to Jerusalem. And in the
myddel of the Vale of Josaphat is a lytel ryver that is y-called *Torrens Cedron*. And
overtwert that ryver lay that tree, of which that Cros was maked, that men yede
855   over. Also in that vale is a cherch of Our Lady, and ther is the tumbe of Our Lady.
And Our Lady was of elde when she deyde 72 yer.

And ney that is a place wher Judas kyssed Our Lord when He was y-take, that
men callen Gessamain. And Crist byleved ther His disciples byfore His Passion,
when he yede to praye and seyde thus: *Pater si fieri potest transeat a me calix iste*. That
860   is to say: "Fader, if hit may be, do let this Passion go fro me."

And ther is the tumbe of Kyng Josaphat, of wham the vale had his name. And
at that oon syde of the vale is Mount Olyvete, and hit is called so for ther greweth
many olyve treis. And hit is heyer than Jerusalem, and fro that hille men may se
fol. 24v   into the stretis of Jerusalem. | And bytwyne that hille and Jerusalem is noght but the
865   Vale of Josaphat, and hit is noght ful large. And on that hille stood Crist when He
went to Hevene, and yit semeth ther the stappes of His lyft foot in the stoon.

And ther is an abbey of blake canons that were somtyme dwellyng ther, but ther
is now a cherche. And a lytel then is a chapel, in which chapel is a stoon on which
Our Lord satte when He prechid to the peple and sayd thus: *Beati pauperes spiritu,*
870   *quoniam ipsorum est regnum celorum.* That is to say: "Blessed be tho that beth poore
in spirit, for her is the kyngdome of Hevene." And ther He taughte His disciples
her Pater Noster. And a litel then is Besfage, fro whom Crist sent Petre to fecche
an asse on Palme Sonday. And toward the est is a chapel that men callen Betonye;
ther dwelled Symon lepre, that herborwed Our Lord and tho that were with Hym

---

837–38 *Natatori Silo*, the Pool of Siloam. **840 pens**, pence; **Fariseis**, Pharisees. **841
synwed**, sinned; **disseyved ryghtfull**, deceived righteous. **845 biried**, buried. **847
Elizabeth**, mother of John the Baptist. **851 lykyng**, pleasant. **852 that₁**, i.e., that mountain.
854 overtwert, across; **yede**, went. **856 elde**, age. **858 Gessamain**, Gethsemane; **byleved**,
left. **861 Josaphat**, Jehosaphat. **862 Olyvete**, Olivet. **863 heyer**, higher. **866 stappes**,
footprints. **867 blake canons**, i.e., Augustinian canons. **871 her**, theirs. **872 Pater Noster**,
Our Father; **Besfage**, Bethphage. **873 Betonye**, Bethany. **874 Symon lepre**, Simon the
leper; **herborwed**, sheltered.

875   of His disciples. And he was y-called Julian, and he was makyd bysshop. And that
      is he that men callen uppon for herborgh.

          In that place God forgaff the synnes of Mari Maudeleyn, and ther she wasshid
      His feet with her teres of her eyen, and wiped hem with her here. And ther was
      Lazar arered, that was dede four daies. And ther is the place wher Our Lady
880   apered to Seynt Thomas after her Assumpcioun, and she gaf to hym her gerdel.
      And ther ney is the stoon uppon which Our Lord sat and prechid many tymes; and
      theruppon shal He sitte on the Day of Dome, as Hymself sayde. And ther ney is the
      Mount of Galilé wher the aposteles were y-gadered when Mary Maudeleyn tolde
      hem of Cristis Rysyng. And bytwyne Mount Olivete and Mount Galilé is a chirche
885   wher the angel tolde Our Lady of her deth.

          Also fro Betonye to Jerico is 5 mile. Jerico was somtyme a litel cité, but hit was
      destruyed and now is ther but a litel toun. That toun toke Josue by miracle of God
      and byddyng of the angel, and destruyed hit and cursyd alle tho that held hit agen.
      Of that cité was Raab, the comune womman, that receyved the messagers of Israel
890   and kepte hem fro peryles. And therfore she hadde a good reward of God, for
fol. 25r Holy | Writte seith thus: *Qui accipit prophetam in nomine prophete, mercedem prophete*
      accipiet. That is to sayn: "He that taketh the prophete in the name of the prophete,
      he shal take mede of a prophete."

          Also fro Betanye men goon to Flom Jordan thorgh wyldernesse, and hit is ney a
895   daies journey estward into a greet hille, wher Our Lord fasted 40 dayes. And the
      devel of Helle temptid Crist and sayde thus: *Dic ut lapides isti panes fiat.* That is to say:
      "Say that thes stones ben maked bred." And ther is an hermytage in the which
      dwelleth a maner of freres that men callen Georgens, for Seynt George funded hem.
      And uppon that hille dwelled Abraham a greet while. Also as men goon to Jerico, in
900   the way seet syke men cryynge thus: *Jhesu, fili David, miserere mei.* That is to seyn:
      "Jhesu, David sone, have mercy on me." And two myle fro Jerico is Flom Jordan.

          And ye shal understande that the Dede See departeth the lond of Jude and of
      Arabye, and that see lasteth fro Sara into Arabie. And that water of that see is ful
      better, and this water casteth out a thyng that is y-called *aspaltoun*, as greet pecis
905   as an hors. And Jerusalem is 200 forlang fro this see, and hit is y-called the Dede
      See, for hit renneth noght; ne noon maner beist may leve therynne, and that hath
      ben assayed many tymes. And no man may drynke of that water, and if eny men
      casteth ire therynne, hit cometh up agen; and if eny men casteth fetheris therynne,
      hit sinketh adoun to gronde, and that is agen kynde.
910   And for synne agen kynde was the cité loste that stode ther. And ther now grow-
      eth trees and berith fruyt of fair colour and semeth rype, but thorgh venjaunce of

---

875 y-called Julian, [later] named Julian. **876 herborgh**, lodging. **877 Mari Maudeleyn**,
Mary Magdalen. **878 eyen**, eyes; **her here**, her hair. **879 Lazar arered**, Lazarus raised. **880
Assumpcioun**, Assumption; **gerdel**, belt. **882 Day of Dome**, Day of Judgment. **884 Rysyng**,
Resurrection. **887 toke Josue**, Joshua captured. **889 Raab**, Rahab; **comune womman**,
prostitute. **893 take mede**, receive the reward. **894 Flom**, River. **897 maked**, made into.
899 a greet while, for a long time. **900 seet**, sat. **902 departeth**, separates. **903 Sara**, Zoar.
904 better, bitter; **aspaltoun**, asphalt. **904–05 as greet pecis as**, in pieces as large as. **905
forlang**, furlongs. **906 beist**, animal; **leve**, live. **907 assayed**, tested. **908 ire**, iron. **909
gronde**, the bottom; **kynde**, nature. **911 venjaunce**, vengeance.

915

fol. 25v

God that cité was brent with fire of Helle. And som men callen that water the Lake of Allfetida, and som men callen hit the Flom of Devel, and som men callen hit the Flom Stynkyng. Ther sonke the 5 citeis all doun, Sodom, Gomor, Aldema, Solome, and Segor, for the synnes of sodomyte that regned on hem. But Segor, thorgh prayers of Loth, was y-saved a greet while, for hit stood uppon a hyll. And men may se moche ther above the water, and men may se the | walles in cler wether.

920

And ther dwelled Loth a greet while, and his doughtres makid hym dronke, and he delede with hem, for they trowed that God wolde have destruyed all the worlde, as He dede at Noeis flood. And therfore they lay by her fader, for men shold be y-bore of hem into the worlde. And if he hadde y-be noght dronke, he hadde noght deled with hem. And at the ryght syde of the se dwellith Lothis wiff in a greet stoon of salt, for that she lokyd ageyn when the cité sanke doun.

925

And ye shal understande that Abraham had a sone that heit Ysaac, and he was circumsysed when he was 8 dayes olde. And therfore Jewes lat circumsise her cheldren at the elde of 8 dayes. And he hadde another sone that men called Ismael, and he was of 14 yer old when he was circumsised, for they were bothe circumsysed uppon oon day. And therfore the Sarasynis let circumsyse her cheldren at 14 yer.

930

935

Also into the Dede See renneth Flom Jordan, and ther hit eyndith. And this Flom Jordan is noght a ful gret river, but ther is moch good fyssh therynne. And hit cometh fro the Mount Libanye fro 2 welles that men callen Jor and Dan, of which the flom taketh his name. And in that oon syde of the rever is the Mount of Gelboe, and ther is a fair playn. And on that other side men gon to the Mount Liban, and the hyll departeth the kyngdomes of Surrye and the contré of Phenes. On that hylle groweth seedes and that berith long apples, as gret as a manis hede.

940

fol. 26r

This Flom Jordan departeth Galilé, and the lond Idonye and the lond of Barron, and hit renneth into a playn that men calleth Meldane and Sermoys. And on that playn is the Temple Job. On this Flom Jordan Our Lord was baptised, and ther was the voys of the Fader y-herde seynge thus: *Hic est filius meus dilectus in quo michi bene complacui ipsium audite.* That is to say: "Her is My Sone that Y love, in wham Y am wel payd; herith | Hym." And the Holy Gost descended uppon Hym in licknesse of a culver, and so was at His baptising the Holy Trinité.

945

And thorgh the Flom Jordan passid the chyldren of Israel al drye, and they sette stones in the myddel of the water in tocknynge of a myracle. Also in that Flom Jordan was Naaman of Surry i-bathed, that was a mesel, and y-helyd was ther. And a lytel then is the cité of Hay, whoch Josue assayled and toke hit also. In the entré of that flom is the Vale Mambre, a fair contré and a plentouous.

950

And ye shal understonde, for to go fro the Dede See estward out of the marche of the Londe of Promission is a strong castel, that men callen Garras other Ser-

---

913 **Flom**, River. 914 **sonke**, sank; **Gomor**, Gomorrah. 915 **sodomyte**, sodomy; **regned on**, flourished in. 916 **Loth**, Lot. 918 **dronke**, drunk. 919 **delede**, had sexual intercourse; **trowed**, believed. 920 **Noeis**, Noah's; **men**, i.e., children. 923 **ageyn**, back. 924 **heit**, was called. 926 **elde**, age. 932 **Libanye**, Lebanon. 935 **Surrye**, Syria. 942 **payd**, satisfied. 943 **culver**, dove. 946 **mesel**, leper. 947 **whoch**, which; **entré**, beginning. 948 **plentouous**, abundant. 949 **marche**, borders.

moyns, that is to say *Ryal Mount* in Frenshe. This castel leet a kyng of Fraunce make, that men callid Baudewyn, that hadde conquered all that londe and hadde y-put hit in hondes of Cristen men to kepe. And under that castel is a fayr toun that is y-called Sabaoth. Ther aboute dwelleth many Cristen men under tribute.

955   And then men goth to Nazareth, of which Our Lord had His name.

[ENVIRONS OF JERUSALEM.] CAPITULUM SEPTIMUM.   [Chapter 7.]

Fro Jerusalem to Nazareth is thre journeys, for men goth thorgh the province of Galilé, thorgh Ramatha and Sophym and by the heyghe hille of Effraym, wher Anna, Samuelis moder, dwelled, and ther Samuel the prophete y-bore.

And then men goth to Sybole, wher the Ark of God was y-kepte under Elye the
960   prophete. Ther makyd the peple of Ebron her sacrifise to Our Lord, and ther spake Our Lord to Samuel. And ther ney by is Gabon and Rama and Benjamyn, of which Holy Writ spekith.

And then men cometh to Sychem, and some men callen hit Sykar. This is in the province of Samaritane, and ther was somtyme a cherche, but hit is cast adoun.
965   And hit is a fair valey and a plenteuous, and ther is a good cité that men callen Neaple. And fro then is a journey to Jerusalem, and therby is the Temple Joseph, Jacobis sone, that was sold into Egipt, for out of Egipt were his bones y-brought in
fol. 26v   leed. And thider cometh Jewes ofte in pilgrimage | with gret devocion. And therby is the cité of Carisoun, wher the Samaritanis maked her sacrifise. And ther nye is
970   the Vale of Dotaym, and ther is the cisterne in which Joseph was y-caste. And hit is 2 myle fro Sykar.

Fro then men goth to Samay, that is y-called Sabaste, which is the chyef cité of that contré. And of that cité were 12 kyndes of Israel. And ther was Seynt John the Baptist graved bytwixte two prophetis, Eliseus and Abdom, but he was byhedid in
975   the castel of Makaryn byside the Dede See. And he was translated with his disciples and y-grave at Samay, but ther Julius Apostata leet take his bones and bren hem, for he was that tyme emperour. But that fynger, the which he shewed Our Lord, seyng thus: *Ecce agnus dei*; that is to say: "Byhold the Lombe of God"; that myght noght be brend, and Seynt Tecle the virgyne let bere hit into the mount, and ther
980   was y-do therto greet worship.

And ther was the hed of Seynt John the Baptiste y-closed in a wall, but Theodosy the emperour let take hit out and fond hit y-wrapped in a cloth al blody, and so he let hit bere to Constantynople. And so hit is yit, the halfendell of the hede, and that other halfendell is at Rome, in the cherche of Seynt Silvestre. And
985   that vestel in which this hede was leed when hit was smyte of, that is at Gene, and men of Gene doth gret worship therto. And somme seyn that Seynt Johnis hede

---

951 *Ryal Mount*, Mount Royal. 952 **Baudewyn**, Baldwin. 957 **heyghe**, high. 958 **Anna**, Hannah. 959 **Sybole**, Shiloh; **Elye**, Eli. 961 **ney by**, nearby. 964 **Samaritane**, Samaritan. 965 **plenteuous**, abundant. 966 **Neaple**, Neopolis, i.e., new city. 967–68 **in leed**, encased in lead. 973 **kyndes**, tribes. 974 **byhedid**, beheaded. 975 **Makaryn**, Machareus; **translated**, transported. 976 **Julius Apostata**, Julian the Apostate. 978 **Lombe**, Lamb. 979 **Seynt Tecle**, St. Thecla. 980 **worship**, honor. 981 **y-closed**, enclosed. 982 **Theodosy**, Theodosius. 984 **halfendell**, half. 985 **vestel**, vessel; **leed**, put. 985 **Gene**, Genoa.

is at Amyas in Pycardy. And that hit sholde be Seynt Johnis hede the Baptiste, Y wot noght, but God wot.

990 Fro Sabaste to Jerusalem is 12 myle. And bytwyne the hilles of the contré is a well that men callen *Fons Jacob*, that is to say "Jacobis Well," which changeth four tymes a yer his colour: somtyme hit is reed, somtyme cleir, somtyme thicke. That men that beth dwellyng therby beth i-called Samaritanis, and they were acounted to the aposteles. And her lawe varieth fro Cristen lawe and Sarasyns, fro Jewes and fro paynemus. And they byleveth wel on God, that all thyng shal deme, and they

fol. 27r leve the Byble after the letter. And they wrappeth | her hedes in reed lynnen cloth
996 for difference of other, for Sarasyns wrappen her hedes in whit lynnen cloth, and Cristen men that dwelleth ther in blew cloth other blak cloth, and Jewes in yelw cloth. In this contré dwelleth many Jewes paynge tribute, as Cristen men doth.

1000 And if ye wole y-wyte the letteris of Jewes, they beth soche. And thes beth the names of her letters, as they callen hem: alpha, běth, gimel, hě, vắu, yắu, ěx, iðth, karryk, lemp, mẽu, m̃, ěn, sameth, ěly, phě, lắd, sðth, fir̃, sðun, tắu, loccirs. Now shal ye have the figures. . . .

And fro this contré that Y spak of, men goth to the playn of Galilé and leveth the hille in that on syde. Galilé is of the province and of the Land of Promission.
1005 And in that province is the lond of Nayme and Capharnaum and Corysaym and Bethsayda. And in Bethsayda was Seynt Peter and Seynt Andrew y-bore. And of Corisaym shal Antecrist come and ther y-bore, as som men sayn. And som men sayn he shal be bore in Babiloyn. And therfor seith the prophecie thus: *De Babilonia columba exiet que totum mundum devorabit.* That is to say: "Of Babyloyn shal a colver come out that shal devoure al the worlde." And this Antecrist shal be
1010 norshed in Bethsaida, and he shal regne in Corysaym. And therfore Holy Wryt seith thus: *Ve tibi Corisan. Ve tibi Bethsayda. Ve tibi Capharum.* That is to say: "Wo be to thee Corysaym! Wo be to thee Bethsayda!" And the Cane of Galilé also is 4 myle fro Nazareth. And of that cité was the womman Cananee of wham the gospel
1015 spekith. And ther Our Lord shewed His ferst miracle at the feste of Architriclyne, when He turned water into wyne at Galilé.

And fro thenne men goth to Nazareth, that was somtyme a gret cité but now hit is a lytel toun, and hit is noght walled. And ther was Our Lady bore, but she was y-gete at Jerusalem. At Nazareth, Joseph toke Our Lady to wyve when she was of 14
1020 yer olde. And ther the angel salved her, when he seyde thus: *Ave Maria, gratia plena*
fol. 27v *dominus tecum.* That is to say: "Hayl be thow, | Mary, ful of grace; God is with thee." And ther was somtyme a greet cherch, and now is ther but a litel closet to receyve the offryng of pilgrimes. And ther is Gabrielis well, wher Our Lord was woned to be bathed when He was litel. At Nazareth was Our Lord norshed. For Nazareth is
1025 to say "flour of gardeyn," and hit may wel be called so, for ther was noryshid the flour of lyff that was Jhesu Crist.

---

987 **Amyas,** Amiens. 988 **wot,** know. 992 **acounted,** known. 994 **deme,** judge. 995 **after,** according to; **wrappeth,** wrap. 999 **y-wyte,** know. 1004 **on,** one; **Land of Promission,** Promised Land. 1007 **Antecrist,** Antichrist. 1010 **colver,** dove. 1011 **norshed,** nurtured. 1013 **Cane,** Cana. 1018–19 **y-gete,** conceived. 1020 **salved,** greeted. 1022 **closet,** room. 1024 **norshed,** nurtured.

1030 　　　And half a myle fro Nazareth is the blood of Our Lord, for the Jewes lad Hym uppon an highe roch to cast Hym doun to sle Hym. But Jhesu Crist passed fro hem and vanshide away, and uppon that roch beth His stappes yit y-sene. And som men sayn, when they beth agast of theves other of enemyes, on this maner: *Jhesu autem transiens per medium illorum ibat. Irruat super eos formido, et cetera. Fiant immobiles, et cetera.*

1035 　　　And ye shal understonde that Our Lady had chelde when she was 15 yer olde, and she dwelled with Hym 32 yer and 3 monthes, and after His Passion she leved 24 yer.

　　　And fro Nazareth to Mount Tabor is 3 myle, and ther Our Lord transfigured Hym byfore Seynt Petre, Seynt John, and Seynt Jame. And ther sey they Crist in 1040 His Godhede and Moyses and Hely the prophete. And tho seyde Seynt Petre in this wyse: *Bonum est hic esse. Faciamus tria tabernacula.* And hit is to say: "Hit is good to be her, make we 3 tabernacles." And Crist bade hem sey hit to no man, unto the tyme that He were arise fro deth to lyve. And upon the same hylle shal foure angels blowe trompes and arere alle men and wymmen that haveth y-be, and beth, 1045 and shal be, fro deth to lyve, and they shal come in body and soule to the Dome. But the Dome shal be gyve in the Vale of Josaphat uppon Pasch day, in such tyme as Our Lord roos fram deth to lyve.

　　　Also a myle fro Tabor is the Mount Ermon, and ther was the cité of Naym. Byfore the gates of the cité, Our Lord arered the wyduwe sone, which had no mo fol. 28r children. And fro thenne men goth to | the cité of Tybourne, that is uppon the See 1051 of Galilé. And thow hit be called a see, yit hit is no see, nother noon arme of the see, for hit is a broke of fressh water. And hit is of leyngthe ney an 100 forlonge and 40 of brede, and therynne is moch good fissh. And uppon that same see, Our Lord yede drie foot. Ther He seyde to Peter, when He yede on the water and was 1055 neygh sonke: *Modice fidei quare dubutasti.* That is to say: "Thou of litel feith, whi hast thou doute?"

　　　In this cité of Tibourne is that table that Crist eete upon with His disciples after His Resurexion. Of which risyng Holy Writ seyth thus: *Et cognoverunt eum in fractione panis.* That is to say: "And ther they knew Hym in brekyng of breed." 1060 　　　And ye shal understande that Flom Jordan bygynneth under the hille of Lyban, and ther bygynneth the Lond of Promission, and hit lasteth to Bersabee in leyngthe to the south and north. And in brede, hit is neye 180 myle.

　　　And amonge the Sarasens in many places dwelleth many Cristen men under tribute. And they beth of diverse maners, and ther beth diverse maneris of monkes, 1065 and they beth all Cristned and haveth divers lawes, but they all byleveth on God the Fader, Sone, and Holy Goost. And yit they diverseth in her articles of our feith. And they ben called Jacobynes, for Seynt Jame converted hem. And Seynt John Baptist baptised hem. And they seyn that men sholde shryve hem to God and

---

1031 stappes, footprints. **1032 agast,** afraid. **1035 had chelde,** gave birth to her child. **1036 leved,** lived. **1039 sey,** saw. **1040 Hely,** Elijah. **1042 her,** here. **1043 arise,** risen. **1044 arere,** raise. **1045 Dome,** Doom (i.e., Last Judgment). **1046 Pasch,** Easter. **1048 Ermon,** Hermon. **1049 arered,** raised; **wyduwe sone,** son of the widow. **1050 Tybourne,** Tiberias; **See,** Sea. **1052 broke,** brook; **forlonge,** furlongs. **1053 brede,** breadth. **1054 yede drie foot,** walked dry-footed. **1055 sonke,** sunk. **1066 diverseth,** differ; **of,** from. **1068 shryve,** confess.

noght to man. For they seyn that God bad noght a man shryve hem to another. For
1070 David seith thus: *Confiteor tibi domine in toto corde meo.* That is to say: "Lord, y-shryve
me to Thee in al my herte." And in another place, David seith thus: *Delictum meum
cognitum tibi feci.* That is to say: "My trespas Y have maked knowen to Thee." And
in another place, David seith: *Deus meus es tu et confitebor tibi.* That is to say: "Thou
art my God and Y shal shryve me to Thee." And in another place, David seith:
1075 *Quoniam cogitacio hominis confitebitur tibi.* That is to say: "Forwhy a mannes thoght
fol. 28v shal | be shreve to Thee."

And they conne wel the Byble and the Sauter book, but they alegge hit noght
in Latyn but in her owen langage. Therfor Seynt Austyn and Seynt Gregore seyth
thus: *Qui scelera sua cogitat et conversus fuerit, veniam sibi credat.* That is to say: "Who
1080 that knoweth his synne and is y-turnd, he may hope to heve forgefnesse." And
Seynt Gregore seith thus: *Dominus pocius mentem quam verba considerat.* That is to
say: "Our Lord taketh more kepe to thoght than to word." And Hillary seith thus:
Longorum temporum crimina in ictu oculi perient si corde fuerit nata contempcio. That is
to say: "Synnes that ben of long tyme shal pershe in twynclyng of an eye, if the
1085 despisyng of hem be y-bore of a mannes herte."

And thus they sey that men sholde shryve hem to God by His owen auctorité
alonliche. And this was the shrift in the ferste tyme, but Seint Peter and the
aposteles and popes which come sithe haveth ordeyned that men shul ben shryve
to prestes, men as hy beth. And for this skyle: for they sey that to a man that hath
1090 a sicknesse, men may geve no good medicyne but they knowe the kynde of the
sicknes, and so they sey that men may geve no convenable penaunce but they know
the synne.

And ther beth other men that beth called Georgenes, which Seynt George converted, and they doth more worship to seyntes of Hevene than other men doth.
1095 And they alle haven her crones y-shave, and the clerkes haveth roonde crones and
lewed men square crones. And they hold the lawe of Grekis. And other men beth
ther that beth called Cristen of girdyng, for they were gerdeles under. And ther
beth many that beth called Nideus, and everich of ham hath som article of our
feith, but everich varieth fram other. And of her variaunce hit were moche to telle,
1100 for ther beth many wonderfull kyndes among hem.

1075 Forwhy, Therefore. **1076 shreve,** confessed. **1077 conne,** know; **Sauter book,**
Psalter; **alegge,** read. **1078 Seynt Austyn,** St. Augustine; **Seynt Gregore,** St. Gregory. **1080
y-turnd,** turned away [from it]; **hope,** expect. **1082 Hillary,** St. Hilary. **1084 pershe,**
perish; **twynclyng,** the twinkling. **1085 despisyng,** rejection. **1086 shryve,** confess. **1087
alonliche,** alone; **ferste,** early. **1088 sithe,** after. **1089 hy,** they; **skyle,** reason. **1090 but,**
unless; **kynde,** nature. **1091 convenable,** appropriate. **1095 crones,** crowns of their heads;
clerkes, educated men; **roonde,** round. **1097 Cristen of girdyng,** belted Christians; **were,**
wear; **gerdeles,** belts. **1098 Nideus,** Nestorians. **1100 wonderfull,** amazing.

A WAY FRO GALILÉ TO JERUSALEM THORGH DAMAS.
CAPITULUM OCTAVUM.   [Chapter 8.]

fol. 29r | Now sithe Y have told of many maners of men that dwelleth in diverse contreis, now Y shal telle, who so wole turne fro the lond of Galilé, that Y spake of eer, he shal go another way thorgh Damas, that is a fair cité and full of good, and ther is plenté of marchaundise. And hit is 3 journeis fro the see and 5 journeis fro Jeru-

1105 salem. But they carieth her marchaundise uppon camels, mules, hors, and drom-edaries, and other maner of beistis. This cité founded Ebreus Damask, that was Abrahamis servant byfore that Josias was y-bore; and he hoped to be Abrahamis eyr, and therfor he called that cité after his name Damas. In that place Caym slow his brother Abel.

1110 And byside Damas is the Mount Syrie. In that cité beth many fucissions to save mennes bodies. And Seynt Poul was a fisician to hele hem bifore that he was converted, and sithe he was ficissian of mannes soules. And Seynt Luke was his disciple to lerne fusike, and many other men.

And fro Damas men cometh by a place that men calleth *Nostre Dame de*
1115 *Sarmany*, the which is cleped Gardmarch, that is 5 myle fro Damas. And hit is uppon a roch, and ther is a fair cherch, and ther dwelleth monkes and nonnes, the which beth Cristen. In that cherche byhynde the highe auter in the wall is a table of tre. In the which wall is an ymage of Our Lady was y-peynted, that many tymes turneth into flessh. But that ymage is now y-sey but a lytel, but evermore, thorgh
1120 the grace of God, that ymage droppeth oyle, as hit were oyle of olyve. And ther is a vestel of marbel that receyveth that oyle, and they hit geveth to pilgrimes, for hit helith hem of many sicknesses. And if hit be y-kept clene all the yer, at the yeres eynde, hit turneth into flessh and blood.

Bytwyne the cité of Sark and the cité of Raphane is a rever that is y-called
1125 Zabatoriye, for on the Saturday hit renneth faste and al the wyke els hit stondeth stille and renneth noght, other els lyte. And ther is another ryver that on the nyght
fol. 29v hit fresith | fast, and on the day no forst is sene.

And so men goth by a cité that is y-called Beruch, and ther men entreth into the see that shal go to Cipre. And they areveth at port de Sure of Tyri and then to
1130 Cipre. Other men goth fro the port to Tyri right and cometh noght to Cipre, and then he shal aryve at som haven in Grece, and so come to this contré by wayes of which Y have tolde byfore.

THE SHORTEST WAY TO JERUSALEM. CAPITULUM NONUM.   [Chapter 9.]

Now Y have told the way lengest and ferrist by which men may go to Baby-loyne, Mount Synay, and many other, and to the Lond of Promission. Now Y wole
1135 telle the ryght way and shortest to Jerusalem. For som men wole noght passe hit for the defaute of costages, and som men for the defaute of companye, and many

1102 **eer**, before. 1103 **Damas**, Damascus; **good**, goods. 1106 **founded Ebreus Damask**, Eleazar of Damascus founded. 1107 **hoped**, expected. 1108 **eyr**, heir; **Caym**, Cain. 1110 **Syrie**, Seir; **fucissions**, physicians. 1113 **fusike**, medicine. 1115 **cleped**, called. 1117–18 **table of tre**, wood panel. 1120 **oyle**, oil. 1121 **vestel**, vessel. 1127 **fresith**, freezes; **forst**, frost. 1128 **Beruch**, Beirut. 1129 **Cipre**, Cyprus; **Tyri**, Tyre. 1130 **right**, directly. 1135 **passe hit**, proceed that way (i.e., the longest way). 1136 **defaute**, lack; **costages**, money.

other causes. And therfore Y shal telle shortly how a man may go with litel costage and short tyme.

    A man that cometh fro the west, as Ingelond, he that goth thorgh France, Bur-
1140 goyne, Lumbardy, and so to Venyse other to Gene, other to som other haven of
that marches, and entreth into a shyppe and goth by see to the ile of Griff, and so
ryveth in Grece, other at Port Murrok, other Valone, other Duras, other at som
other haven, and goth to londe and resteth hym. And then goth agen to see and
ryveth in Cipre, and come noght into the ile of Rodes, and aryveth at Famagost,
1145 that is the chif haven of Cipre, other ellis at Lamaton. And then entre into the
shippe ageyn and passeth bysyde the haven of Tyre and come noght to londe. And
so he passeth by alle the havenes of the costes tylle he come to Jafphe, that is the
ney haven to Jerusalem, for hit is 27 myle bytwyne.

    And so fro Japhe men goth to the cité of Rames, and that is but a lytel thenne,
1150 and hit is a fair cité. And bysyde that cité is a cherch of Our Lady, wher Our Lord
shewed Hym to her in thre licknes, the which bytockneth the Trinité. And ther neye
is a cherch of George, wher his hed was y-smyte of. And then men goth to the castel
fol. 30r of Chynay and then to the Mount Joye. And fro | thenne, pylgrimes may ferst se to
Jerusalem, and then to the Mount Madyn and then forth the way to Jerusalem.

ANOTHER WAY TO JERUSALEM. CAPITULUM DECIMUM.   [Chapter 10.]

1155 For as moche as meny men mowe noght suffre the savour of the see but is lever
to go by londe, thow hit be more peyne, a man shal go to oon of thes havenes of
Lombardy, as Venyse other another. And he passe to Grece, other to Port Marrok
other another, and he shal go to Constantynople. And then he shal passe the water
that is called the Bras of Seynt Jorge, and that is an arme of the see. And fro thenne
1160 he shal go forth to Pylverall, and so to the castel of Synople, and so to Capados,
which is a greet contré, and ther beth many gret hilles. And he shal go thorgh
Torkye and to the cité of Nyke, the which they wonne fro the emperour of Constantynople. And hit is a fair cité and wel y-walled. And ther is a ryver that men callen
the Lay. And ther men goth by the alpes of Morraunt, and by the valeys of Molbryn-
1165 or, and by valeys of Ernax and so to Aunteoch the Betre, that sitteth on the ryght
honde. Ther aboute beth many goode hilles and many fair wodes and wilde beestes.

    And he that wole go another way, he shal go by the playnes of Romayn,
costande by the Romayn See. On that coost is a fayr castel, that men called
Florach. And when a man is out of these hilles, he passeth thorgh Marrock and
1170 Artoys, wher is a greet brygge over the rever of Ferne, that men callen Fasser.

    And bysyde the cité of Damas is a ryver that men callen Albane. At the passage
of this ryver, Seynt Eustace lost his two sones when he hadde lost his wyff. And hit
goth thorgh the playn of Archades and so to the Reed See. And som men goth to
the cité of Phenne, and so to the cité of Ferne. And thenne to Aunteoch, and hit
1175 is a fair cité and well y-walled. For hit is two myle longe at eche pylour. And ther

---

1140 **Gene**, Genoa. 1141 **marches**, region. 1142 **ryveth**, arrives. 1147 **costes**, coasts;
Jafphe, Jaffa. 1151 **licknes**, likenesses. 1152 **George**, St. George. 1155 **mowe**, may;
savour, smell; **is lever**, prefer. 1159 **Bras of Seynt Jorge**, Arm of St. George. 1162
Torkye, Turkey; **Nyke**, Nicea. 1165 **Aunteoch**, Antioch. 1167 **Romayn**, Romany. 1168
costande, sailing along the coast. 1170 **brygge**, bridge. 1175 **pylour**, i.e., city boundary.

fol. 30v   is a brygge, and at ech | pyler of the brygge is a fair tour. This cité is the beste that
            is in the kyngdome of Surri.

                 Fro Aunteoch men shal go to the cité of Lacuth, and so to the cité of Gelboe,
            and so to Turtouse. And therby is the londe of Chaumbre, and ther is a strong
1180   castel that is y-called Maubek. And fro Turtouse men goth to Triple on the see, and
            so to Vacres. And ther beth two weyes to Jerusalem. On the lyft syde men goth thus
            to Damas by Flom Jordan. And on the ryght syde men goth thorgh the lond of
            Flagme, and so to the cité Cayphas, of which Cayphas was lord, and som men callen
            hit the castel of Pyllerynes. And fro thens is 4 dayes jorneis to Jerusalem, for to go
1185   thorgh Sesarye Philippum and Japhe and Rames and Emaux, and so to Jerusalem.

A Wey All by Lond to Jerusalem. Capitulum undecimum.   [Chapter 11.]

                 Now have Y tolde yow som weyes by londe and watres how men may go to Jeru-
            salem. And thogh hit be so that ther beth many other weyes that men may go by,
            after the contreis that men cometh fro, and at the laste they cometh to oon eynde.
            And yit ther is a wey all by londe to Jerusalem, and pass no see out of France other
1190   Flandres. But that wey is ful longe and perelous of gret travel, and therfore men
            goth by that wey ful fewe. And he that wole go by that wey, he shal go thorgh Al-
            mayne, Spruse, and so to Tartaryse.

                 This Tartarie is y-holde of the gret Cane, of wham Y shal speke afterward, for
            thider last his lordship, and the lord of Tartarye payeth tribute to hym. This is a ful
1195   wicked lond, and a ful sondy londe, and lytel fruyt-beryng therynne. For ther grow-
            eth but lytel corne, ne benes, ne wyne, ne pesyn, but bestes beth ther gret plenté.
            And therfor they etith but flessh withoute brede, and they soupeth the broth, and
            they drynketh mylk of all maner bestes. And thei etyth cattes, ratons, and meese,
            and all maner wylde bestes. And they haveth litel wode, for they make her mete
fol. 31r   with hors mocke | and of other bestes y-dryed. Princes and other lordes etith but
1201   ones upon a day and ryght litel. And they beth foul peple and of yvel kynde.

                 In somer ther beth many stormes and thondres that sleith moch folk and
            bestes, and hit cometh sodeynly. Ther is gret colde and as sodeynly gret hete. The
            prince that governeth that lond is called Raco, and he dwelleth at the cité of Orda.
1205   And forsothe ther wole no good man dwelle, for hit is good to sowe neteles and
            other wedys, but other good non, as Y have herd say — for Y was never ther.

                 But Y was in londes that marcheth therto, as the londe of Rossye, Nyvelond, the
            kyngdome of Crokowe, Lettow, and the kyngdom of Grasten, and many other
            places. But Y went never that way to Jerusalem, for Y have understonde that men
1210   may noght go wel that way but in wynter, for water and marys that beth ther, whiche
            men may noght passe, but yf they have forst right hard and that hit be snow above.
            For were noght the snow, ther myght no man go.

1180 Triple, Tripoli.   **1185 Sesarye Philippum**, Cesarea Philippi. **1190 perelous**,
dangerous; **travel**, difficulty.   **1191–92 Almayne**, Germany.   **1192 Spruse**, Prussia;
Tartaryse, Tartary. **1193 y-holde of**, controlled by; **Cane**, Khan. **1194 last**, extends. **1195
sondy**, sandy. **1196 corne**, wheat; **pesyn**, peas. **1197 soupeth**, sup. **1198 ratons**, rats;
meese, mice. **1199 make**, cook. **1200 mocke**, dung. **1205 neteles**, nettles. **1207 Rossye**,
Russia. **1208 Lettow**, Lithuania. **1210 marys**, marshes. **1211 but yf**, unless; **forst**, frost.

And ye shal understonde that a man shal go thre journeis fro Pruys to passe this way, tyl he come to the lond of Sarasyns that men dwelleth ynne. And thow hit
1215   be so that Cristen men passe eche yer ther forth, they caryeth with hem vitayles, for they shal fynde noon there, but a maner of thyng that is y-called skleys. And they make her cariage uppon dreys. And as longe as her vitayles lasteth, they mowe dwelle ther, but no lenger. But when the spyes of the contré seith that Cristen men cometh, they renneth to toune and crieth loude, "*Kerra, Kerra!*" And also sone as
1220   they kepith hem, they do hem vylonye.

And ye shal understonde that hit is hatter ther than here, and also colder. And therfor every man hath a styve in his hous, and therynne he eetyth and drynketh and doth what hym lyketh. For that londe is at the north syde of the worlde, which comenly is coldest. The sonne cometh noght ther, ne shyneth but litel. And that
fol. 31v   lond in som place is so cold that ther may no man dwelle ther. | And at the south
1226   syde of the worlde, in som place hit is so hoot that ther may no man dwelle, for the sonne geveth so gret hete in the contrees.

TRUTHE OF SARASYNS. CAPITULUM DUODECIMUM.   [Chapter 12.]

For as moch as Y tolde of Sarasyns and of her londes, yf ye wole Y shal yow telle a party of her lawes and of her faith, as her book telleth, which is called *Akkaron*. And
1230   som men calleth hit the book *Mesap*, and som *Arne*, in dyverse maner of langage. The whiche book Macamete gaf to hem, in which he wrote, among other thynges, as Y have seen and radde many tymes, and hit saith that a man that is good shal go to Paradys, and a man that is wycked shal go to Helle — and that byleveth all the Sarasyns. And if a man aske what thyng Paradys is, they speke and seyn hit is a place
1235   ful of delytes, wher a man shal fynde all maner of fruytes of the yer, and ryvers rennyng with mylk and hony and wyne and fressh water. And they shal have ther fair houses, as they have deserved. And thilke houses beth y-maked of precious stones, goolde, and selver. And ech man shal have 10 wyves, all maydens, and he shal lygge by hem, and they shal ever be maydens, and so they byleveth.
1240   And they spekyth ofte of the Virgyne Marye and of the Incarnacioun that Mary was lerid of an angel. And that Gabriel seyde to her that she was chose of alle other fro the bygynnynge of the world, and that witnesseth her book *Ackaron*, and that Gabriel tolde to her of the Incarnacion of Jhesu Crist, and that she conceyved and bare a child and was mayde afterward. And they seyde that Jhesu Crist spake as
1245   sone as He was bore, and that He was a very prophete in word, in dede: meke and ryghtwys to all men, and withoute vice.

And they sey when the angel told her of the Incarnacion, that she hadde gret drede, for she was yonge. And ther was oon in that contré that delid with sorceryes
fol. 32r   that was called Tabina, which with enchauntement coude make hymself lyke to | an
1250   angel, and he lay ofte tymes with maydens. And therfore Mari was aferde of the angel, for she wende hit had y-be Tabina. And she conjured the angel and bade

1213 Pruys, Prussia. **1215 vitayles**, food. **1217 cariage**, carriages; **dreys**, sleds; **mowe**, may. **1220 kepith**, capture; **vylonye**, harm. **1221 hatter**, hotter. **1222 styve**, heated room. **1229 party**, part; *Akkaron*, the Koran. **1231 Macamete**, Mohammed. **1236 ther**, i.e., in Paradise. **1241 lerid of**, taught by. **1246 ryghtwys**, righteous. **1248 delid**, dealt; **sorceryes**, witchcraft. **1251 wende**, thought.

hym say if he were Tabina. And the angel bade her that she sholde have no drede, for he was very messager of God.

And also her book seith that she hadde child under a palme tre, and therfore
1255   she was ashamed, and gradde, and seyde that she wolde be dede. And so anoon that childe spak and seyde: *Ne timeas Maria*. That is to say: "Have no drede, Marie." And in many other places speketh her book *Ackaron* that Jhesu Crist spak also sone as He was born. And that book telleth that Jhesu Crist was God Almyghty to be en-sample to all men, and that God shal deme all men, the goode to Hevene and the
1260   wicked to Helle. And that Jhesu Crist was the beste prophete that ever was, and that He was verry prophete, which gaf sight to the blynde and heled mesalles, and reysed dede men, and yede all quyke to Hevene. And if they may fynde a book of gospelles, namely with *Missus est angelus Gabriel*, they do hit gret worship; and fast-eth oon monthe in that yer, and they eten but on the nyght, and then they kepeth
1265   hem fro her wyves. But they that beth sike, they beth noght constrayned to that fast.

And that book speketh of Jewes and seith that they beth wickid folke, for they wole noght byleve that Jhesu Crist is God. And they seith that Jewes lieth on Our Lady and on her Sone Jhesu, seynge that they dede Hym noght on the Cros.

And for Sarasyns byleveth so neygh our fay, they beth lightly converted when
1270   men telle hem the lawe of Crist. And they seth they wyteth well by her prophecies that the lawe of Machamete shal be destrued and faile as doth the lawe of Jewes, and that Cristen lawe shal laste unto the worldes eynde. And if a man aske wher-ynne thei byleve, they sey thus: how thei byleve in God, maker of Hevene and of
fol. 32v   erthe and of all other thynges, and withoute Hym is nothyng y-do, and in the | Day
1275   of Dome, when ech man shal be demed after his deservyng, and that al thyng is sooth that Crist seyde by the mouth of the prophetes.

Also Macamete bade in his *Ackaron* that ech man shold have 2 wyves, other 3, other 4, but now they have 9, and as meny lemmans as they like. And if any of her wyves do amys to her hosebondes, he may put her out of his hous and take
1280   another, but hym byhoveth to geve her som of his godes.

Also when men spekith of the Fader, Sone, and Holy Gost, they sey tho beth 3 persons and noght oo God, for her *Ackaron* spekith noght therof, for he toucheth noght of the Trinité. And they sey that God spake, and elles He was dombe; and that He hath a gost, other elles He were noght on lyve. And they sey that Moyses
1285   and Abraham were wel with God, for they speke with Hym. And they say also that Macamete was ryght messager of God. And they have many good articles of our fay, and they knowe moche of Holy Wrytte. For tho that beth understondyng of Scripture and of prophecies, all they hem wryteth in her owen langage. But they hit understonde noght, but after the lettre and noght gostly. And therfore Seynt
1290   Poul seith thus: *Littera occidit, spiritus autem vivificat*. That is to say: "The lettre sleeth and the gost maketh quyke."

1254 her, their (i.e., the Saracens'). **1255 gradde**, wept. **1259 deme**, judge. **1261 mesalles**, lepers. **1262 quyke**, alive. **1265 constrayned**, compelled. **1267 on**, about. **1269 fay**, faith; **lightly**, easily. **1270 wyteth**, know. **1275 Dome**, Judgment; **demed**, judged. **1277 *Ackaron***, Koran. **1278 lemmans**, lovers. **1280 hym byhoveth**, it is necessary for him; **godes**, goods. **1282 oo**, one. **1284 gost**, spirit; **on lyve**, alive. **1287 fay**, faith; **tho**, those. **1289 after the lettre**, literally; **gostly**, spiritually. **1291 maketh quyke**, gives life.

And the Sarasens seith that Jewes beth wicked, for they kepe noght her lawe that Moyses toke hem; also Cristen men beth wicked peple, for they kepe noght the 10 Commaundementz that Jhesu Crist sende to hem.

1295   And therfore Y shal telle yow a tale. Y was with the soudan in his chambre uppon a day, and he lete voyde the chambre of all maner men, for he seide that he wolde speke with me in counseil. And he asked of me how Cristen men hem governed in her contré.

And Y seyde, "Ryght well, thanked be God."

1300   And he seyde, "Sikerly, nay, for youre prestes maketh no force of Godis servise. For they sholde geve ensaumple to men to do well, and they gyve wickid ensaumple.

fol. 33r   And when | youre peple sholde go to holy cherche on the holy day to serve God, they go to taverne and to marchaundyse, and lyve in glotonye and covetyse day and nyght, and ete and drynke as bestes that wyte noght when they have ynow.

1305   Also Cristen men," he seyde, "enforseth hem to fighte togedres and ech to bygyle other. Also," he seyde, "they beth so prout that they wyte noght what thei may werth: now longe clothes, now short clothes, now strait clothes, now wyde clothes.

"And they sholde be symple," he seyde, "and meke and trywe, and do almes dede as Jhesu dyde, in wham they byleveth. And they beth so covetous," he seyde,

1310   "that for a lytel sylver, they wole selle wiff and childe and sostre. And a man take another mannes wyf, and no man holdeth wel his feith to other. And for her owen synnes," he seyde, "hath Cristen men lost al the lond the which that we holdeth, and for youre synnes hath your God gyve these londes to us, and noght thorgh oure streyngthe. For we wyte well," he seyde, "when ye serveth well your God, that

1315   He wole helpe yow, so that no man shal do ageyn yow. And ye wyte well by youre prophecies that Cristen men shal wynne agen thes londes, when they serveth wel her God. But while they lyven so yvel as they doon, we have no drede of hem, for her God wole noght help hem."

And then Y asked of hym how he wiste the state of Cristen men so well. And he

1320   seyde he knew hit ful well, bothe of comens and of lordes by his messagers, whiche he sende thorgh all londes, as they were marchauntes with precious stones and other marchaundises, to knowe the maner of every lond. And thenne he leet calle agen all the lordes into his chambre. And thenne he shewed to me foure that were gret lordes in that contré, the which devised my contré and other contreis of

1325   Cristendom, as they had be men of that same contré. And they spak Frenssh ryght wel and the soudan also. And than had Y gret mervayll of that sclaundre of Cristen men. For they that sholde be turned by our good techyng and ensample uppon Cristen feithe, be withdrawe thorgh oure yvel ensample of lyvenge. And therfore

fol. 33v | hit is no wonder that they callen us wicked men. But the Sarasyns beth trywe, for

1330   they kepe truly the comaundementz of her *Ackaron*.

And ye shal understonde that Machamete was y-bore in Arabye, and he was ferst a poore man and kepid hors and ran after marchauntz. And so he cam into

Egipt with marchauntz, and Egipt was that tyme Cristen. And ther was a chapel neygh Arabye and ther was an heremyte. And when he com to the chapel that was
1335 but a litell hous and lowe, the entré bygan to be as gret as a gate of a paleys. And that was the ferst mervayle that Machamete byfell in his youthe.

Then after bygan Machamete to be ryche and wys, and he was a gret asterlaberer. And sithe he was keper of the lond of the prins Coradan, and he governed hit ful wisly in soch maner that when the prins was dede, he weddid the lady, which
1340 men called Quardrich. And Machamete hadde ful ofte the fallyng yvell, wherfore the lady was wroth that she hadde y-take hym to her lord. But he makyde her to understonde that ech tyme that he fyll, so the angel Gabriel spak to hym and for the gret bryghtnes of hym he fyll adoun.

This Machamete regned in Arabye the yer of Our Lord 600 and 20 yer. And
1345 he was of the kynde of Ysmael, that was Abrahamis sone, which that he gat of Agar his chamberer. And therfor som Sarasyns beth called Ysmaelites, and som Agariens of Agar. And other beth called properly Sarasyns of Sara, and som beth called Moabites, and som beth called Amonites after two sones of Loth.

And so Machamete loved well a good man, an hermyte, that dwelled in
1350 wildernysse a myle fro the mount of Synay in the way as men goth fro Arabye to Galdé and Indee, a dayes journe fro the see wher marchauntes of Venyse cometh. And Machamete wende so ofte to that hermyte that all his men were wroth with hym. For he herde gladly that heremite preche, and he leet all his men walke that nyght. And his men thoughte that they wold that this heremyte wer dede. So hit
fol. 34r byfell upon a nyght that Machamete was ful dronke | of good wyne, and he fyl on
1356 slepe. And his men toke his owne swerde out of his shethe, whiles that he slepe, and slow the heremyte. And then they put up his swerd al blody. And on the morwe, when he fond the heremyte dede, he was ful wroth and wold have y-do his men to deth. But they seyde, all with oon assent, that he hymself slow hym when
1360 he was dronke, and they shewed hym his swerd al blody. And then he leved hem that they seyde soth.

And then he cursed wyn and all tho that drynketh wyn. But som drynketh hit prevely; and if he drynke hit openly, he shal be repreved. But they drynk good beverage and swet and noryshynge, which is makid of calamele, of that is sugre y-
1365 maked. Also hit falleth somtyme that Cristen men bycometh Sarasyns, other for povert other som other skyll. And therfore Larchesleven, that is receyvour of Cristen men, when he receyveth hem, he seith thus: *Ra elles ella Machamete reozes alla.* That is to say: "Ther is no God but on, and Machamete his messager."

And sith Y have told yow a party of her lawe and her customes, now shal Y say
1370 of her lettres, which Y have, with her names and her maner of figuris, what they beth: almei, bethath, chathi, ephoti, delphoy, fothi, garaphi, hochym, iocchi,

---

1334 he, i.e., Mohammed. **1335 entré**, entrance. **1336 Machamete byfell**, happened to Mohammed. **1337–38 asterlaberer**, user of an astrolabe. **1338 prins**, prince. **1340 fallyng yvell**, epilepsy. **1341 wroth**, angry. **1345 kynde**, tribe; **Agar**, Hagar. **1346 chamberer**, servant. **1350 Synay**, Sinai. **1352 wende**, went. **1353 leet all his men walke**, made all his men stay awake. **1357 put up**, put away. **1360 leved**, believed. **1361 soth**, the truth. **1363 prevely**, privately. **1364 calamele**, sugarcane. **1365 falleth**, happens. **1366 skyll**, reason; **Larchesleven**, a Saracen religious leader. **1368 on**, one.

kaůthi, loᵵhym, mᵛlach, nᵃhabot, oᴘthi, poᵲir, zȯth, ruᵜhelat, sȧlachi, tᵃthimus, uᴵthon, axᵍros, yᵲthoy, azȯtchi, iotiᵽyn, zechetus. Thes beth the letters, now shal Y telle the figures. . .

1375   And they have in her langage mo lettres than we have, for as moche as they speketh in her throtes. And we have in our langage two lettres in Englyssh mo than they have in her ABC, that is to wyte þ and ȝ, that men calleth thorn and yogh.

DYVERSETEIS OF PEPLE AND OF CONTREIS.
CAPITULUM TERCIUMDECIMUM.   [Chapter 13.]

And sithen Y have devysed byfor the Holy Londe and contrees ther aboute, and
fol. 34v   many weyes and to the Mount Synay, | and to Babyloyne, and other places, now wole
1380   Y telle of yles and dyverse peple and bestes. For ther beth many diverse peple and bestes and contrees, which beth departed by the foure flodes that cometh out of Paradys Terrestre.

For Mesopotanye and the kyngdom of Caldé and Arabye beth bytwyne the flodes of Tygre and Eufrates. And also the kyngdom of Mody and of Perce beth
1385   bytwyne the flode of Tygre and Nyle. The kyngdome of Syrri and Palastyn and Fimes beth bytwyne Eufrates and the See Metterane, and hit is of leyngthe fro Marrok to the see of Spayne and into the Greet See, and so lasteth hit byyonde Constantynople, 43 myle of Lombardye into the Gret See, Occian.

And ye shal understande that in the contré beth many iles and londes, of which
1390   hit were moche to telle all. But som Y shal speke. For he that wole go to Tartarye, other Perce, other Caldee, other Inde, he shal entre into the see at Gene, other Venyse, other at another havene by that coste, and so passe the see and aryve at Trapasond, that is a good cité that was somtyme called *Le Port de Pounce*. And ther is the kyng of Percens and Medoyns and also of many other marches.

1395   In this cité lith Attonas, that was bysshop of Elisaundre that makide the psalme *Quicumque vult*. This man was a gret doctour and mayster of dyvinité, for he spak so deep in divinité and of the Godhede, he was accused to the pope of Rome that he was an herityk — that was his heresie, for that was his feith. And when the pope saw that, he seyde that therynne was all our feith. He leit delyver hym anoon out
1400   of prison. And the pope commaunded that psalme to be seyd every day at prime and helde Atthonas a good Cristen man. But he wolde never go to his bysshoprych agen, for they accused hym of heresye.

Trapasond was somtyme y-holde of the emperour of Constantynople, but a gret
fol. 35r   man that he send to kepe hit ageyn the Turkes held hit hymself and | called hym
1405   emperour of Trapasond.

And fro then men goth to Litel Admonye. In that contré is an olde castel that is uppon a roch that is y-called the castel of Sperver. And ther men fyndeth an

---

1378 **sithen**, since. 1380 **yles**, places. 1381 **flodes**, rivers. 1382 **Paradys Terrestre**, the Earthly Paradise. 1383 **Mesopotanye**, Mesopotamia; **Caldé**, Chaldea. 1384 **Tygre**, Tigris; **Mody**, Media; **Perce**, Persia. 1385 **Syrri**, Syria; **Palastyn**, Palestine. 1386 **Fimes**, Phoenicia; **See Metterane**, Mediterranean Sea. 1387 **Marrok**, Morocco; **Greet See**, Black Sea; **byyonde**, beyond. 1388 **myle of Lombardye**, Lombard miles. 1391 **Gene**, Genoa. 1392 **coste**, coast. 1393 **Trapasond**, Trebizond. 1394 **marches**, regions. 1395 **Attonas**, Athanasius; **Elisaundre**, Alexandria.

hauke on a perche sittyng right wel y-maked, and a fair lady of fayre kepeth that
hauke. And he that wole wake this hauke 7 dayes and 7 nyght (and som seith 3
1410   dayes and 3 nyght) alone withoute companye and withoute slepe, this fayre lady
shal come to hym at 7 dayes (other the 3 dayes) eynde, and she wole graunte hym
the ferst thyng that he wole aske of worldly thyng. For hit hath y-be ofte asayed
and y-preved.

And somtyme hit fill that a kyng of Ermonye, that was a doughty man, waked
1415   on a tyme this hauke. And at the 7 dayes ende, the lady com to hym and bade aske,
for he hadde wel y-do his dever. And the kyng sayde that he was a gret lorde and
in good pees and rych ynow, so that he wolde aske nothyng but the lady, to have
his will of her. And she seyde to hym that he was a fole, for he wist noght what he
askyd, for she was noght worldly. And the kyng seyde he wolde have nothyng elles.
1420   And she seyde to hym, "Siththen that ye wole aske nothyng elles," she wolde
graunte hym som other thyng and noght that.

And so she sayde thus: "Sire kyng, to thee, and to all other that cometh after
thee, ye shul have werre withoute pees unto the nynthe degré, and ye shal be in
subjeccioun of youre enemyes, and ye shal have gret nede to good and to catell.
1425   For ye aske thyng out of reson, for ye may have me noght, for Y am a spyritte."
And fro that tyme all kynges of Ermonye have y-be in werre and needfull and
under tribute of Sarasyns.

Also a pore man somtyme wold wake that hauke, and he askid of the lady that
he myght be ryche and happy in catell and marchaundyse. And the lady graunted
1430   hym, but she seyde that he askyd his undoyng, for greet pruyde that he shold have
therof. But he that shal wake hath gret nede to kepe hym fro slep, for if he slepeth,
fol. 35v   he | is lost. But this is noght the right way but for that mervayll.

And fra Trapasond men goth to the Gret Ermonye, to a cité that men calle
Artyron. And so to a hille that is y-called Sabissatel, and ther is another hille that
1435   men calle Airach, but the Jewes calle hit Thane, and ther resteth Archa Noe, and
yit hit is uppon that hille. And a man may see hit in fair wether and cler. And that
hille is 7 myle heygh. And som men seyth that they have be ther and put her
fyngres in the hole wher the devel went out when Noe seyde *Benedicité*. But a man
may noght wel go theder uppon that hille for snow that lith alway uppon that hille
1440   wynter and somer. For ther cometh never man sithe Noe was, but a monk that
thorgh the grace of God went thider and broughte a plancke, that is yit at the
abbey at the hille foot. For he hadde gret desyre to go uppon that hille, and he
aforsed hym therto. And when he was at the thrydde part of the hylle upward, he
was so wery he myght no ferther, and restyd hym ther and slepte. And when he
1445   woke he was doun at the hille foot. And thenne he prayde to God devoutly that He
wolde suffre hym go uppe. And an angel seyde to hym that he sholde go uppe, and

1408 fayre, faerie (i.e., the supernatural world). **1409 wake**, keep awake. **1412 asayed**,
tested. **1415 bade aske**, told him to ask. **1416 dever**, task. **1418 fole**, fool. **1419 noght
worldly**, not of this world. **1423–24 in subjeccioun of**, ruled by. **1424 good**, goods. **1425
out of reson**, unreasonable. **1426 needfull**, poor. **1428 wake**, keep awake. **1435 Archa
Noe**, Noah's Ark. **1436 yit**, still. **1439 theder**, thither. **1441 plancke**, plank [from the
Ark]. **1443 aforsed hym**, forced himself; **at the thrydde part of the hylle upward**, a third
of the way up the hill.

so he dide and broughte the planke. And suche com never man ther, and therfore they that seith that they have y-be ther, they gabbe.

1450   Fro thenne men goth to a cité that men calleth Tauzyre, and that is a fayr cité and a good. And bysyde that cité is an hille of salt, and therof ech man taketh what he wol. And ther dwelleth many Cristen men under tribute of Sarasyns. Fro thenne men goth to many tounes, citeis, and castelles many journeys toward Ynde, and cometh to a cité that is y-called Cassache. And ther mette thre kynges togedre and went to make present to Our Lord. And fro that cité men goth to a cité that is y-

1455 called Cardabago. And paynemys saith that Cristen men may noght dwelle ther, but they deye sone and they wyte noght why.

    And fro thenne men goth thorgh many contreis, citeis, and tounes, of which hit

fol. 36r were moch to telle, | tyl they come to a cité that is called Carnaa, that was woned to be so gret that the walles aboute were of 25 myle. And the walles beth y-sene yit,

1460 but hit is noght inhabited with men. And ther eyndeth the londe of the emperure of Peryse. On the ryght syde of that cité of Carnaa men entreth into the lond of Job, which is a good londe and a plenteuous.

    In this lond is the cité of Thomar. Job was a paynym, and he was Coffraces sone, and he held that lond as prince therof. And he was so ryche that he knew noght the

1465 hundred part of his good. And sithe he was so pore that he hadde no good but the grace of God. And afterward God makyd hym so ryche than he ever was byfore. And afterward he was kyng of Ydoyne and of Ysau. And thenne he was called Jobab and lyved kyng an 180 yer, and Job when he deyde was of elde 248 yer. And ther beth hilles wher men fyndeth manna, that is y-called bred of angelys that is a white

1470 thyng, ryght swete and more swetter than sugre other hony. And hit cometh of the dewe of hevene and falleth on the herbes and congelith and wexeth white.

    This lond of Job marcheth to the lond of Caldee, that is a gret lond and full of peple. And wymmen beth ther ryght lothlych and yvel y-clothed. And they go barfoot with an yvel cote, large and wyde and short to the kneys, and long slevys

1475 to the foot. And they have gret here and hangeth long aboute her sholdres.

    And then is a lond of Amasoyn. In that lond dwelleth no man but all wymmen, as men sayn, for they wole have no lordship of no man. For somtyme was a kyng in that lond, and men dwellid ther as men dede in other contreis. And he hadde a wyff. And hit byfell that the kyng made werre with hem of Zechie, and he was y-

1480 called Solopenuce, and he was slayn in batayll and all the good blood of his lond. And the quene, when she herde that and other ladyes also, that the kyng and her lordes wer slayn, they gadred hem togedre and slow all the other men that were

fol. 36v left at hom in the lond, and syth that tyme | dwelled no man ther.

    And when they wole have company of men, they sendeth for hem into another

1485 contré that is neygh to her lond. And then men cometh and beth ther 7 other 8 dayes, other also long as the wymmen liketh, and then they go agen. And if they have knave chyldren, they sendeth hem to her fadres when they con eete, go, and speke. And if they have mayde cheldryn, they kepe hem wel. And tho that beth of

---

1447 **suche**, i.e., otherwise. **1448 gabbe**, lie. **1453 thre kynges**, i.e., the Wise Men. **1454 to make present**, to give gifts. **1462 plenteuous**, abundant. **1465 sithe**, after. **1472 marcheth**, borders on. **1473 lothlych**, loathly. **1475 gret here**, big hair. **1476 Amasoyn**, Amazonia. **1480 good blood**, highborn men. **1487 knave**, male; **con**, are able to.

1490

1495

1500

1505

1510
fol. 37r

1515

1520

1525

gentil blood, they brenne the left pappe awey, for beryng of a shyld. And if they be of lower blood, they brenne the ryght pappe, for shetyng with a bowe. For the wymmen of that lond beth all good werryours and beth ofte y-souded with other lordes. And the quene governeth that lond well, for that lond is all closed with water.

Byside Amasoyne is a good lond and profetable that is y-called Turmaget. And for the greet profyte therof, Kyng Alysaundre let make ther a cité, that is y-called Alysaundre.

And in the other syde of Caldee, toward the south, is Ethiope, a gret lond. In this lond in the south syde the peple is ryght black. In that side is a welle, that on the day the water is so colde that no man may drynk hit, and on the nyght hit is so hoot that no man may suffre hit. In this lond revers and waters beth all trobel and somdel salt for the gret heet.

In Ethiope beth soch peple that han but oon foot, and they goo so faste that hit is mervayl. And that foot is so large that hit maketh shade and covert to his body for the sonne. In that lond is the cité of Saba, of which oon of the thre kynges was that soughte Our Lord. He was kyng ther.

Fro Ethiop men goth to Ynde, and hit is y-called Ynde the Gretter, and hit is departed in thre parties, that is to say, Ynde the Moore, that is a full hot londe. And Ynde the Lasse that is a tempered londe. And the thridde party is toward the north, and ther hit is aryght colde. So that for gret forst the water wexith into cristal, and uppon that wexeth the good dyamaunde, that is a trobul colour. And that dyamaunde is so hard that no man may breke hym. Other diamaundes men fyndeth in Arabye, that beth noght so goode, that beth | more nessh. And some beth in Cipre, and somme beth in Macydoyn, but the beste beth in Ynde. And somme beth y-founde in a mas, ther men fyndeth goolde fro the myne, and tho beth as hard as eny in Ynde.

Also men fyndeth good dyamaundes uppon the roche of adamaundes in the see, as hit were hasel notes. And tho beth all square and poynted of her owen kynde, and they groweth togodres, the maule and the femaule. And they beth noryshed with the dewe of hevene, and they engendreth comunely and bryngeth forth other smale dyamaundes, that multeplieth and groweth all yeres. And Y have many tymes asayd that if a man kepe hem with a lytel of the roch, which he groweth uppon, and wete hym with Mayis dewe, they shal growe ech yer, and the smale shal wexe greet. And a man shal bere a dyamaunde uppon his lyft syde, and thenne hit is more vertu than elles, for the streyngthe of her growyng is toward the north, and that is the lift syde of the worlde.

And if ye wole knowe the vertu of the dyamaund, Y shal telle yow, as men of that contré sayn. To hym that berith this dyamaund aboute hym, hit geveth hym

---

1489 pappe, breast; **for beryng of a shyld**, to carry a shield. **1490 shetyng**, shooting. **1491 werryours**, warriors; **y-souded**, united. **1492 closed**, enclosed. **1494 profyte**, good. **1494 Kyng Alysaundre**, Alexander the Great. **1499 trobel**, turgid. **1500 somdel salt**, somewhat salty. **1502 mervayl**, a marvel; **covert**, covering. **1506 parties**, parts. **1507 tempered**, temperate. **1508 forst**, frost. **1509 dyamaunde**, diamond; **trobul**, murky. **1511 nessh**, soft. **1512 Cipre**, Cyprus; **Macydoyn**, Macedonia. **1513 mas**, mass; **myne**, mine. **1515 adamaundes**, lodestones. **1516 hasel notes**, hazelnuts. **1517 maule**, male; **femaule**, female. **1520 asayd**, tested. **1523 vertu**, power. **1524 lift**, left.

hardynesse, hit kepith the lymes of his body hole. And hit gyveth victorye of his enemyes, and a mannes cause be trywe. Hit saveth a mannes wytte. Hit kepith a man fro stryff, fro ryot, fro yvell dremes, and fro soceryes and enchauntementz.

1530   Also none wylde bestes shal greve hym, ne assayle hym.

Also the dyamaund shal be geve frely, withoute coveytyng other beggyng, and then hit is of more vertu. Hit helith hym that is lunatyk and hym that is y-traveyled with a devell, of venym and of poyson, if a man be brought in presens of the dyamaund. And if eny other stoon be y-brought in presens of the dyamaund, anoon

1535   hit wexith moist and bygynneth to swete.

And also a man may asay hym wel in this maner. Tak a stoon that is y-cleped adamaund, that is the shipmanis stone, that draweth the nedel to hym. And men ley the dyamaund uppon the adamaund, and then ley a nedle byfore the ada-

fol. 37v   maund, and if the dyamaund | be good and vertuous, the adamant may noght drawe
1540   the nedle to hym whiles the dyamaunt lith ther. And this is the preve that they doth byyonde see. But hit falleth ofte that the good dyamant losith his vertu many tymes, and they conne make his vertu com agen.

Ther is a water that renneth thorgh the lond that men calleth Ynde; in that water men fyndeth elys of 20 foot long. In Ynde beth mo than 5 mille yles that men

1545   dwelleth ynne. And in ech of tho beth many citeis and moch peple, for men of Ynde beth of condicioun that they passeth noght out of her lond comonlych. For they dwelleth under a planete that men clepith Saturne, and that planete maketh his torn by the 12 signes in a monthe. And for Saturne is of so late steryng, therfore men that dwelleth under hym and that clymate haveth no good wyll to mech

1550   styryng aboute. And in our contré is all the contrarye, for we beth in a clymate that is of the mone and of leyght styryng, and that is the planete of way. And therfore hit gyveth us wyll to be moch steryng and to go into diverse contreis of the worlde, for hit passeth aboute the worlde more leyghtlych than another planete.

Also thorgh Ynde men goth to the Gret See, that is y-called Oxean, and then

1555   they fynde ther the yle of Ermes, whider marchauntz of Venyse, and of Gene, and of partyes of Cristendom cometh to bygge marchaundise. And hit is so hoot ther that mennys ballockys hongeth doun to her shankes. And men of that contré byndeth hem full straytly uppe, and they do hem anoynte with oynementz y-maked therfore, other elles myght they noght lyve in that lond.

1560   And other men and wymmen lyen al naked in ryvers and wateris fro undren of the day tyl hit be passed noon. And they lye all in water but her face, for gret hete that is ther. In this yle beth shippes withoute nayles of yre other bondes of yre, for the roch of the adamaund that beth in that see wolde drawe the shippes to hem.

1527 **hole**, whole. **1528 and**, if. **1532 y-traveyled**, oppressed. **1535 swete**, sweat. **1537 adamaund**, lodestone; **draweth**, attracts; **nedel**, needle. **1539 vertuous**, powerful. **1540 preve**, test. **1541 byyonde**, beyond the; **falleth**, happens. **1544 elys**, eels; **mille**, thousand. **1548 torn**, orbit; **signes**, astrological signs; **late steryng**, slow moving. **1549 good wyll**, desire. **1549–50 mech styryng**, much traveling. **1550 our contré**, i.e., England. **1551 leyght**, quick; **way**, travel. **1553 leyghtlych**, quickly. **1555 Gene**, Genoa. **1556 partyes**, regions; **bygge**, buy. **1557 ballockys**, testicles; **shankes**, legs. **1558 byndeth**, bind; **straytly**, tightly; **oynementz**, ointments. **1559 therfore**, for that purpose. **1560 undren**, about 9 a.m. **1562 yre**, iron; **bondes**, bands. **1563 drawe**, attract.

Fro this yle men goth by the see to the yle of Cana, wher is gret plenté of corne

fol. 38r
1566

and wyne. And the kyng of this yle was somtyme so myghty that he helde | werre
with Kyng Alysaundre. And men of this yle han dyverse lawes, for somme worshippeth the sonne, and somme the fyre, and somme addres, and som trees, and som
the ferst thyng that they mete on the morwenynge, and som worshippeth simulacres and som ydoles. For bytwyne simulacres and ydoles is differens, for sim-

1570

ulacres beth ymages y-maked to licknes of what thyng a man wol. For som ymage
hath thre hedes: on of man, another of an hors, and on of an oxe or other best that
a man wole.

And ye shal understande that they that worshipeth simulacres, they worshipe
hem for som worthy men that were somtyme, as Hercules, other soch other whiche

1575

dede many mervayles in her tymes. For they seyn they woot wel they beth noght
God of kynde, that maked all thyng, but they beth ryght wel with God for mervayles that they doth. And so they sayn of the sonne, for hit chaungeth ofte tymes
of the yer and geveth hete to norssh all thynges of the erthe. And for hit is of so
gret profyte, they sey they wot well that hit is wel with God, and that God loveth

1580

hit wel more than eny other, and therfore they worshippeth hit. And thus saith
thay of fure, for hit is profitable. And thus maketh thay skyles why they worshipe
other planetes and thynges.

And ydoles beth of alle quyke bestes. And of alle ydoles they sayn the oxe is best
and holiest that is in the erthe, and most profitable than eny other best. And

1585

therfore they make her god that oon half man and that other half an oxe, for man
is the best creature that ever God makyd. And they do worship to eddres and to
other bestes that they mete ferst on the morwe.

In this yle of Cana beth many wylde bestes and ratons. Ratons of that contré
beth also gret as houndes her, and they take hem with mastyves, for cattes may

1590

noght take hem. Fro thenne men goon to a cité that is called Sarchie, and hit is a
good cité and wel y-dyght.

And fro thenne to the londe of Bomk and ther is the cité of Polomee, and

fol. 38v

under that cité is an hille that men callen | Polombe, and therof taketh that cité his
name. And at the foot of this hille is a fair well and hath a swet savour of all maner

1595

of spices, and ech oure of the day hit changeth his savour diversly. And whoso
drynketh thries a day of that well, he shal be maked hole of alle maner sycknesses
that he hath. For Y have dronke of that well, and me thynketh yit Y fare the better.
Som men callen hit the well of youthe, for they that drynketh therof semeth
evermore yonge and leven withoute gret syknesse. And they say that the well

1600

cometh fro Paradise, for hit is vertuous. In that contré groweth gyngyner, and
thyder cometh marchauntz for spyces.

1564 corne, wheat. **1567 addres**, adders. **1568 mete on the morwenynge**, encounter in
the morning. **1568–69 simulacres**, images. **1570 what thyng a man wol**, whatever thing
one chooses. **1571 on**, one. **1574 were somtyme**, lived previously. **1576 kynde**, nature;
ryght wel with, pleasing to. **1581 fure**, fire; **skyles**, reasons. **1583 quyke**, living. **1586
eddres**, adders. **1588 ratons**, rats. **1589 her**, here; **mastyves**, mastiffs. **1595 oure**, hour.
1596 hole, whole (i.e., healthy). **1599 leven**, live. **1600 vertuous**, virtuous; **gyngyner**,
ginger.

In this contré men worshipeth the oxe for his gret meknesse and profyt that is on hym. And they make the oxe to travayle but 6 other 7 yer, and then they ete hym. And the kyng of that lond hath evermore an oxe with hym. And he that

1605 kepith hym, taketh his fees for his kepyng, and also he gadreth his uryne and his donge in a vestel of goold and berith hit to her prelate, that they calleth Archi-protapaton. And the prelate bereth hit to the kyng and maketh theron a gret blessyng. And then the kyng putteth his hondes therynne, and thenne they calle hit *gaule gaule*. And he anoyneth his frount and his brest therwith. And they do

1610 therto moch worship and seyn that they shal be fulfeld thorgh vertu of the oxe, and that he is y-makyd holy thorgh the vertu of the oxe. And when the kyng hath thus y-do, then do other lordes so, and then other men, as they ben of degré. When they may have eny remanent y-left therof, they doth hit into tresorye.

In this lond her ydoles beth half man and half oxe. In these ydoles beth wycked

1615 gostes and speketh to hem and geveth to hem answer of all thyng that they aske. Byfore these ydoles they sleyn her cheldren and sprengeth her blood uppon the ydoles and so make they sacrifyse.

And if any man dey in that lond they brenne hym in toknyng of penaunce, and he were y-layd in the erthe he sholde suffre no penaunce for etyng of wormes. And

fol. 39r | if hys wyff have none cheldren, they brenne her with hym. And they seyn that hit

1621 is good resoun that she make hym companye in the other worlde, as she dede in this worlde. And if she have cheldren, she shal lyve with hem, if that she wole. And if the wyff deye byfore the man, they brenne her and the man, if that he wole.

Fro this londe men goth many contreis and journees to a contré that is y-called

1625 Mabaron. And that is a gret contré and a gret kyngdome, and ther beth many fair citees and tounes. In this londe lyth Seynt Thomas in flessh in a fair tumbe in the cité of Calamye and the arme with the honde that he putte in Our Lordes syde when He was y-ryse fro deth to lyve, when Crist seyde thus: *Noli esse incredulus sed fidelis.* That is to say: "Be thow noght of wanhope but trywe." That same honde lyth

1630 yit withoute the tumbe al bare ther, and with that hand they geve ther her juge-ment and her domes in that contré. For if stryff other debate be bytwyne two parties, they lete wryte her ryght and her mater in two bylles, and they beth putte in Seynt Thomas hande. And anoon the hand cast away that bylle that is fals and holdeth that other that is ryghtfull. And therfore men cometh fro ferre contrees

1635 to have jugementz of causes that beth in doute.

In the cherche of Seynt Thomas is a greet ymage and that is a simulacre, and hit is wel y-dyght with precious stones and perles. And to that ymage men cometh fro ferre contrees with gret devocioun in pylgrimage. And som of tho that cometh in pylgrimage bereth sharp knyves in her hondes, and as they goth by the way they

1640 kytte her owen shankes and her thyes, that the blood may com out for the love of

---

1602 profyt, good. **1603 travayle**, work. **1605 gadreth**, collects. **1606 donge**, dung; **vestel**, vessel; **prelate**, churchman of superior rank. **1610 fulfeld thorgh vertu**, fulfilled by the power. **1612 as they ben of degré**, according to their rank. **1615 gostes**, spirits. **1616 sleyn**, kill; **sprengeth**, sprinkle. **1618 in toknyng**, as a sign. **1621 good resoun**, right. **1627 honde**, hand. **1628 y-ryse**, risen. **1629 thow**, thou; **wanhope**, despair; **trywe**, faithful. **1630 bare**, uncovered. **1632 ryght**, claim; **mater**, argument; **bylles**, formal statements. **1634 ryghtfull**, honest. **1640 kytte**, cut; **shankes**, legs; **thyes**, thighs.

that ymage. And thay sey that he is holy that wole deye for his goddes sake. And som of tho pylgrymes, fro that tyme that they goon out of her hous, at ech thrydde pase they knelith adoun tyl they come to this ymage. And when they come ther, they have ensense, other som other sweet thyng, to ensense therwith that ymage, 1645 as we wole do to Goddis body.

fol. 39v And byfore the cherche of this ymage | is a stocke ful of water, and in that stock the pylgrimes casten her goold and selver, precious stones, and perles withoute nombre instede of her offrynges. And when the cherche hath nede of helpe, anoon they take hit up of that stock to amendement of the cherch.

1650 And ye shal understonde, when gret festes beth of this ydole, as dedicacioun of the cherch other the crounyng of the ydole, all the contré is assembled theder. And men setteth this ydole in gret worship in a chayre, with precious stones wel y-dyght with ryche clothes of goolde. And other, that ledith hym with solempnité aboute the cité, thay beth rychely aparayled. And byfore this chare goth ferst in 1655 processioun all the maydenes of the contré, two and two togedre. And after hem goth pylgrimes that beth y-come fro ferre contrees, of which pylgrimes, som falle adoun byfore that chare and lete the wheles go over hem, and so they beth dede, and som have ther her armes and sholdres to-broke. And this doth they for love of her ydole, that they sholde have the more joye.

1660 And overthwert and nexte byfore the chare goth all the mynstralles of that contré, as hit were withoute nombre, with many diverse melodyes. And when they ben come agayn to the cherch, they sette uppe the ydole in his trone. And for worship of this ydole two men, other thre, ben slayn with sharp knyves and with her good wylle. And as a man thenketh in our contré that he hath gret worship if 1665 he have a holy man to his kyn, so they say that tho that ben slayn ben seyntes, and they beth wryten in her letenyes. And when they ben thus dede, her frendes leet brenne her bodyes, and let take the askes, and let kepe hem ful welle as relykes. For they seyn that hit is holy thyng, and they have no doute of no peryle the whyle they have tho askes.

1670 For to go fro this londe and this contré 52 journeys, ther is a londe that men callen Lamoryse. And ther is gret hete, and the custome ther of men and wymmen goon all naked. And they skorneth hem that goth clothed. For they say that God

fol. 40r maked Adam and Eve naked and that men sholde | have no shame of that thyng that God makyd, for nothyng is foull that He makyde. And they belyve in God that 1675 makyde all the worlde. And ther is no womman y-wedded, but beth all in comune. And they say that God comaunded to Adam and Eve and to all that come of hem and seyde thus: *Crescite et multiplicamini et replete terram*. That is to say: " wexeth and be multeplied and fulfyll the erthe." And no man may say "this is my wyff," ne no womman, "this is myn husbonde." And when they have chyldren, they geve hem 1680 to wham they wole of men haveth delyd with hem.

1643 pase, step. **1644 ensense**, incense. **1645 Goddis body**, i.e., the Host. **1646 stocke**, basin. **1652 chayre**, chariot. **1653 solempnité**, ceremony. **1657 wheles**, wheels. **1658 to-broke**, broken. **1659 joye**, i.e., joy in heaven. **1660 overthwert**, opposite. **1662 trone**, throne. **1664 good wylle**, consent; **worship**, honor. **1666 letenyes**, litanies. **1667 askes**, ashes; **relykes**, relics. **1668 hit**, i.e., such a relic; **doute**, fear. **1675 in comune**, in common. **1680 haveth delyd**, who have had sex.

Also that lond is all in comune, for that a man hath in oon yer another man hath another yer. Also all goodes and cornes of that contré beth in comune, for ther is nothyng under loke. As ryche is oon man as another. But they have an yvel custome: they eten gladloker mannes flessh than other flessh, and thyder bryngeth marchauntes her cheldren to selle. And tho that ben fatte, they ete hem, and the other they kepe and fede hem tylle they ben fatte, and then they ete hem.

In this lond nother in many other aboute, men may noght se the sterre that is y-clepid Transmontane, which standeth evene north and stereth never, by which shipmen beth y-lad, for hit is noght seyn toward the south. But ther is another sterre, which is y-clepid Anteryke, and that is evene agenst that other sterre. And by that sterre shipmen beth y-ladde toward the south, for that is noght y-seye toward the north. And therfore men may wel se that the lond and the see ys all round, for partyes of the firmament which sheweth in oo place and apereth noght in another place. And that may men preve thus: for yf a man myght fynde shypyng and men wolde go to see, men myght go all aboute the worlde above and bynethe. And preve Y thus after that Y have y-seye. For Y have be in Braban and y-seye the astrelabre of the sterre Transmontayne, and hit is 54 degreez hey in Almayne, and toward Beme hit hath 59 degreez, and more north hit hath 62 degreez in heyth and som munytes.

And ye shal understonde that agenst the sterre in the north is the sterre Anteryke. These two sterres styreth nevermore, and by hem turneth | the firmament as a wheel in a extre, so that thees two sterres departeth all the firmament in two partyes. And thenne went Y toward the south and Y fond that in Lybie hit hath in heythe 18 degreez and somme munytes, of which munytes 60 maketh a degree. And so passyng by lond and by see toward contrees that Y have spoke byfore, and other londes and yles agenst hem, they fond this Anteryke of 33 degreez and 16 munytes. This beth 4 score and 15 degreez and ney half a munyte. And so hit lacketh bote 80 and ner half degré: thenne have Y sen all the firmament.

And therfore Y sey sykerly that a man myght go all the worlde aboute, above and bynethe, and com agen to his owen contré, he that hadde shipyng, and alway he sholde fynde many londes and yles as beth in thylke contré. For ye wot wel that thes men that dwelleth ryght under Anteryke beth foot agenst foot of these that dwelleth under Transmontayn as wel as we. And thes men that dwelleth agenst us beth foot agenst foot, for alle partyes of the erthe have her contraryes of thynges which beth agenst hem.

And ye shal understonde that the lond of Prester John, emperour of Ynde, is under us. For if a man shal go fro Skotlond other Ingelond toward Jerusalem, he shal go ever upward, for our londe is in the lowest partye of the west, and the lond of Prester John is in the lowest partye of the est. And they have day when we have nyght, and nyght when we have day. And as moch as a man ryseth upward out of

1685

1690

1695

1700
fol. 40v

1705

1710

1715

1720

our contré toward Jerusalem, as moche shal he go donward toward the lond of
Prester John fro Jerusalem, and that is for all the erthe is round.

    Now ye have y-hurd telle that Jerusalem is in the myddel of the worlde, and
that may wel be y-preved thus: for and a man ther take a sper and set hit evene in
1725   the erthe at mydday, when the nyght and the day is y-lyche longe, the sper maketh
no shadowe. And David bereth wytnesse when he seyth thus: *Deus operatus est salu-*
fol. 41r *tem in medio terre.* That is to say: "God hath | y-wrought hele in the myddel of the
erthe." And therfore they that goth out of oure contrees of the west toward Jerusalem, as many journeyes as they make to go theder upward, as many journeys shal
1730   they make to go into the lond of Prester John donward fro Jerusalem. And so he
may go into thes yles, evene round all the roundnesse of the erthe and of the see,
tyl he come evene under us.

    And therfore Y have y-thought many tymes of a tale that Y hurde when Y was
yong, how a worthy man of oure contré wente a tyme to se the worlde. And he
1735   passyde Ynde and these iles byyonde Ynde, where beth mo than 5000. And he
wende so longe by londe and by see seynge aboute the worlde, and he fonde an yle
where he herde his owen speche, and dryvynge beestys saynge soch wordes as men
dyde in his owen contré, of whych he hadde gret mervayle for he wiste noght how
that myghte be. But Y say he hadde y-go so longe on londe and see, goynge aboute
1740   the worlde, that he was y-come into his owen marches. But for he myghte have no
passage ferther, he turned agayn as he com, and so he hadde a gret travayl. And
hit byfyl afterward that he wente into Northway in a tempest of wynde on the see,
and droff hym so that he aryved in an yle. And when he was ther, hym thoughte
that hit was the yle the whych he hadde y-be on byfore, where he hurde speke his
1745   owen speche as the men drof beestys. And that myghte ryght wel be, of all hyt be
that simple men of connyng trowe hit nought, that men may go under the erthe.

    For as us thinketh that thes beth under us, so thenketh hem that we beth under
hem. For if a man myghte falle fro the erthe into the firmament, by more skyle the
erthe and the see that beth so hevy sholde falle into the firmament, but that may
1750   noght be. And therfore God saith thus: *Non timeas me suspendi terram ex nihilo.* That
is to say: "Have no drede that Y have the erthe honged of noght."

    And if be al possible that a man may go al aboute the erthe, neverthelasse of
1000 men, oon ne sholde noght take the nexte way to his owen contré, for ther
fol. 41v beth so many wayes | that a man myght fayle, but if hit were the special grace of
1755   God. For the erthe is gret and long, and hit holdeth in roundnesse aboute, above
and bynethe, 20,400 and 25 myle, after the opynion of olde wyse men that seyn
hit, which Y wole noght repreve. But after my lytel wyt, me thenkyth, save her
grace, that hit is more aboute.

    And for to understonde better that Y wol say, Y ymagine a figure wher is a gret
1760   compas, and aboute the poynt of that compas, that is y-cleped centre, by another
lytel compas departed by lymes in many partyes, and that thes lymes meteth to-

---

1724 y-preved, proved; **and**, if. **1727 hele**, salvation. **1736 wende**, went; **seynge**, seeing.
1741 travayl, hardship. **1743 droff**, it drove. **1745–46 of all hyt be that**, even though. **1746
simple men of connyng**, men of simple understanding. **1748 by more skyle**, more
reasonably. **1751 of noght**, from nothing. **1752 if be al**, though it is. **1757 repreve**, gain-
say. **1758 more aboute**, bigger around. **1759 that**, what. **1760 by**, is. **1761 lymes**, limbs.

gadre on the centre, so that as manye partyes other lemes as al the greet compas hath be on lytel compas, thow al the space be the lasse.

1765   Now by the greet compas set forth the firmament, the which by astronomyers is departed in 12 signes, and ech signe is departed in 30 degrees. This is 300 and 60 degres that is aboute. Now be the erthe departed in as meny partyes as the firmament and everych of these annswereth to a degré of the firmament. Thes beth in al 700 and 20. Now be thes in all multiplie 300 tymes and 60, and hit shal amounte in al 21,000 myle and 5, ech myle of 8 forlanges, as myles beth in other

1770   contrees. And also moche hath the erthe in compas and in roundenysse al aboute, after myn opynyon and myn understondyng. And ye shal understonde, after opyn-ion of olde wyse philosofres and astronomers, that Ingelond, Skotlond, Walys, ne Yrlond beth noght rekened in the heythe of the erthe, as hit semeth wel by all bookes of astronomye. For the heythe of the erthe is departed in 7 planetes,

1775   whiche beth y-clepid clymates. And these cuntreez that Y spake of beth not in these clymates, for they beth dounnward so toward the west. And also thes yles of Ynde which beth evene agenst us beth noght recknid in tho climates, for they beth toward the est so lowe. And climates goth aboute al the worlde.

    And ney thes yle of Lamory, which Y spak of, is another yle that men clepeth
fol. 42r   Somaber. Men of that yle and wymmen leet merke hem in the visage | with an hoot
1781   yre that they beth knowe fro other peple, for they holdeth hemself the worthiest of the worlde. And they have werre evermore with tho men that beth naked, of which Y spake afore.

    But ther is another gret yle that men calleth Java, and the kyng of that contré
1785   hath under hym 7 kynges, for he is myghty and stronge. In that yle groweth alle maner of spices more plenté than in another place, as gyngyner, clowes, canel, notemyge, maces, and other spyces, and ye shal understonde that the notemyge bereth the maces. Al thyng is ther in plenté save wyn.

    The kyng of this londe hath a riche palays, for alle the greces in the halle and
1790   in the chambre, oon is goold, another is sylver, and all the walles ben y-coveryd and y-plated with goold and sylver. And in the plates ben y-write storyes of kynges and of knyghtes and batayles. And the pavement of the chambre is of goold and sylver. And no man wole trowe the rychesse that is ther but if he hadde y-seyn hit.

    The kyng of this yle is so myghty that he hath overcome the Gret Cane of
1795   Catay, that is the myghtiest emperour of the worlde. For they beth moch at werre, for the Cane wolde make hym holde of hym his londes and to be his soget under hym, and he wole noght.

    And for to go forth by see, men fyndeth an yle that is y-called Salamasse. And som men callen hit Patro, that is a gret kyngdome with many faire citees. In this
1800   lond groweth trees that bereth meele, of which men maketh brede fayr and white and of good savoure, and hit semeth as hit were of whete. And ther also beth other trees that bereth fenym, agayn which is no medicyne but oon, and that is to take

---

1763 the lasse, smaller. 1769 forlanges, furlongs. 1770 also, as. 1774 heythe, height. 1775 y-cliped, called. 1780 merke hem, mark themselves. 1780–81 hoot yre that, hot iron so that. 1786 gyngyner, ginger; clowes, cloves; canel, cinnamon. 1787 notemyge, nutmeg; maces, mace. 1789 greces, steps. 1793 y-seyn, seen. 1796 soget, subject. 1802 fenym, venom.

the leves of that same tre and stampe hem with water and drynke hit, other elles
he shal be dede sodeynly, for tryacle may noght help hym. And if ye wole wyte how
1805 the trees bereth meele, Y shal yow telle. Ferst men heweth hit with an ax aboute
the foot of the tree, doun by the erthe, so that the rynde be pershid in many places.
fol. 42v And then cometh out a lycour that is thicke, which they take in a vestell | and set hit
in the sonne to dryghe, and when hit is dryghe they do hit to the mylle to grynde
hit, and then hit is fayr meele and whyte. And hony and fenym is y-drawe out of
1810 trees in the same maner and y-do into a vestell.

In that ile is a dede see that is a water that hath no ground. And if anythinge
falleth therynne, hit shal never be founde. By that see groweth grete cannes that
beth soch reedes, and under her rootes men may fynde many precious stones of
vertu. For he that bereth oon of thes stones uppon hym, ther may non yre der hym
1815 ne drawe blood of hym. And therfore tho that haven of thylke stones fighteth ryght
hardely. And her enemyes that knoweth hem and the maneres of hem, they
maketh hem quarelles sharp withoute yre, and so they slee hem.

Than is ther another ile that is y-called Calonache, which is a good londe and
plenteuous. And the kyng of that londe hath as many wyves as he wole, and he lyth
1820 never by oon of hem but oons. And that lond hath a mervayle that is noght in
another lond: for alle the maner fisshes of the see cometh oon tyme of the yer, ech
maner of fissh after other, and leith hem neygh the londe and som on the londe,
and ther they lyen 3 dayes. And men of that londe cometh and taketh of hem what
hem lyst, and then goth that maner of fyssh away. And then cometh another maner
1825 of fyssh and lyth ther other thre dayes, and men taketh of hem also. And thus doth
alle maner of fysshes tylle all have ben ther, and so men taketh of hem what they
wole. And men wot noght what is the cause, but they say that tho fysshes cometh
theder to do worship to the kynge, as for most worthy kynge of the worlde, for he
hath so many wyves and geteth so many chyldren.

1830 Also ther beth snayles so greet that in somme of her shelles men may be y-
herborwed, as in a lytel hous. And if a man deye on that contré, they grave his wyff
with hym al quyke, and saith hit is good skyle that heo make company in the other
worlde, as she dude in this.

Than is ther another ile that men callen Goffalles. Men of that yle, when her
fol. 43r fren|des beth syke that they wene that he shal deye, they take hym and hong hym
1836 al quyke an a tree, and sayn that hit is beter that bryddes that beth angelys of God
ete hym than wormes ete hym.

Fro thenne men gon to an ile, and tho beth men of wicked kynde for they
norsheth houndes to strangly men. And when her frendes beth sike and they hope
1840 that he shal deye, they lete houndes strangly hem. For hy wole noght that they
deye kyndely deeth, for than sholde he suffre to greet penaunce, as they say. And
when they beth thus strangled, than ete they his flessh instede of feneson.

1803 **stampe**, mash. 1804 **tryacle**, treacle. 1806 **rynde**, bark; **pershid**, pierced. 1807
vestell, vessel. 1808 **do**, take. 1811 **ground**, bottom. 1812 **cannes**, canes. 1814 **yre der**,
iron harm. 1815 **haven of**, have any of. 1817 **quarelles**, arrows. 1820 **oons**, once. 1824
hem lyst, they wish. 1830–31 **y-herborwed**, sheltered. 1832 **quyke**, alive; **skyle**, wisdom;
heo, she. 1833 **dude**, did. 1835 **wene**, believe. 1836 **an**, on. 1839 **norsheth**, raise;
strangly, kill; **hope**, expect. 1840 **hy**, they. 1841 **kyndely**, natural. 1842 **feneson**, venison.

And then men goon to the ile of Melke. And ther men ben of wicked kynde, for they have no delyte but for to fyghte and sle men, for they drynkyn gladly mannes **1845** bloode. And he that may sle most men, he is at most name among hem. And if two men be at the debate and they be makyd at oon, hem byhoveth to drynke every otheris blood other elles the acoorde is noght.

Than is ther another ile that is y-called Tracota, wher men beth as beestes and noght resenable, for they eten eddres and they speke noght but make soch noyse **1850** as eddres don.

And they make noon fors of no rychesse, but of oon stone that hath 40 colouris that is y-called traconyghte. And they knowe noght the vertu of that stone, but they coveyte hym for the gret fayrenesse of hym.

Fro that ile men goon to another yle that is y-called Natumeran. Men and **1855** wymmen of that contré hath houndes hedes, and they ben resonable. And they worshipeth an oxe for her god, and they gon all naked save a lytel cloth byfore her prevyteis. And they ben good men to fyght, and they beren a gret targe with wham they coveryn all her body, and a sper in her honde. And if they take any man in batayl, they sende hym to her kyng, which is a gret lord and devout in his faith. **1860** For he hath aboute his necke on a corde thre hundred perlys orient in maner of pater-noster of aumbre. And as we say oure *Pater Noster* and *Ave Maria*, so this kyng saith ech day 300 prayers byfore his god or he ete any mete. And he bereth also aboute his necke a rubye orient fyne and good that is neye a foot long. For whenne **fol. 43v** they chese her kyng they geveth | hym that rubye to bere in his hond, and so they **1865** lede hym rydyng all aboute the cité. And therfore he bereth that rubye evermore aboute his necke, for if he bare noght that rubye hy ne wolde no lenger hold hym kyng. And the Greet Cane of Catay hath moch coveyted that rubye, but he myght never have hit for no werre ne for no catelle.

And then is ther another ile that men callen Dodyn, that is a gret yle. And ther **1870** beth many diversytees of men, and they have wicked maneres, for the fadres eteth the sones, and the sones the fadres, and the housbond the wyff, and the wyff the housbond, and ech so of other. And if hit be so that the fader be syke, other the moder, other any of her frendes, the sone anoon goth to the prest of the lawe and prayeth hym that he aske of the god, that is her ydole, if his fader other moder **1875** shal deye of that sycknesse other lyve. And then the prest and the sone knelith adoun byfore the ydole devoutly and asken of hym and he annswerith hem. And if he say that he shal lyve, thenne they kepe hym wel. And if he sey that he shal deyghe, then cometh the prest with the sone and with the wyff other with what frend hit be to hym that is syke, and they ley her hondes over his mouth to stop his **1880** breth. And so they sle hym, and then they hewe his body all to peeces. They preye all his frendes to come and ete of hym that is dede and they maketh a greet feste. And when they have y-ete his flessh, they berieth the bones. And all tho of his

---

1845 at most name, most famous. **1846 makyd at oon**, reconciled. **1846–47 every otheris**, each other's. **1849 resenable**, reasonable; **eddres**, adders. **1851 make noon fors of**, do not care for. **1857 prevyteis**, genitals; **targe**, shield. **1860 perlys orient**, oriental pearls. **1861 pater-noster of aumbre**, amber-beaded rosary; *Pater Noster*, "Our Father" prayer; *Ave Maria*, "Hail Mary" prayer. **1862 or**, before. **1863 rubye orient**, oriental ruby. **1864 chese**, choose. **1866 hy**, they. **1873 prest**, priest. **1880 preye**, invite.

frendes that were noght ther to ete of hym haven gret vylonye, so that they never-
more ben y-holde his frendes.

1885   The kyng of that ile is a gret lord and myghty, and he hath under hym 54 iles,
and ech of hem hath a kyng. And in som of thes yles beth men that haveth but oon
eye, and that is in the myddes of her forhede, and they ete noght but raw flessh.
And in another ile dwelleth men that haveth noon heed, and her eyen beth in her
shuldres, and her mouth in her brest.

1890   And in another ile beth men that haveth a plat visage withoute nose and eye,
fol. 44r   but they have two smale holes instede of eyen, and | they have a plat mouth lyples.

    And in another ile beth peple that beth bothe man and womman, and have
membres of bothe. And when they wole they use bothe, that on at on tyme and that
other at another tyme. And they gete children when they usen the mannes
1895   membres, and they bereth children when they use the membre of the womman.

    Many other maner of peple beth theraboute, of wham hit were to moche to
telle. And for to passe forth, men cometh into an ile wher men beth ryght smale,
and they have a litel hole instede of her mouth, and they mowe noght ete. But
when they sholde ete other drynke, they souke hit thorgh a pype that is holgh
1900   thorghout.

THE LAND OF MANCY. CAPITULUM QUARTUMDECIMUM.   [Chapter 14.]

    For to go fro this ile toward the see of Occian estward many journeys, a man
shal fynde the kyngdome of Mancy, and that is in Ynde. And hit is the best lond,
and most delitable, and most plenteuous of alle good that is in the power of man.
In this lond dwelleth Cristen men and Sarasyns, for hit is a gret londe, for ther-
1905   ynne beth two thousand citees and other many tounes. Ther goth no man on beg-
gynge, for ther is no poure man. And tho men have thynne beerdes as cattes. And
ther beth fayre wymmen, and therfore som men callen hit the lond of Albanye, for
the whyte peple that is therynne. And ther is a gret cité that is y-called Latorym,
and hit is moche more than Parys.

1910   In that lond ben breddes twyes as moche as in any other place of the worlde.
And ther is good chepe of vitayles, and ther is gret plenté of gret eddres, of which
they make gret festes and ete hem in gret solempnytees. For though a man make
a feste and dyghte all maner of metes that beth most deynté, but he ordeyne some
eddres and geve hem to mete, they have no thanke for all her feste.

1915   In this contré beth white hennes, but they have no fetheris but woll, as sheep
in our lond. And wymmen that beth y-wedded bereth crounes uppon her hede to
be knowe fro other.

    Fro this cité men goth many journeyes to another cité that is y-called Cessay,
fol. 44v   that is the most cité of the worlde. For hit is 50 myle a|boute the walles and ther
1920   beth many good gates, and at every gate is a good tour in which men dwelleth to

---

1883 haven gret vylonye, are scorned. **1884 ben y-holde**, are considered. **1887 myddes**,
middle. **1888 eyen**, eyes. **1890 plat visage**, flat face. **1891 lyples**, lipless. **1893 membres**,
genitals. **1899 holgh**, hollow. **1901 Occian**, Ocean. **1906 poure**, poor. **1909 more**, larger.
1910 breddes, birds; **moche**, large. **1911 chepe**, trade; **vitayles**, food. **1912 solempnytees**,
rituals. **1913 dyghte**, make; **deynté**, fine (delicious); **ordeyne**, order. **1914 geve hem to
mete**, offer them for dinner. **1915 woll**, wool. **1919 most**, largest.

kepe hit fro the Gret Cane, for hit marcheth uppon his lond. And at that oon syde of that cité renneth a good rever. And ther dwelleth Cristen men and other many, for ther is a good contré and a plenteuous. And ther groweth right good wyne that men callen begoun. In this cité was woned the kyng of Mancy for to dwelle.

1925   And so men goth by this ryver tyl they come to an abbey of monkes a lytel fro that cité. And that abbey is a gret gardeyn and a fair, in the which beth many trees of diverse frutes. And ther beth many mervelous herbes and other thynges that Y shal telle of. In that gardeyn beth many bestes, as baboyn, marmesettes, apes, and other. And when the covent hath ete among hem, they take the relyfe and bere hit

1930   to the garden and smyteth ons with a cleket of sylver which he holdeth in his honde. And sone therafter cometh the beestes out and any other, neygh 3000 other 4000, and he geveth hit hem in fair sylver fessel. And when they have ete, he smyteth that cleket agayn, and all the beestes goon agayn wher they come fro.

And they say that thilke beestes beth soules of men that beth dede. And the fair

1935   beestes beth soules of lordes, and the foule beestes beth soules of other men. And Y asked hym if hit were noght betre to geve that relyve to pore men. And they seyde ther was no pore man in that contré, and though yit were hit more almes to geve hit to thilke soules that suffred ther her penaunce than to hem that may go and travayle for her mete.

1940   And fro thenne cometh men to the cité of Chibence, wher was ferst the sege of the kyng of Mancy. In this cité beth 40 brygges of stoon bothe fair and good.

THE LONDE OF THE GRET CANE OF CATAY.
CAPITULUM QUINTUMDECIMUM.   [Chapter 15.]

Fro the cité of Chibence they passen over a gret ryver of fressh water, and hit is ney 3 myle brood. And then men entren into the londe of the Gret Cane. This ryver goth thorgh the lond of pegmans, wher men beth of litel stature, for they ben

fol. 45r   but thre spanne longe. And they beth | ryght fair, and they beth weddede when they
1946   beth but half yeres olde. These smale men travelen noght, but they have among hem gret men, as we beth, to travele for hem. And they have greet skorne of gret men, as we have of hem. And they lyveth but 8 yer, and he that lyveth so longe is y-holde ryght oolde ther.

1950   And thenne men goth thorgh many contreis to a ryver that is y-called Caro-masan, which renneth thorgh Catay and doth many tymes moche harme when he waxeth greet. And Catay is a gret contré and good, and ful of good and of mar-chaundise. Theder cometh marchaundes every yer to fecche spices and other marchaundises, more comunely than they doth to another contré. And ye shal

1955   understonde that marchauntes that cometh fro Venyse and fro Gene, other fro eny other places of Lumbardie other Romayn, they goth by see. And by londe hit is 11 monthes and more or they come to Catay.

1921 marcheth uppon, borders on. **1928 baboyn**, baboons. **1929 covent**, convent; **relyfe**, remnant. **1930 cleket**, clapper. **1932 hem**, to them; **fessel**, vessel. **1937 though yit**, still. **1939 travayle**, work. **1940 thenne**, thence; **sege**, seat. **1944 pegmans**, pygmies. **1945 spanne**, handspans. **1946 travelen**, work. **1952 good$_2$**, goods. **1953 marchaundes**, merchants.

And toward the est is an old cité in the province of Catay. And byside that cité the Tartaryns haveth y-maked another cité that they callen Cadom, that hath 12

1960   gates, and bytwyne two gates evermore is a myle, so that the two citees, the olde and the nywe, is aboute more than 14 myle. In this cité is the sege of the Gret Cane in a ryght fair palays. And the garden is uppon an hille uppon which is a fair palays, and hit is the fairest that may be founde in any contré. And aboute that hille beth many trees berynge many diverse of fruytes. And aboute the hille is a

1965   gret ryver and a gret diche. And ther fast by beth many ryvers and vynes uppon ech syde. And in tho vyne and ryvers beth gret plenté of fissh and of wilde foules, which the Gret Cane may take with his haukes and go noght out of his palays.

The halle of that palays is rychely dight, for withynne the halle beth 24 pylers of goolde, and alle the walles beth y-covered with rych skynnes of beestes that men

1970   callen panters, which ben fair and well smellyng. And for tho skynnes smelleth so

fol. 45v   well, no wicked smel may come in that palays. And tho skynnes ben as | reed as blood, and they shyneth so agayn the sonne that unnethe any man may beholde hem. And men preesen tho skynnes for as moche hit were goold.

And at the over eynde of the halle is a trone of the emperour, right heygh. And

1975   ther he sitte at his mete, at a table that is well y-bordured with goolde, and that bordure is ful of precious stones and gret perles. And the greces the which he goth uppon to his trone beth of diverse precious stones bordured with goolde. And at the lift syde of his trone is the sege of his wiff, a gre lower than he sitteth, and that is of jasper bordured with goolde. And the sege of his secunde wyff is a gre lowere than

1980   his ferst wyff, and that is also bordured with goolde. And the sege of the thridde wyff is a gre lower than the secunde, for alway he hath thre wyves with hym, wherso he be. Besyde thes wyves on the same syde sitteth ladyes of kynne, ech lower than other as they beth wedded and of degré. And all tho that beth y-wedded haveth a contrefeit of a mannes foot uppon her hedes, half a foot longe and all y-maked with

1985   precious stones wel and rychely, in tocknyng that they ben in subjeccioun to man and under mannes foot. And they that beth noght wedded have no soch tocknynge.

And in the right side of the emperour sytteth ferst his eldest sone, that shal be his eyre. And also he sitteth a degré lower than the emperour, in soch maner as the emperes sitteth, and by hym other lordes of kynne, ech lower than other as they

1990   ben of degré. And the emperour hath his table by hymself, that is of goolde and of precious stones and of white cristall other of yolgh bordured with goold. And ech of his wyves haveth a table by herself. And under the emperouris table sitteth 4 clerkes, and writeth al that he saith, good other ylle.

And at gret festes, above the emperouris table and all the other tables in the

fol. 46r   hall, is a vyne y-maked of fyn goold | that goth aboute the halle. And hit hath many

1996   branches y-like to the grapes of a vyne. Som beth white, som beth yolgh, som beth reed, som beth black. All the rede beth rubyes other cremans other alabans, the

---

1961 **aboute**, i.e., in circumference; **sege**, seat. 1964 **diverse**, diverse [kinds]. 1965 **fast by**, close by. 1968 **dight**, adorned. 1970 **panters**, panthers; **for**, because. 1972 **unnethe**, hardly. 1973 **preesen**, prize; **for as moche hit were goold**, as if they were gold. 1974 **over**, uppermost. 1975 **y-bordured**, bordered. 1976 **greces**, steps. 1978 **sege**, seat; **gre**, degree. 1982 **kynne**, good family. 1984 **contrefeit**, likeness. 1991 **yolgh**, yellow. 1997 **cremans**, possibly light garnets; **alabans**, albandines.

white beth of byrrel other cristall, the yolghe beth of topaces, the grene beth of emeraudes and crisolites, the blacke beth of oniches and geraundes.

2000   And this vine is thus y-maked of precious stones as properly that hit semeth that hit were a vyne growynge of the erthe. And byfore the borde of the emperour stondeth gret lordes, and no man so hardy to speke to hym but if he speke ferst, but hit be mynstralles to make solas to the emperour. And all the vessel, the which is y-served in halle and chambre, beth of precious stones, and namely at that table

2005   ther the lord sitteth: that is to say of jasper, cristal, amatist, and of fyne goold. And the coppes ben of emeraudes, sapheres, topaces, pydos and other maner stones. They have no deynté of sylver vessel, but they make of sylver greces, pylers, pament to halle and to chambre.

        And ye shal understonde that myne felawes and Y were soudeours with hym 16

2010   monthes agayn the kyng of Mancy. And the cause was for Y hadde gret desyre to se the nobleye of the contré, if hit were y-shewed as we herde speke of. And for-sothe we fond hit rycchere and nobleour and more solempne than was told to us. And we sholde never have y-leved hit but if we hadde y-sey hit.

        But ye shal understonde that the mete and the drynke is more honeste in that

2015   contré than in any other, for alle the comons eteth noght elles but flessh of all maner beestes. And whan they have ete, they wype her hondes upon her lappes, and they ete but ons a day.

WHY HE IS Y-CLEPED THE GRET CANE. CAPITULUM SEXTUMDECIMUM. [CHAPTER 16.]

        And why he was called the Gret Cane Y shal telle yow. For ye wyte well that al the worlde was destruyed with Noeis flood, outtake Noe and his wyff and his chil-

fol. 46v   dren. Noe had 3 children: Sem, | Cham and Japhet. And Cham was he that un-
2021   keverede his fader and skorned hym when he slepe, and therfore he was acursed. And Japhet covered his fader agayn. Thes thre bretheryn hadde all the londe for to parte. Cham toke the best partie estwarde that is called Assye, and Sem toke Affrik, and Japhet toke Europe. Cham was the myghtiest and the richest of his

2025   brethren, and of hym bycom the paynymes and the dyverse maner of men of yles, som hedles and other men defigured. And for this Cham, the emperour called hem after hym "Cham," and lord of all.

        But ye shal understonde that the emperour of Cathay is called "Cana" and noght "Cham," and for this skyle. Hit is noght longe that al Tartarye was in sub-

2030   jeccioun to other naciouns aboute, and they were maked herdmen to kepe beestes. And among hem were 7 lynages of diverse kyndes. The ferst was called Tartarye and that is the beste. The secunde lynage is y-cleped Tangoth, the 3 Eurace, the 4 Valayr, the 5 Semeth, the 6 Menchi, the 7 Sobeth. Thes ben holde of the Gret Cane of Cathay.

1998 **byrrel**, beryl; **topaces**, topazes. 1999 **oniches**, onyx; **geraundes**, possibly dark garnets. 2000 **as properly**, so well. 2001 **borde**, table. 2006 **coppes**, cups; **pydos**, peridots. 2007 **deynté**, appreciation; **greces**, steps. 2008 **pament**, floors. 2009 **soudeours**, soldiers. 2011 **nobleye**, worthiness; **y-shewed**, shown. 2013 **y-leved**, believed; **y-sey**, seen. 2014 **honeste**, temperate. 2019 **Noeis**, Noah's; **outtake**, except. 2023 **parte**, divide between them. 2025 **bycom**, descended; **paynymes**, pagans. 2026 **hedles**, headless. 2027 **hem**, themselves. 2029 **skyle**, reason. 2031 **lynages**, families (tribes). 2032 **lynage**, family, (tribe).

2035   Now byfill hit so that in the ferst lynage was an old man, and he was noght ryche, and men called hym Changyse. This man lay and slepe uppon a bed in a nyght, and ther com to hym a knyght all white, sittynge uppon a white stede, and seyde to hym, "Chane, slepest thow? God that is almyghty sende me to thee, and hit is His will that thow seye to thyn 7 lynages that thow be her emperour, for to

2040 conquere alle the londes that ben aboute yow. And they shal be in youre subjeccioun, as ye have be in heres." And when hit was day he roos up and wente to his 7 lynages and sayde thes wordes, and they skorned hym and sayde he was a fole. And the secunde nyght the same knyght com to the 7 lynages and bad hem in Goddes byhalf to make Chaungise her emperour, "and ye shal be out of all subjec-

2045 cioun, and ye shal have other londes aboute yow in subjeccioun." And uppon the morwe they chese Chaungice to her emperour, and dede to hym all worship that they myght do, and called hym Chane, as the white knyghte sayde. They wolde do all that he bad hem do.

fol. 47r   And tho he makede many statutes and lawes which he cal | led Isacan. The ferste
2050 statute was that they sholde be obedient to Almyghty God and lyve that He shal delyvere hem out of all thraldom, and that they sholde calle uppon Hym in all her nede. Another statute was that alle men that myghte armes bere sholde be armed and numbred, and to every 20 sholde be a mayster, and to every 100 a maister, and to every 1000 a mayster. And thenne he commaunded to alle the grettest of

2055 principalles of the 7 lynages that they sholde forsake all that they hadde in heritage and lordship, and they sholde be wel payed if that he wolde geve hem of his grace. And they dede so. Anoon he bade that every man sholde brynge his eldest sone byfor hym, and that every man sle his owene sone with his owene hondes and smyte of her hedes. And anoon they dede so. And when he sey they maked no

2060 lettyng of that he bade hem do, thenne he bade hem folwe his baner. And so he put in subjeccioun alle the londes aboute hym.

     And hit byfell uppon a day that the Chane rode with a fewe of his men to se the londe that he had wonne, and he mette with a gret companye of his enemyes. And ther he was cast adoun of his hors and his hors y-slayn. And when his men saw hym

2065 at the erthe, they wende he hadde be ded, and fled away, and her enemyes pursued after. And when the Chane saw his enemyes wer fer he yede and hyd hym in a bossh, for the wode was thicke. And his enemyes come agayn fro that chace. They sought among the wode and they fond many men, but hym noght. And as they come by the place ther he was, they saw a bryd sitte uppon a tre, which bryd men

2070 callen an oule. And he sat above his hed uppon that tre, and then they sayde ther was no man for the bryd was ther, and so went thay away. And thus was the Chane y-saved fro the deeth, and so wente he away by nyghte to his owen men, which were fayn of his comynge. And fro that tyme hyderward men of that contré have y-do gret worship to that bryd, and more than to any other.

2075   And thenne he assembled all his men and rood uppon his enemyes and de-
fol. 47v struyed hem. And when | he hadde wonne all the londes to Mount Belyan, the white

2037 **stede**, horse. **2041 be**, been. **2042 fole**, fool. **2043 bad**, ordered. **2046 chese**, chose; **to**, as. **2049 tho**, then. **2050 lyve**, believe. **2051 thraldom**, servitude. **2053 numbred**, counted; **mayster**, leader. **2059–60 maked no lettyng of**, did not refuse. **2065 wende**, thought. **2066 fer**, far away. **2067 bossh**, bush. **2073 fayn of**, joyful at.

knyght come to hym in a vision and sayde, "Chane, the wyll of God is that thow passe the Mount Belyan, and thow shalt wynne many londes. And for ther is no ryght passage, go thow to Mount Belyan that is uppon the see and knele 9 tymes
2080 theruppon agayn the est in the worship of God, and He wole shewe to thee a way how thow shalt passe." And the Cane dede so, and anoon the see that touchid the hille withdrow hym and shewed a fair way of 9 foot brode bytwyne the hille and the see. And so he passed and alle his men, and so wan he the lond of Cathay, that is the most lond of the worlde. And for tho 9 knelynges and the 9 foot of way, the
2085 Chane and the men of Tartarye haveth the numbre of 9 in gret worship.

And when he had y-wonne the lond of Cathay, he deyde. And thenne regned after hym Chicoto Chane, his eldest sone. And his eldest brother went to wynne hym lond in other contrees. And they wonne the londe of Spruys and Russyghe and het hym Chane also. But they of Chatay is the grettest Cane, for he is the
2090 grettest lord of the worlde. And so he calleth hym in his lettres when he seith thus: *Chane filius dei excelsi universam terram colencium summus imperator et dominus dominancium.* That is to say: "Chane, Goddes sone, emperour of alle tho that tylieth lond, and lord of all lordes." And the wryting aboute his gret seel saith thus: *Deus in celo, Chanus super terram eius fortitudo omnium hominum imperator.* That is to say:
2095 "God in Hevene, Chane uppon erthe His strengthe, emperour of all men." And the writyng aboute his prevy seel is this: *Dei fortitudo omnium hominum imperatoris sigillum.* That is to say: "The streynthe of God, seel of His pryvé seel, the emperour of alle men." And thow hit be so that they be noght Cristen, yit the Chane and the Tartaryns byleveth on Allmyghty God.

ARAY OF THE COURT OF THE GRET CHANE.
CAPITULUM SEPTIMUMDECIMUM. [Chapter 17.]
2100 Now Y have told yow why he is cleped the Gret Chane. Now shal Y telle yow the governaynge of his court when they make gret festes, and that is principaly at 4
fol. 48r tymes of the yer. The ferste feste is of his berynge, | the secunde is when he was bore to the temple to be circumcised, the thrid is of his ydoles when they bygan ferst to speke, the 4 when his ydoles bygan ferst to do miracles. And at thes tymes
2105 he hath his men wel araed by thousandes and hundredes, and every man woot wel what he shal do. For ther beth ferst ordeyned 4000 riche barones to ordeyne the feste and to serve the emperoure. And thes barones haveth crounes of goolde wel y-dyght with perles and precious stones, and they beth all y-clothed in clothes of goold and cammaka ful richely. And they may wel have soch clothes, for ther they
2110 beth of lasse prys then wollen clothes ben her. And thes 4000 barones beth departed on 4 parties, and every party is y-clothed in dyverse colour ful richely. And when the ferst 1000 is passed and haveth shewed hem, then cometh the secunde 1000, and so the thridde, and so the ferthe. And noon of hem speketh a word.

2078 for, because. **2083 wan**, won. **2084 most**, largest. **2089 het hym**, called themselves. **2092 tylieth**, till. **2093 gret seel**, imperial seal. **2096 prevy**, private. **2102 beryng**, birth. **2105 araed**, arrayed. **2109 cammaka**, a silk-like fabric. **2110 prys**, price. **2112 shewed hem**, shown themselves.

2115 And by that emperouris syde at the emperouris table sitteth many philosophers and of many sciences, of astronomye, nigromancy, geometrye, piromancy, and other many sciences and som haveth after hem astrelabers of goold and of precious stones full of sond other coles brennyng. Som have orlages wel y-dight and richely, and other maner instrumentes of her sciences. And at certeyn oures when they seith tyme, they say to men that stondeth byfore hem, "Maketh pees," and

2120 then tho men that stondeth byfore crieth loude, that all tho in the hall may here, "Now beth stylle a while!" And then speketh oon of the philosophers and saeth thus: "Every man do reverence and loute to the emperour, that is Goddes sone and lord of all lordes and of all the worlde, for now hit is tyme." And then all men louteth and kneleth to hym on the erthe. And then byddeth the philosophers hem

2125 aryse up agayn. And at other oures other philosophers biddeth hem all put her fynger in her earis, and they do so. And at another oure, another philosophere

fol. 48v byddeth that alle men sholde ley her hondes on her mouth, | and they do so. And so after he byddeth hem take away, and they do so. And thus fro oure to oure they byddeth diverse thynges.

2130 And Y asked prevyly what hit sholde mene. And oon of tho maystres sayde that the loutynge and the knelynge on erthe at that tyme was tockne that all tho men that kneled so sholde evermore be trywe to the emperour: that for no geftes, ne for no heste they sholde never be traytour to hym. And the puttyng of the fynger in the earis hath this tocknynge: that never oon of tho men sholde her noon yvell

2135 y-spoke of the emperour, of fader ne of of moder ne of noon other, but he telle hit to the emperour other to his consayle.

And ye shal understonde that no man dightteth nothyng to the emperour, ne breed, ne drynke, ne clothes, ne noon other thyng necessarye, but at certeyn tymes and oures whoche philosophers telleth. And if any man wole werry ageyn the em-

2140 perour, in what contré so hit be, these philosophers wite hit sone and telleth the emperour and his consaile, and sendeth men thyder to make an eynde.

Also he hath many men to kepe bryddes, as gerfaucons, sperhaukes, faucon gentel, laurettes, sacres, paupenjayes spekyng, and other maner of foules. And he hath 11,000 olyfauntz and baboynes, marmusettes. And he hath fusicions to loke

2145 urines, of which 3000 ben Cristen men and 20 Sarasens. But he tretith more with Cristen men than with Sarasyns, and therwith in his court beth many barones and other that beth Cristen, and other that beth converted to our faith thorghe prechynge of good Cristen men that dwelleth ther. But ther beth many that wole noght that men wite that they ben Cristen men. And he hath in his chambre a pyler of

2150 goold, in which is a rubye and a charbocle which is a foot long, and that geveth lyght all nyght to all the chambre. And he hath many other precious stones and rubyes, but that is the grettest and the beste.

2116 astrelabers, astrolabes. **2117 orlages**, clocks. **2119 seith tyme**, see it is time. **2122 loute**, bow. **2130 prevyly**, privately; **maystres**, masters. **2133 heste**, behest. **2134 tocknynge**, significance. **2137 dightteth**, gives. **2138 but**, except. **2139 wole werry**, wants to make war. **2140 wite**, know. **2142 bryddes**, birds. **2142–43 faucon gentel**, falcons of excellent breed. **2143 laurettes**, lanners (a type of Mediterranean falcon); **sacres**, sakers (female lanners); **paupenjayes**, parrots. **2144 olyfauntz**, elephants; **fusicions**, physicians; **loke**, study. **2145 tretith**, has dealings. **2150 charbocle**, carbuncle.

This emperour dwelleth in the somer toward the north, in a cité that men callen Camelat. Ther is ryght an hoot londe, and ther dwellith he for the most

fol. 49r
2156
partye. And when this Gret Cane shal ryde | fro oon contré to another they or-deyneth 4 ostes of peple, of which the ferst goth afore hym a dayes journey. For that oste lith a nyght ther he shal lye another morwe, and ther is good plenté of vitayles. And another gooth on the ryght syde, and another on the lift syde, and on every oste is moch peple. And then cometh the ferthe oste byhynde hym a bowe
2160
draught, and therin beth mo men than of eny of the other.

And ye shal understonde that the emperour rydeth uppon an hors, but if he wole wende to any place with privé mayne he rydeth in a chare with 4 whelys. And theruppon is y-maked a chambre of tre that men calleth *lignum aloes*, that cometh out of Paradys Terrestre, and that chamber is covered withynne with plates of fyn
2165
goold and precious stones and perles. And foure olefantes and 4 stedes goth ther-ynne. And 5 other 6 gret lordes rydeth aboute the chare so that noon other man shal com ney hym but he calle hem. And on the same maner rydeth the quene with an ost by another syde, and the emperouris sone in the same aray. And they have so moch peple that hit is mervayle to se.

2170
Also the lond of the Gret Chane is departed in 12 provinces, and every prov-ince hath mo than 2000 citees and other good tounes many. And every province hath a kyng. Also when the emperour rideth thorwe the contré and passeth thorgh citees and tounes, every man maketh fire byfore his dore in the street, and they caste encense other som other good thyng to geve good smell to the emperour.
2175
And if men of religion which ben Cristen dwelle ney wher he shal passe, they mete hym with procession. And they have a crosse and holy water byfore hem, and they synge thus, *Veni creator spiritus*, with a loud vois. And when he seeth hem come, he commaundeth the lordes that rydeth ney hym to make way, that the religious men may come to hym. And when he seeth the cros, he dooth of his hatte, whiche is wel
2180
maked and rychely with precious stones and gret perles, and then he louteth to the
fol. 49v
cros. And he that is priour other prelat | of that religious goth and seith orisons byfore hym and geveth hym his beneson with the crosse, and he louteth to his beneson devoutly.

And then the same prelate geveth hym of som fruyt of the numbre of 9 in a
2185
plate of goold. For the maner is so ther, that no strange man shal come byfore the emperour but he geve hym somthyng, after the olde lawe that seith thus: *Nemo accedat in conspectu meo vacuus*. That is to say: "No man come in my sight voyde." And thes religious men goon forth fro the emperour, so that no man of the oste defouleth hem. Also the religious men that dwelleth ney wher the emperesse other
2190
the emperouris sone shal come and do in the same manere, for this Gret Chane is the grettest lord of the worlde. For Prester John is noght so gret as he, ne the soudan of Babyloyn, ne the emperour of Perce ne of Grece.

2153 somer, summer. **2156 ostes**, hosts. **2159–60 bowe draught**, the length of a bowshot. **2162 wole wende**, wants to go; **with privé mayne**, in secret. **2168 aray**, array. **2179 dooth of**, takes off. **2180 louteth**, bows. **2181 priour**, prior; **prelat**, churchmen of superior rank; **religious**, order. **2183 beneson**, blessing. **2187 voyde**, empty-handed.

This peple byleveth on God that makide all the worlde, and yit have they idoles of goold and sylver. And to thes idoles they offre the formest mylk of her beestes.

2195   And this Gret Chane hath 3 wyves, and the ferst most principal was Prester Johnis doughter.

Also men of this contré bygynnen to do all her thynges in the nywe mone, and they worship moche the sonne and the mone. And they hold hit gret synne to breke a bone with another, and to shede mylk on the erthe other any other licour

2200   that men may drynke. And the most synne that they may do is to pisse in house wher they dwellen. And he that pissith on his hous shal be slayn. And of all thes synnes they shryve hem to her prestes, and for her penaunce they geve sylver. And that place wher men haveth thus y-pissed byhoveth to be halwed, other elles may they noght come ther. And when they han doon her penaunce, they shal passe

2205   thorgh a fyre, for to make hem clene of her synnes.

And when men of that contré have eten, they wype her hondes on her lappes, for they have none bordes but byfore gret lordes. Also when they have eten, they

fol. 50r   put her disshes and her doblers | unwassh into the potte other caudren. And the flessh they leven when they have eten, till they ete another tyme. They leve hit

2210   stylle in the crocke. And rich men drynken mylke of mares other asses and other beestes. And another drynke ther is that is maked of mylke and water togedre, for they have no wyne nother ale.

And when thay goon to werre, ful wysly every of hem bereth two bowes other thre, and many arwes, and a gret axe. And knyghtes and gentyles have shorte

2215   swerdes. And whoso fleith on batayle, they sle hym. And they beth ever aboute to brynge all londes in subjeccioun to hem. For they saith that her prophecies seyth that they shal be overcome by shot of archers, and that they shull be turnd to her lawe, but they wyte never what men tho sholde be.

And that is gret peryle to pursue the Tartaryns when they flee, for they wole

2220   shet byhynde hem and sle also well as byfore. For they have smale eyen and litel berdes, and they comunely ben fals, for they holdeth noght that they byheit.

And when a man shal deie among hem, they stryke a sper on the erthe bysides hym. And when he draweth to the deeth, thei goon alle out of the house tyll he be deed, and then they putte hym in the erthe in the feld. And when the emperour

2225   the Gret Chane is dede, they sette hym in a chaire amyddes the toun and setteth byfore hym a table y-helid with a cloth, and flessh theruppon and other metys, and a coppe full of mylke of a mare. And they set a mare with her fole bysyde hem, and an hors y-sadelid and brydelid. And they leggen uppon the hors goold and selver. And then they make a gret grave, and hym and all these other thynges they putte

2230   ynne the grave togedre. And they say when he cometh to another worlde, he shal noght be withoute an hous, an hors, and other thynges. And the mare shal geve hym mylke and bryng forth mo hors, tylle he be wel astored in the other worlde.

2194 **formest mylk of her beestes**, first milk from their beasts. **2197 nywe mone**, new moon. **2202 shryve hem**, confess themselves. **2203 halwed**, ritually purified. **2207 bordes**, table linens. **2208 doblers**, plates. **2214 gentyles**, gentlemen. **2215 fleith on**, flees in. **2217–18 turnd to her lawe**, converted to their religion. **2218 wyte never**, do not know. **2220 shet**, shoot; **also**, as. **2221 byheit**, promised. **2226 y-helid**, covered. **2228 leggen**, lay. **2232 astored**, provided for.

For they byleve when they ben dede that they sholde ete and drynke in another worlde, and have solas of her wyves as they have. And after that hit is layd on erthe, no man be hardy to speke of hym byfore | his frendes.

fol. 50v

2236　　And when the emperour the Gret Chane is thus dede, the 7 lynages goth to-gedre, and they chese his sone other the nexte of his blood, and they sey thus: "We wole and we praye and we ordeyn that thow be our lord and our emperour." And

2240　　he answereth thus: "If ye wole that Y regne uppon yow, every of yow that Y commaunde shal do, and if Y bydde that eny shal be slayn he shal be slayn anoon." And they answeren all with oon vois, and saeth thus: "All that ye bydde shal be doon." Then saeth the Chane the emperour: "Fro this tyme now herafter, myn word shal be sheryng as my swerd." And then they sette hym on a chaire and crouneth hym. And then all the citees and good tounes senden hym presentes, so

2245　　that he shal have that same day more then a cartfull of goold and selver and pre-cious stones, and other many jewelles. And lordes seyndeth hym hors and riche clothes of camacas and tartaryns and many other.

This lond of Chatay is in Asye the Depe, and this lond marcheth westward uppon the kyngdom of Percey, the which was somtyme oon of the 3 kynges that

2250　　went to present Our Lord in Bethleem.

In the lond of Corasen, which is in the lond of Catay on the north syde, is gret plenté of good but ther is no wyne, which lond hath at the est syde a gret wilder-nesse that lasteth more than 100 journeys. And the leste cité of that lond is called Corasayn, and after that cité is that lond called. And men of this contré beth good

2255　　werryours and ryght hardy.

And ther ney is the kyngdom of Coman, that is the most kyngdome of the worlde. But hit is noght habited, for on a place in that lond is so gret cold that no man may dwelle ther, and in another place is so gret hete that no man ther may dwelle. And ther beth so many flyen that a man woot noght in what syde he may

2260　　turne hym. In this lond men lyen in tentes, and they brenne mucke of beestes for defaute of wode. This lond descendeth toward Spruys and Rossye and Turkye. In

fol. 51r　this lond renneth the ryver of Ethel, which is oon of the grettest | ryvers of the worlde. And hit is every yer y-froze so hard that men fight theruppon in gret batayle both on hors and on foote, mo than 100,000 of men at ones. And a lytel fro

2265　　that ryver is the Gret See of Oxean, that men calle Maure, and in this Maure is gret plenté of fyssh.

And then to Caspize, and at Caspyze beth ful strayte passages to go toward Ynde. And therfore Kyng Alisaundre let make ther a cité that is y-called Alisaun-dre, to kepe that passage so that no man shal passe but he have leve. And now that

2270　　cité is called Port de Feare.

And the principal cité of Coman is called Sarochize. This is oon of the 3 wayes that gooth to Inde, bot in this way may noght many men go togedre but in wynter. This passage is called Barkent. And another way is for to go to the londe Turkes-ton thorgh Perce, and in this way beth many journeyes and wildernesse. And the

2235 **be hardy**, dares. **2238 wole**, will. **2243 sheryng**, sharp. **2247 camacas**, silk-like fabric. **2248 Asye the Depe**, Deepest Asia. **2257 habited**, inhabited. **2259 flyen**, flies. **2260 mucke**, manure. **2265 Oxean**, Ocean; **Maure**, the Black Sea. **2270 Port de Feare**, Gate of Iron.

2275   3 way that comth fro Cosmanne and gooth thorgh the Gret See and the kyngdom
         of Abcare. And ye shal understonde that alle thes kyngdomes and londes into Pers
         ben y-holde of the Gret Chan of Chatay, and other many mo. And therfore he is
         a gret lord of men and of londes.

THE LOND OF PERS. CAPITULUM OCTAVUMDECIMUM.   [Chapter 18.]

              Now Y have devised the londes and the kyngdomes toward the north to com fro
2280   the lond of Cathay unto the londes of Spruys, wher Cristen men dwelleth. Now shal
         Y telle of other londes and kyngdoms comyng fro Chatay, comyng fro the Gregyssh
         See wher Cristen men dwelleth. And for as moche as hit is nexte to the Gret Chane
         of Chatay, the emperour of Perce is grettest lord, therfore Y shal speke of hym. And
         ye shal understonde that he hath two kyngdoms. That oon bygynneth toward the est,
2285   toward the kyngdom of Turkeston, and hit lasteth estward to the see of Caspise, and
         southward to the lond of Ynde. And this lond is good and playn and wel y-manned
         and of many citeis, but the two citees that ben most principale ben y-cleped Battria
fol. 51v and Sorman Gramang. And that other kyngdom | of Perce lasteth fro the rever of
         Fyson to the Gret Ermonye, and northward to the see of Caspyse, and so forth to the
2290   lond of Ynde. And this is aplentuous lond and good. And in this kyngdom beth thre
         principal citees: Nessabor, Saphan, and Sarmasse.
              And Sarmasse is in the lond of Ermonye, in which wer somtyme foure kyng-
         doms. And Perce lasteth westward to Turky in leyngthe, and in brede lesteth fro
         the cité of Alisaundre, that now is y-called Port de Feare, unto the lond of Medy.
2295   In this Ermonye beth many fayre citees, but ther Canryssy is most of name.
              This lond of Medy is a lond but noght brood, that bygynneth estward to the
         lond of Perce and Inde the Lasse, and lasteth toward the kyngdom of Caldee, and
         northward lasteth to the Lytel Ermonye. The beste citees of that lond ben y-called
         Garaghe and Karmen.
2300   And then is the kyngdom of Gorge, that bygynneth estward at the gret hylle
         that is y-called Abyor. This lasteth fro Turky to the Gret See and this lond of Medy
         and of the Gret Ermonye. And in this lond beth two kynges, on of Akas and
         another of Gorge. But he of Gorge is in subjeccioun to the Gret Chane, but he of
         Akas hath a strong contré, and he defendith hym wel fro his enemyes.
2305   In this lond of Akas is a gret mervayl, for ther is a gret contré that is ney 3
         journeys aboute, and hit is y-called Hamson. And that contré is covered al with
         derknes so that is no lyght. And men ther der noght go in that contré for hit is so
         derke. And yit men of that contré that beth ther sayen that they may here somtyme
         therynne voys of men, and of hors, and of cockes crowyng, and therfore men
2310   wyteth wel that men dwellen therynne. And they say that hit is derknesse that
         cometh thorgh miracle of God that He shewed for Cristen men. For hit was som-
         tyme a wicked emperour of Perce that men called him Saures, and he pursued
         Cristen men to destruye hem, and for to make hem do sacrifise to his fals goddes.
2314   And at that tyme in that contré dwelled many Cristen men, which forsooke her |
fol. 52r good and her catell and all rychesses, and wolde go into Grece. And when they

2281 Gregyssh, Greek. **2286 playn**, flat. **2295 of name**, famous. **2307 derknes**, darkness.
2309 voys, voices.

were all on a gret playn that men callen Megone, the emperour and his men pursued hem so faste that alle the Cristen men setten hem on her kneys and prayed
to God that He wolde help hem. Afterward ther come a thicke cloude, and overclapped hem, the emperour and all his oste, so that they myght never go away, and
2320   somme dwelleth ther yit in that derknesse. And the Cristen men went wher they
wolde, and therfore they myghte sey thus: *A Domino factum est istud et est mirabile in
oculis nostris.* That is to say: "Of Our Lorde this is y-do, and that is mervayl in our
eyen." Also out of this derk londe comth a ryver, that men may se by takyng of
good that men dwelleth therynne.
2325   And then the nexte is the lond of Turkye, that marcheth to the Gret Ermonye.
And therynne beth many contrees, as Capas, Saure, Brike, Quecissioun, Pytan, and
Geneth. In ech of these beth many good citees. And hit is a playn lond and fewe
hilles and fewe ryvers, and hit is plenteuous of vuryk and rychasse. Than is the
kyngdome of Mesopotayn, that bygynneth estward at the flum of Tygre at a cité
2330   that men calleth Morcelle. And hit lasteth westward to the Fame Eufrates, to a cité
that men callen Rochaus, and fro the Heye Ermonye unto the Lasse. And hit is a
good lond and a playn, and hit marcheth to the lond of Caldee. And the lond of
Ethiope marcheth estward to the gret wyldernesse, and westward to the lond of
Nubyse, and southward to the kyngdome of Maritane, and northward to the Rede
2335   See. And this Maritane, that lasteth fro the hilles of Ethiope into Lybye the Heye,
and hit marcheth into Nubye wher dwellen Cristen men. And then is Nubye the
Heye and the Lowe, which that lasteth to the gret see of Spayne.

THE KYNDOM OF CALDEE. CAPITULUM NOVEMDECIMUM.   [Chapter 19.]

             Now have Y spoke and y-told of many contreis of this side and of the kyngdom
Catay, of which many beth obesshant to the Gret Chane. Now then Y shal speke
fol. 52v   of londes and of contrees and yles that beth yende Catay. And | whoso shal goo fro
2341   Chatay to Ynde the Heye and the Lowe, he shal go thorgh a kyngdom that men
callen Caldee, and that is a gret lond. And ther groweth fruyt as hit were goordes.
And when hit is rype, men sher hit asondre. And they fynde therynne as hit were
a beest of flessh, blod, and boon, and as hit were a lytel lombe withouten wolle.
2345   And they eten that beest and the fruyt also, and that is a gret mervayle. Neverthe-
les Y seyde to hem that Y helde that no gret mervayle, for Y sayde that in my
contré beth trees that bereth fruyt that bycometh bryddes fleynge, and tho beth
good to ete. And they had gret mervayle of this. In this lond and in many other
aboute beth trees that berith clowes and notemyges, canel and other spices. And
2350   ther beth vynes that bereth gret grapes, that a strong man shal be besy to bere a
clustre therof.
             In that same lond, Jewes ben enclosid in the hilles of Caspyze, that men callen
Uber. And thilke Jewes ben of the kynde of Gog Magog, and they may noght com
out at no syde. Ther wer enclosed 22 kynges with other peple that dwelled byfore

2318–19 **overclapped**, enshrouded. **2319 oste**, host. **2322 y-do**, done. **2327 playn**, flat.
2328 vuryk and rychasse, wealth and riches (?). **2329 flum**, river. **2330 Fame**, River.
2339 obesshant, obeisant. **2340 beth yende**, are beyond. **2343 sher**, shear. **2344 lombe**,
lamb; **wolle**, wool. **2349 clowes**, cloves; **notemyges**, nutmegs; **canel**, cinnamon. **2350**
besy, hard-pressed. **2353 kynde**, kin.

2355 bytwyne the hilles of Siche. For the kyng Alisaundre chased hem thider among
thilke hilles, for he trowed to have enclosed hem ther thorgh worchyng of men, but
he myght noght. And tho he prayde to God that He wolde fulfylle that he hadde
bygonne, and God herd his prayer and enclosed the hilles togedre so that the Jewes
dwelleth ther as they were y-loke in a castel. And ther beth hilles alle aboute hem
2360 but at oon syde, and ther is the see of Caspize. And som man myght aske, "Syth ther
is a see at oon syde, why go they noght out ther?" But that Y answer and say, though
hit be so y-called a see, hit is no see but a stonk stondyng among hilles, and hit is
the grettest stonk of alle the worlde. And if they went over that see, they wyte noght
wher to aryve, for they conne noght speke but her owen langage.
2365 And somtyme hit is so that som of the Jewes gon over the hilles. But many may
noght passe ther togedre, for the hilles beth so gret and so heye. And men say in
fol. 53r the | contré aboute that in the tyme of Antecrist thay shulleth do mych harme to
Cristen men. And therfore all the Jewes that dwelleth aboute in the worlde lerneth
to speke Ebreu, for thilke Jewes that dwelleth among thilke spekith none thyng but
2370 Ebreu. And then shal these Jewes speke Ebreu to hem as Y trowe, and lede hem
to Cristendome for to destruye men of Cristendom. For these Jewes sayen they
wyte wel that the Jewes that dwelleth among thilke hilles shulleth come oute, and
Cristen men shal be in her subjeccioun as they ben now under Cristen men.
And if ye wole wyte how they shal fynde the passage out, as Y have understonde
2375 Y shal say yow. In the tyme of Antecrist, a fox shal make his den in the same place
wher Kyng Alisaundre leet make the gates. And he shal worche in the erthe that
he shal go thorgh out tyl that he come among the Jewes. And when they seyn this
fox they shal have gret mervayle of hym, for they sawe never none soch a beest.
And they shul chace this fox and pursue hym til he be fled into his hole that he
2380 come fro. And then shul the Jewes grave after hym as he went til they fynde the
gates, which ben makyd with gret stones wel y-dight with sement. And they shal
breke these gates, and so shal thay come out.
Then is the lond of Bakarie wher beth wicked men and felle. In that lond beth
trees that bereth wolle as hit were of sheep, of which they make hem clothis. In this
2385 lond beth many griffons, mo than in other londes. And som men sayen that they
have the body byfore as an egle and byhynde as a lyon, and hit is so. But the grif-
fol. 53v fons haveth a body gretter than 8 and strenger than an 100 | egles, for he wole bere
fleynge to his neste a gret horse and a man uppon hym y-armed, other two oxen
y-yoked togedre as they go at the plow. And he hath gret nayles and long on his
2390 feet, as hit were hornes of oxen, and of thilke nayles they make coppes to drynke
of, and of his rybbes they make bowes to shet with.

2356 worchyng, the work. 2359 y-loke, locked. 2360 Syth, Since. 2362 stonk, swamp.
2367 Antecrist, Antichrist. 2369 Ebreu, Hebrew; thilke₂, these same [hills]. 2370 trowe,
believe. 2375 say yow, tell you. 2376 worche, work; that, [so] that. 2377 seyn, see. 2380
grave, dig. 2381 y-dight, constructed. 2384 wolle, wool. 2386 egle, eagle; lyon, lion.
2391 shet, shoot.

THE LOND OF PRESTER JOHN. CAPITULUM VICESIMUM.   [Chapter 20.]

Fro this lond of Bacarie, men goon many journeys to the lond of Prester John, that is the emperour of Ynde, that men callen his lond Pentoxorie. This emperour Prester John hath many good citees and tounes and many gret iles and large, for
2395   the lond of Ynde is departed in iles by cause of the gret floodes that cometh out of Paradis. And also in the see beth many gret iles. And the best cité of Pentoxorie is y-called Nyse, for that is a noble cité and a ryche.

Prester John hath under hym many kynges and many diverse peeple. And his lond is good and ryche, but noght so ryche as the lond of the Gret Chane. For
2400   marchauntes cometh noght so moche thider as they doon to the lond of the Gret Chane, for hit is longer way. And also they fyndeth in the ile of Catay all that they have nede to, as spices, clothes of goolde, and of other thyng. And thow hit be beter chepe in the lond of Prester John, yit they leve hit for the lenger way and gret periles of the see. For in the see beth many places wher ben many roches of
2405   adamaundes, which of his owene kynde draweth yre to hym. For Y went ones in that see, and Y say as hit had y-be a gret ile of trees growyng as stockes. And oure
fol. 54r   shipmen sayde that thilke trees were of shippes | mastes that sayled on the see, and so abode the shippes ther thorgh vertu of the adamaund.

The lond of Prester John is longe, and marchauntes cometh thider thorgh the
2410   lond of Perce and cometh to a cité that is y-called Ermes, for a philosopher that men called Ermes founded hit. And then is another cité that is y-called Soboth. And ther is lytel whete and barlich, and therfore they eten ryse and mylke and chese and other fruytes. And ther ben gret plenté of popynjayes, as ben in other contreyes of larkes.

2415   This emperour Prester John weddeth communely the doghter of the Gret Chane, and the Gret Chane his doghter. In this lond beth many precious stones so gret and brode that they make vessel therof, as platers, coppes, and other thynges. This Prester John is Cristen and a gret party of his lond also, but they have noght alle the articles of our feith. For they byleve wel on the Fader, Sone,
2420   and Holy Gost, and they make noon fors of no catel. And Prester John hath under hym 72 provinces other contreys, and ech hath a kynge, and thilke kynges haveth other kynges under hem.

And in this lond beth many mervailes, for in that lond is the Gravel See, that is al sonde and gravel and no water, and ebbeth and floweth with gret wawes as the
2425   see dooth. And hit resteth never, ne no man may passe that see with shippe neyther noon other wyse. And in that see men fyndeth good fissh of other shap than is in other sees, and of good savour and good to ete. In that contré is a playn among hilles. In the playn groweth trees that at sonne rysing every day bygynneth to growe. And so they groweth til mydday and berith fruyt, but men der noght ete
2430   therof for hit is maner of ire. And after mydday hit turneth agayn to the erthe, so that when the sonne is doune hit is nothyng y-sene.

2403 **chepe**, bargaining; **for**, because of. 2405 **adamaundes**, adamant (lodestone); **yre**, iron. 2406 **as stockes**, like stalks. 2408 **vertu**, power. 2412 **barlich**, barley; **ryse**, rice. 2413 **pop-ynjayes**, parrots. 2415 **communely**, usually. 2420 **make noon fors of**, do not care for. 2425 **neyther**, nor. 2426 **wyse**, way. 2430 **ire**, iron. 2431 **nothyng y-sene**, not seen.

fol. 54v   In that contré beth | many popinjayes spekyng, the which spekith of her owen
            kynde as pertly as doth men.
                When this emperour Prester John weyndith to batayle he hath no baner tofore
2435   hym. But he hath thre crosses y-bore byfore hym, oon of fyne goold, and thilke beth
            wel y-dight with precious stones. And for kepyng of every crosse beth ordeyned a
            thousand men of armes and mo than 100,000 of foot men, in the maner as men
            kepeth a standard in batayle. And when he rideth in another maner in lond of pees,
            then hath he y-bore byfore hym a crosse of tree, noght y-peynted and withoute
2440   goold and sylver and precious stones. And hit is all playn in tokneynge that Our
            Lord deyed on a crosse of tre. And also he hath y-bore byfore hym a plate of goold
            full of erthe, in tokenynge that his lordship and his noble aray is noght and shal
            turne into erthe agayne. And also another vessel is y-bore byfore hym ful of jewels
            and goold and precious stones, in tocknynge of his nobley and his myght.
2445   Prester John dwelleth at the cité of Suse, and ther is his chief palays. And above
            the chief tour beth two pomelles of goolde all rounde, and eyther of tho hath two
            charbocles gret and large that shyneth ryght cleer uppon the nyght. And the chief
            gates of that palays beth of precious stones that men calle sardyn, and the bordure
            of barres beth of yvour, and the wyndowes of the halle and chamber of cristal. And
2450   the tables which they ete uppon beth of emeraudes somme, and som of mastyk,
            and somme of goold and other precious stones. And the pelers that bereth these
            tables beth also of precious stones.
                And the greces uppon the which he goth to his mete and to his sege wher he
fol. 55r   sitteth, oon is of mastyk, another of cristal, another of | jaspe, and other precious
2455   stones. And alle the greces ben y-bordured with fyne goolde and wel y-dyght with
            gret pyleres and precious stones. The pylers in the chambre beth of fyne goold
            with many charbocles that geveth gret lyght, and ther brenneth also in his cham-
            bre every nyght 12 gret vesselles of cristal ful of baume, to geve good smel in the
            chambre. The forme of his bed is ful of safyres and wel y-boonde with goolde, to
2460   make hym slepe wel and to destruye lecherye. For he wole noght lye by his wyves
            but thries in the yer, and all for getyng of children.

ARAY OF THE COURT OF PRESTER JOHN.
CAPITULUM VICESIMUM PRIMUM.   [Chapter 21.]

                Also he hath a faire palays at the cité of Nyse, wher he dwelleth when hym
            liketh. And he hath every day in his court mo than 30,000 persones, withoute stran-
            gers that cometh and gooth. But 30,000 ther is, and in the coort of the Gret Chane
2465   of Cathay spendeth noght so moche as hys doth, for 12,000 men he hath evermore.
            And he hath 7 kynges in his court to serve hym and every of ham serveth a monthe
            aboute. And with every kyng serveth every day 72 dukes and 300 erles. And every
            day eteth in his court 12 erchebysshoppes and 12 other bysshoppes. The patriarke

---

2432–33 of her owen kynde, by nature. **2433 pertly,** clearly. **2434 weyndith,** goes. **2438
of pees,** at peace. **2439 tree,** wood. **2442 noght,** nothing. **2446 pomelles,** rounded knobs.
2447 charbocles, carbuncles. **2448 sardyn,** sardonyx; **bordure,** border. **2449 yvour,** ivory.
2450 mastyk, resin. **2451 pelers,** pillars. **2453 greces,** steps; **sege,** seat. **2454 jaspe,**
jasper. **2458 baume,** aromatic balm. **2459 forme,** frame; **y-boonde,** bound. **2463
withoute,** not counting. **2465 he,** i.e., the Great Khan. **2466 every of ham,** each of them.

2470 of Seynt Thomas is as he were a pope and erchebysshop, bysshop, and abbot, and ther beth alle the kynges. And som of these lordes ben maistres of the halle, and som of chambre, som stywardes, som marchalles, and som other offecers, and therfore he is ful ryal.

In this lond was somtyme a ryche man that men called Catholonabeus, and he had a fayre castel uppon an hylle and a strong. And he had y-lete make a good
2475 walle all aboute the hille, and withynne was a fair gardeyn in which were many fair trees beryng all maner fruyt that he myghte fynde. And he let plante therynne of
fol. 55v alle maner herbes and of good smel. And ther were many fayre | welles therby, and by hem were y-maked many fayre halles and chambres, wel y-dyght with goold and asure. And he hadde y-leet make bryddes and beestis that turned aboute by gynne
2480 in an orlage, and songe as they had be quyke. And he had in his gardeynes may-dens of 15 yer olde, the fairest that he myghte fynde, and knave children of the same elde, and they were clothed in clothes of goolde and he sayde that thay were angeles. And he had y-maked a condite under erthe so that when he wolde, that condyte shold renne somtyme mylke, somtyme wyne, and somtyme hony. And this
2485 place is called Paradis. And when any yong bacheler of that contré, knyght other squyer, cometh to hym for to solacy hym and disporte hym, he ledith hym into his Paradis and showeth hym all these diverse thynges and his damyselles and hys welles, and he dyd smyte hys instrumentz of musyke in a heye tour that may noght be seye, and he seyde they were angeles of God and that place is Paradys that God
2490 graunted to hym that beleved, when He sayde thus: *Dabo vobis terram fluentem lac et mel.* That is to say: "I shal gyve yow londe flowyng mylke and hony."

And a lytel fro that place, on the lyft syde by the ryver of Fison, is a gret mer-vayle. Ther is a valeye bytwyxte two hilles that is 4 myle long. Som men calle hit the Valeye Enchaunted, and som men calle hit the Valey of Fendes, and som men
2495 calle hit the Valey Perlous. And that valey beth many gret tempestes and gret noyses and thondres every day and every nyght. This valey is all full of develes and hath y-be allway. And men say ther that hit is an entré to Helle. In this valey is moche goold and sylver, wherfore many Cristen men and other gooth theder for covetyse, to have of that goold and sylver. But fewe of hem cometh out agayn, for
fol. 56r they beth anoon astrangled | with fendes.
2501   And in the myddel of that valeye uppon a roch is a visage and the heed of the devel bodylich, ryght hydous and dredful to se. And ther is nothyng y-sene but the hede to the shuldres, but ther is no man in the worlde, Cristen ne other, so hardy but that he sholde have gret drede to se hit. And his eyen beth so staryng and
2505 sprynclynge of fire of diverse coloures and he chaungeth so ofte his contenaunce that no man der come nye hym for all the worldes good. And out of his mouth and his nose cometh gret plenté of fyre. But alway a good Cristen man that is stable in his feith may go thorghout that valey wel ynow withoute harme, if he be clene y-shryve and blesse hym with the signe of the crosse.

2472 **ful ryal**, very royal. 2479 **asure**, azure; **gynne**, engine. 2480 **orlage**, clock. 2481 **knave**, male. 2483 **condite**, conduit. 2486 **solacy hym**, solace himself. 2489 **seye**, seen. 2494 **Fendes**, Fiends. 2495 **Perlous**, Perilous; **And**, In. 2496 **thondres**, thunders. 2499 **covetyse**, greed. 2500 **astrangled with**, killed by. 2502 **devel bodylich**, devil incarnate. 2505 **sprynclynge**, sparkling. 2508–09 **clene y-shryve**, well confessed.

2510   And when my felawes and Y were in that valey we had ful gret drede and som of myn felawes acorded to go that way and som noght. And ther were in oure company 2 freres menoures of Lumbardye, and they sayde if eny of us wolde go theryn they wolde also. And then uppon trist of hem we sayde that we wolde go. And we leet synge a Messe, and were y-shryve and houseled, and so went we yn 14.

2515   And when we come out we were but 10, and wiste noght whoder oure felawes were y-lost other turned agen, for we saw no more of hem. And som of oure felawes that wolde noght go yn with us went aboute by another way and were ther byfore us.

      And we say many wonder syghtes in that valey: goold, sylver, precious stones, gret plenté as us thoughte. But whether hit was as we semed we wyte noght, for Y

2520   touched none. For the fendes beth so sotel that they make many tyme thynges to seme other then they ben. And we were ofte y-cast adoun into the erthe with wynde

fol. 56v   and thondre and tempestes. But God halpe us alway and so | that we passed thorgh the valey withoute harm, thanked be Our Lord God.

      And byyonde that valey is a gret ile wher that peple ben as gret as gyauntes of

2525   28 other 30 foot longe. And they have no clothyng but beestes skynnes. And tho ete no breed but raw flessh, and drynketh mylke, and they eteth gladloker flessh of men than of other. And men sayde that byyonde that yle was another yle wher beth gretter gyauntz, for they beth of 45 other 50 foot longe, and som seyde of 50 cubites longe, but Y sey hem noght.

2530   And another ile is ther wher ben wicked and lither wymmen. And tho have stones in her eyen, and tho han soch a kynde that if they byholdeth any man with wrathe, they sleeth hym with her lokynge.

      Another ile is ther of faire peple, wher the custome is soche that the ferste nyght that they ben y-wedded they telleth that hit is y-ordeyned therto a man, and

2535   let hym lye by her wyves to have her maydenhode. And they geve hym gret hire for his travayle. And thilke men ben called *gadlybyriens*. For men of that contré holden hit a gret peryle to have a wommanis maydenhod. And if hit be so that her hosbande fynde her a mayde when he cometh to her, the hosband shal playne hym to the lawe that he hath noght do his dever, and he shal be gryvouslich pursued.

2540   After oon nyght they kepen her wyves well, that they speke noght with thilke man.

      And Y asked what was the cause why they had that costome, and they seyde somtyme men lay by her wyves ferst, and som of tho wyves had eddres in her bodies that touched her hosbandes yerd in her bodyes. So were many men slayn. Therfore leet thay other men have her maydenhode for drede of deth, or thei put

2545   hemself in aventure.

      Another ile is ther wher they chesen the kyng and they chesen hym noght for

fol. 57r   his ry|chesse ne for his nobleye, but he that is of good condiciouns and most ryghtwys and trywest to juge every man of his trespas, litel other mochel, riche

---

2513 trist, trust. **2514 y-shryve**, confessed; **houseled**, given communion. **2515 whoder**, whether. **2518 say**, saw. **2519 we semed**, it seemed to us. **2524 gyauntes**, giants. **2526 gladloker**, more gladly. **2529 sey**, saw. **2530 lither**, evil. **2534 hit is y-ordeyned therto a man**, there is a man specially designated. **2535 gret hire**, good pay. **2536 travayle**, work. **2538 playne hym**, make a complaint. **2539 he**, i.e., the gadlybyrien; **dever**, task; **gryvouslich**, grievously. **2543 yerd**, penis. **2544 or**, before. **2545 aventure**, danger. **2548 ryghtwys**, righteous; **trywest**, fairest.

2550   other poore. And that kyng may do no man to deth withoute conseil of his barons and that they alle be assent therto. And if hit be so that the kyng do a gret trespas, as to sle a man other soch another, he shal be dede. But he shal noght be slayne, but they shal defende and forbede that no man be so hardy to make hym companye, and nother speke with hym, nother come to hym, ne gyve hym no mete ne drynke, and thus he shal deighe.

2555   In this lond and many other of Inde beth many cocthrylles, that is a maner of a long eddre. And on the nyght they dwell in wateres, and uppon the day in the londe amonge roches. These eddres sleeth men and eteth hem gryntynge, and they have no tonge.

     In this contré and many other, they sowen the seed of coton every yer. And hit
2560   groweth as hit were smale trees and bereth coton.

     In Arabye beth many bryddes and som men callen hem gyrsaunt, that is a wel fayr beest, and hit is heyer than a gret courser other a stede, but his necke is neygh 20 cubites longe, and his cruper and his tayle is lyke to an hert and he may loke over an high hous. And ther beth many camelions, that is a lytel beest that eteth
2565   ne drynketh never. And he changeth his coloures ofte, for somtyme he is of oo colour and somtyme of another. And he may chaunge hym into alle colouris but blak and reed. And ther beth many wilde swyn of many colouris, and as gret as an oxe, and hy beth all splotted as hit were founes. And ther beth lyons al white, and
fol. 57v   ther beth other beestes as gret as stedes that men callen | lonhorauns, and som men
2570   callen hem tontys. And they beth blake, and they have 3 long hornes in her front as sheryng as a sharp swerd, and he chasseth and sleeth the olyfaunt. And ther beth many other beestes.

     And ther is another gret ile and plenteuous where beth good men and trywe and of good lyff after her feith. And though they be noght Cristen, yit of lawe of
2575   kynde they beth full of good vertues. And they fleeth alle vices of synnes and of malis, for they beth noght envyous, ne proute, ne covetous, ne glotons, nother lechours. And they do to no man but as they wolde they dede to hym. And they fulfelleth the 10 Commaundementes. They make noon fors of no rychesse. They swereth noght but ye and nay, for they say tho that swereth, he wole bygyle his
2580   neyghbore. And som calle this ile Bragme, and som men calle hit the Ile of Feith. And thorgh this yle renneth a gret ryver, the which men calle Tebe. And generallich alle men in this yle and other neygh beth ryght trewe, and trewer and ryghtwyser than in another contré.

     In this ile ben none thefes, none morthereres, nother comen wymmen, no
2585   lechoures, ne beggeres. And for they beth so trywe and so good, ther is no tempest, ne no werre, no hunger, ne none other tribulacioun. And so hit semeth wel that God loveth hem, and that He is wel apayed of her levynge. And they leven so

---

2549 conseil, counsel. **2552 defende**, forbid. **2555 cocthrylles**, crocodiles. **2557 gryntynge**, groaning. **2561 gyrsaunt**, giraffes. **2562 heyer**, taller; **courser**, charger. **2563 cruper**, hindquarters; **hert**, deer. **2568 hy**, they; **founes**, fawns. **2569 stedes**, horses; **lonhorauns**, rhinoceroses. **2571 sheryng**, cutting; **olyfaunt**, elephant. **2574 lyff**, life. **2574–75 of lawe of kynde**, according to natural law. **2576 proute**, proud. **2578 make noon fors of**, care nothing for. **2584 thefes**, thieves; **morthereres**, murderers; **comen wymmen**, prostitutes. **2587 apayed of her levynge**, pleased by their way of life.

honestly in mete and drynke that they lyven ryght longe, and many of hem deyen withoute sycknesse, for kynde fayleth hem for ylde.

2590   And Kyng Alisaundre sende somtyme thider for to wynne that londe, and they sende hym letteres agayn and seyde thus: "What is ynow to a man that all the worlde may noght suffyse? Thow shalt fynde nothyng in us why thow sholdest werre on us, when we have no rychesse nother tresour, and all the catel and goodes

fol. 58r | of our contré ben in comune. Our mete and our drynke is our tresour and ryches-

2595 ses. And instede of goold and sylver, we have pees and acorde and good lyff alone. And we have but oon cloth uppon us, and our wyves beth noght araed rychely to pleysyng of men, for we hold hit a gret foly a man to dyght his body to make hym seme fayrere than hit is. We have evermore y-be in pees til now that thow wylt desert us. We have a kyng among us, noght for lawe ne for demyng of no man, for

2600 ther is no trespas among us, but al onlich to lere us and to be obedient to hym. And so myght thow noght take noght fro us but our good pees." And when Kyng Alisaunder saw this letter, he thoughte that he sholde do moche harm if he sturbled hem, and so he sende to hem that they sholde kepe wel her good maners and have no drede of hym.

2605   Another ile ther is that is y-called Synople, wher also beth good peple and trywe and ful of good feith, and beth moch lyke of lyveng to the peple byforesayde. And they goth all naked. And into that ile com Kyng Alisaundre, and when he saw her good feith and trywe, he sayde he wolde do hem no harme, and bade hem asken of hym what they wolde have. And they answered that they had rychesse

2610 ynow when they had mete and drynke to susteyne her bodyes. And they seyde the rychesse of the worlde is noght worth. But if hit were so that he myght graunte hem that they sholde never deye, of that they wolde pray hym. And Kyng Alis- aundre seyde he myght noght do that, for he was dedelych hymself and sholde deye as they sholde.

2615   Then sayde they, "Why art thow so proute and woldest wynne all the worlde

fol. 58v and have in thyn subjeccioun as hit were a god, and thow hast no terme | of thyn lyf? And thow wolt have all the rychasse of the worlde, which shal forsake thee or thow forsake hit. And thow shalt bere noght with thee, but hit shal by leve byhynde thee to other. But as thow were y-bore naked, thow shalt be y-do yn erthe." And so Kyng

2620 Alisaundre was gretly astoned of this aunswer.

    Although hit be so that they have noght alle the articles of our feith, yit Y trowe that God love hem neverthelasse for her good purpoos, and that they take her the same degré as He dide of Jope that was a paynem, the which He helde hym for His triwe servaunt, and many other. And Y trowe that God loveth all thilke that loveth

2625 Hym and serveth Hym meckly and trywly, and despised vaynglory of the worlde as thes men dide, and as Jope dyde.

2587–88 they leven so honestly in mete and drynke, they eat and drink so moderately. **2589 ylde**, old age. **2596 araed**, arrayed. **2597 dyght**, adorn. **2599 desert**, disinherit (take from). **2600 al onlich**, only; **lere**, teach. **2603 sturbled**, disturbed. **2606 lyveng**, living. **2611 noght worth**, worth nothing. **2613 dedelych**, mortal. **2616 as hit were a god, and thow hast no terme of thyn lyf**, as if you were a god, whose life would never end. **2617 or**, before. **2618 by leve**, be left. **2622 purpoos**, intentions. **2622–23 they take her the same degré as He dide of Jope**, they get the same consideration He gave to Job. **2625 meckly**, meekly.

And therfor Our Lord saeth thus: *Ponam eis multiplices leges meas.* That is to say: "I shal put to hem my lawes manyfold." And the godespell saeth thus: *Alias oves habeo que non sunt ex hoc ovili.* That is to say: "I have other sheep that beth noght

2630   of this foold."

And therto acordeth a visioun of Seynt Petre which he saw at Japhe, when the angel com fro Hevene and brought with hym of alle maner of beestis, eddres, and briddes, and seyde to Seynt Petre, "Tak and ete." And Petre sayde, "I ate never of bestes unclene." And tho the angel saide thus: *Non dicas inmunda que deus mundavit.*

2635   That is to say: "Calle thow noght thilke thinges unclene which God hath clensed." This was y-do in tocknyng that men sholde have no man in dispite for hire diverse lyvenge, for we wyteth noght wham God loveth most, and wham he hateth most.

And another ile is ther which they calle Pytan. Men of this ile tylyeth no corn

fol. 59r   lond, for they | ete noght. And they ben smale men, but noght so smale as ben
2640   pigmans. These men lyven with the smel and savour of wild apples. And when they goth fer out of contré they berith apples with hem, for also sone as they leveth the savour of the apples they deye. And they ben noght ful resonable, but as bestes. And then is another ile wher the peple ben all in fetheris as bryddes, but the face and the palmes of her hondes. These men goth as well uppon the see as uppon the

2645   londe. And they eten flessh all raw. In this ile is a gret ryver that is two myle brod and an half, that men callen Ranymar.

And byyende that is a gret wyldernesse, as men sayn that han be ther, in the which men sayn ben trees of the sonne and of the mone that spake to Kyng Alisaundre and told hym of his dedes. And men sayn that peple that kepith thes

2650   trees and eteth of the fruyt, they lyven 400 other 500 yeres, thorgh myght of that fruyt. And we wold have go theder, but Y trowe a hundred thousand men of armes sholde noght passe that wyldernesse for wylde bestes, as dragones and other.

In this yle beth many olyfauntz white and blew withoute nombre, unicornes, and lyons of many coloures. Many other yles beth in the lond of Prester John that

2655   were to longe to telle, and ther is myche rychesse and many precious stones.

WHY HE IS Y-CLIPED PRESTER JOHN.
CAPITULUM VICESIMUM SECUNDUM.   [Chapter 22.]

I trowe som of yow have y-herd telle whi he is y-called Prester John, but for tho that wyte noght, Y shal say. Ther was somtyme an emperour that was a noble prince and a doughty, and he hadde many Cristen knyghtes with hym. And this emperour thought he wolde y-se the maner of Cristen men and the servise in

2660   cherche of Cristen men. And tho was Cristendome and Cristen cherches in Tur-
fol. 59v   kye, Surry, Tartarye, Jerusalem, Palestyne, Araby, and | all the lond of Egypte. And this emperour come with a Cristen knyght into a cherche of Egipte uppon the Saturday uppon Witsoneday, when the bysshope makyde orders, and he byheld the servise. And he asked of the knyght what peple tho sholde be that stood byfore the

2665   bysshope. And the knyght seyde tho sholde be prestes. And tho he seyde he wolde no more be called "kyng," ne "emperour," but "prest." And also he wolde have the

---

2628 godespell, gospel. **2638 tylyeth**, till. **2640 pigmans**, pygmies. **2643 but**, except. **2663 makyde orders**, ordained priests.

name of hym that come out ferst at the dore of the prestes, which man was y-called
John. And so he wold be called "Prester John," and so haveth all the emperoures
sithe be y-called.

2670   In that lond ben Cristen men of good feith, and they have prestes to syng her
Masse, and they make her sacrament as men of Grece doth. But they say noght so
many thinges as our prestes doth, for they say noght but as the aposteles, Seynt
Petre and Seynt Thomas and other, sayde. When they synge Messes, they seith
ferst *Pater Noster* and the wordes which Goddes body is makid with. For we have
2675   many addiciouns which that popes han y-ordeynd, which men of that contré knoweth noght.

And more estward beth two yles. That oon is y-called Orrel and that other is y-
called Argete, of wham all the lond is myne of goold and sylver. In this ile men
may se none sterres cler shynyng but a sterre that is y-called Canapos. And ther
2680   men may noght se the mone but in the laste quarter.

In that ile is a gret hille of goold that pismeres kepeth, and they fynyth the
goold. And the pismeres beth as gret as houndes her, so that no man may come
ther for drede of hem, so that men may gete of that goolde but by queyntise.
Therfore when hit is ryght warme tho pismeres hideth hem in the erthe fro undre
Pynson   of the day to none, and then | men of the countré take camellys and dromaderyes
2686   and other bestes, and goo theder and charge theym with golde and go awey fast
or the pyssmyres come oute of the erthe. And other tymes whan it is nat so hote,
that the pissmyres hyde them nat, they take meres that have foles, and they lay
upon these meres two vesselles as it were two smale barelis tome and the mouthe
2690   upwardes and dryve theym theder, and holden their foles at home. And whan the
pyssmyres sene theyse vesselles, for they have of kynde to leve nothynge tome, they
fylle these vesselles of golde. And whan men trowe that the vesselles ar full, they
take the foles and brynge theym as nere as they dare, and they whyne and the
meres here theym. And as sone they come to ther foles, and so men take the gold
2695   so than. For these pyssemyres woll suffre bestes to goo amonge theym but no men.

Beyonde the iles of the lond of Prester John and his lordship of wyldernesse,
to goo right est men shall nat fynde but hylles, great roches, and other myrke
londe where no man may see on day ne on nyght, as men of the countré say. And
this wyldernes and myrke londe lasteth to Paradyse Terrestre where Adam and Eve
2700   were sette, but they were there but a lytell whyle. And that is towarde the est at be-
gynnynge of the erthe, but that is nat oure est that we call where the sonne rysethe
in those countrees towarde Paradyse. Than it is mydnight in oure countré, for the
roundnesse of the erthe. For Oure Lord made the erthe all rounde in myddes of
firmament.

2705   Of Paradyse can I nat speke propirly for I have nat be there, and that angoreth
me. But that I have herde I shal say you. Men say that Paradyse Terrestre is the
hyghest londe of the worlde, and it is so high that it toucheth nere to the sercle of

---

2678 myne, a mine. **2679 sterres**, stars. **2681 pismeres**, ants; **fynyth**, refine. **2683
queyntise**, cunning. **2684–85 fro undre of the day to none**, from mid-morning to midday.
2686 charge, load. **2687 or**, before. **2688 meres**, mares; **foles**, foals. **2689 tome**, empty.
2695 than, then. **2697 est**, east; **myrke**, dark.

the mone, for it is so highe that Noes flode myght nat come therto, the whyche covered all the erthe aboute. And this Paradyse Terrestre is enclosed all aboute
2710 with a walle, and that wall is all covered with mosse, as it semethe that men may se no stone ne nothynge ellis wherof it is. And the hyghest place of Paradyse, in the mydes of it, is one wall that casteth oute the foure flodes that renne thorowe dyvers londes. The first flode is called Physon or Ganges, and that renneth thorough Ynde. In that ryver are many precious stones and moche *lignum aloes* and gravell
2715 of golde. Another is called Nylus or Gyron, and that rennethe thorough Ethiope and Egypt. The thirde is called Tygre, and that renneth thorough Assary and Er-mony the Grete. And the forth is called Eufrates, that rennethe thorough Ermony and Persy. And men say that all the swete and fresshe water of the world take theyr springynge of theym.
2720   The first ryver is called Physon: that is to say a gaderynge of many ryvers togeder and falle into that ryver. And som call it Canges, for a kynge that was in Ynde that men called Tangeras, for it renneth thorough hys lond. And this ryvere is in som place clere, in som place troble, in som place hote, in som place colde. The secounde ryvere is called Nylus or Gyron, for it is ever troble. For Gyron is to
2725 say "troble." The third ryver is called Tygris. That is to say "fast rennynge," for it renneth faster than any of the other, and so is a best that men call tygrys for he renneth fast. The forth ryver is called Eufrates, that is to say "well brennynge," for there groweth many gode thynges upon the ryver.
    And ye shall understonde that no man lyvynge may go unto that Paradyse. For
2730 by land he may nat go for wylde bestes which ar in the wyldernes, and for hylles and roches where no man may passe. Ne by those ryvers may no man passe, for they come with so greate course and so great wawes that no shyp may go ne sayle ageyne theym. Many greate lordes have asayed many tymes to go by those ryvers to Paradyse, but they myght nat spede in their wey. For som dyed for wery of
2735 rowynge, som wex blynde, and som deefe for noyse of the waters. So no man may passe there but thorough special grace of God.
    And for I can tell you no more of that place I shall say you of that I have sene in these Iles of the londe of Prester John, and they ar under the erthe to us. And other iles ar there, whoso wolde pursue them, for to environ the erthe whoso had
2740 grace of God to holde the wey, he myght come right too the same countrees that he were come of and come fro, and so go aboute the erthe. And for it were to longe tyme and also many perylles too pas, fewe men assay to go so, and yet might be done.
    And therfore men came fro these iles to other iles coostynge of the lordshyp of
2745 Prester John. And men come in the comynge to one ile that men call Cassoy. And that countré is nere sexty journes longe, and more than 50 of brede. That is the best londe that is in those countrees save Chatay. And if marchauntes come theder as comonly as they do unto Chatay it shuld be better than Chatay, for it is so thyk of cytees and townes that whan a man gothe oute of a cyté he seth as sone another

2708 **mone**, moon. 2712 **mydes**, middle; **flodes**, rivers. 2723 **troble**, murky. 2726 **best**, beast; **tygrys**, tiger. 2727 **brennynge**, burning. 2731 **for**, because. 2732 **wawes**, waves. 2733 **asayed**, tried. 2734 **wery**, weariness. 2744 **coostynge**, lying off the coast. 2745 **comynge**, traveling. 2746 **brede**, breadth.

2750   on eche syde. There is greate plenté of spyces and other godes. The kynge of this
        yle is full ryche and myghty, and he holdeth his londe of the Great Chane, for that
        is one of the 12 provynces that the Greate Chane hath under hym withoute his
        owne londe.
              Fro thys Ile men goo to another kyngdom that men call Ryboth, and that is also
2755   under the Greate Chane. This is a gode countré and plenteuous of corne, wyne, and
        other thynges. Men of this londe have none houses, but they dwell in tentes made
        of tre. And the pryncipall cyté is all blacke, made of blake stones and whyte, and all
        the stretes are paved with suche stones. And in that cyté is no man so hardy to spyll
        blode of man ne beest, for worshyp of a mawmet that is worshypped there. In that
2760   cyté dwelle the pope of their lawe that they call Lobassy, and he gyveth all dignytee
        and benefyses that fall to the mawmet. And men of relygyon and men that have
        churches in that countré ar obedyente to hym as men ar here to the pope.
              In this Ile they have a custume thoroughe all the countré that whan a mans
        fader is dede they woll do hym greate worship. They send after all his frendes, re-
2765   ligious prestes, and other many, and they bere the body to an hyll with great joy
        and myrth. And whan it is there the grettest prelate smyteth of his hede and layeth
        it upon a greate plate of golde or sylver and he gyveth it to his son, and the son
        takethe it too his other frendes, syngynge and saynge many orysons. And than the
fol. 60r prestys and the religyous cutte | the flessh of the body into peces and sayeth
2770   orisones. And briddes of the contré cometh thider, for they knoweth the custome,
        and they flieth aboute hem as egles and other briddes eteth, and eteth the flesshe.
        And the prestes casteth the flessh to hem, and they berith hit a little thenne and
        eteth hit. And as prestes in oure contré as her among us singes for soules *Subvenite*
        sancti dei, that is to say, "Helpeth Sentes of God," so thes prestes singen ther with
2775   heye vois in her langage, "Byholdeth how good a man this was, that angels of God
        cometh to fecche hym and berith hym to Paradys." And thenketh the sone that he
        is gretly y-worshiped when bryddes have y-yete his fader. And wher beth most
        plenté of thes briddes, he hath most worship.
              And then cometh the sone hom with alle his frendes and maketh hem a gret
2780   feste. And the sone leteth make clene his fadir his heed. And the flessh of the
        heed, he sherith hit and yif hit to his moste special frendes, every man a litel, for
        a gret denté. And of the skulle of the hed the sone leteth make a coppe, and therof
        drynketh he al his lyfftyme in rememoraunce of his fader.
              And fro thenne to go 10 journeys thorgh the lond of the Gret Chane is a wel
2785   good ile and a gret kyngdom. And the kyng is ful myghty and he hath a ful noble
        lyvyng and ryche, after the maner of the contré. For he hath 50 damesels to serve
        hym every day at his mete and abedde, and doth what he wole. And when he sittith
        at the table, they bringeth hym his mete, and everi tyme fyve messes togedre, and
        singeth in the bryngyng a good song. And they kytteth his meete and put hit in his

---

2752 withoute, outside. **2757 tre**, wood. **2759 mawmet**, idol. **2764 send after**, call together. **2766 smyteth of**, chops off. **2768 orysons**, prayers. **2777 y-worshiped**, honored.
2780 his fadir his heed, father's head. **2781 sherith**, carves; **yif**, gives. **2782 denté**,
delicacy. **2783 lyfftyme**, lifetime. **2786 lyvyng**, way of life. **2788 messes**, servings. **2789
kytteth**, cut.

2790   mouth, for he kytteth noght, but holdeth his hondes byfore hym uppon the table,
        for he hath so longe nayles that he may noght holde.

fol. 60v   And hit is a gret nobleye in that contré | to have longe nayles, and therfor they
        letteth her nayles growe as longe as they wolleth. And som leteth hem growe so
        longe til they wole come al aboute her hondes, and that thenketh hem a gret
2795   nobley and gret gentrise. And the gentrise of a womman ther is to have smale feet,
        and therfor also sone as they beth y-bore, they byndeth her feet so strayt that they
        may noght wexe as they sholde.

             And this kyng hath a wel fair palays and a riche wher he dwelleth, of which the
        walle is two myle aboute. And therin beth many faire gardens. And all the pave-
2800   ment of the halle and chambre is of goold and sylver. And in the myddel of oon
        of the gardens is a litel hulle wheruppon is a litel place y-maked with toures and
        pynacles al of goold. And ther he wole sytte ofte to take the eyr and disport, for hit
        is y-maked for noght elles.

             Fro this lond may men go thorgh the lond of the Gret Chane. And ye shal under-
2805   stonde that alle thes men that Y have spoke of that beth resonable haveth some ar-
        ticles of our feith. And they troweth in God of kynde that maked all the worlde, and
        Him clipe they "God of kynde" as her prophecie saieth: *Et metuant eum omnes fines
        terre.* That is to say: "And alle eyndes of the erthe shal drede Hym." And in another
        place thus: *Omnes gentes servient ei.* That is to say: "All people shal serve to Hym."

2810   But they conne noght propurly speke of God but as her kyndely witte techith
        hem, for they spekith noght of the Sone nother the Holy Goost as they sholde do.
        But they kunne wel speke of the Bible, and specialich of Genesis and of the booke
        of Moyses. And they sayeth thes thynges which thei worshepith beth none godes,
2814   but they worshipe hem for the gret | vertues that beth on hem, whiche thei say may
fol. 61r noght be withoute special grace of God.

             And of simulacres and mamettes that they saith that alle men haveth simulacres
        and mamettes, for they saith that Cristen men haveth images of Our Lady and of
        other. But they wit noght that we worshipeth noght thes images of stoon nother of
        tre for hemself, but the seyntes for wham they beth y-maked. For as the letter
2820   techith clerkes how thei shal trowe, so images and pentours techeth lewed men to
        worshipe the seyntes for wham they beth y-maked.

             They saith also that the angel of God spekith to hem in her mametis, and that
        they doth miracles. They say sooth. They haveth an angel wythynne hem, but ther
        beth two maner of angels, the gode and the wickede: as men of Grece saith, *Chaco*
2825   and *Calo.* Chaco is yvel and Calo is good. But this is no good angel but yvel, that
        is in the mamettis to bygile hem and for to maynteyne hem in her mametrye.

             Ther beth many other contrees and mervayles which Y have noght y-seye, and
        therfor Y can noght speke propurly of hem. And also on contrees wher Y have y-be
        beth many mervailes of which Y speke noght, for hit were to longe tale. And also
2830   Y wole say no more of mervayles that beth ther, so that other men that wendeth
        theder may fynde many nywe thynges to say, of whiche Y have noght tolde nother

---

2792 nobleye, sign of nobility. **2795 gentrise**, show of status. **2796 strayt**, tightly. **2797 wexe**, grow. **2801 hulle**, hill; **toures**, towers. **2802 eyr**, air. **2807 clipe**, call. **2810 but**, except; **kyndely witte**, common sense. **2816 mamettes**, idols. **2817 Our Lady**, the Virgin Mary. **2818 wit**, understand. **2819 tre**, wood. **2820 pentours**, paintings; **lewed**, unlettered.

y-spoke. For many man hath gret likyng and desire to hyre nywe thynges. And Y, John Maundevyle, knyght, that wente out of my contré and passide the see the yer of Our Lord 1332 — and Y have y-passed thorgh many londes, contrees, and iles and am now come to reste — Y have compyled this book and lat write | hit the yer of Our Lord 1366, at 24 yer after my departyng fro my contré, for Y was travelynge 34 yer.

fol. 61v
2836

And for as moche as many man troweth noght but that they se with her owen eye other that they may conseyve with her kyndely witte, therfore Y maked my way in my tornyng homwarde to Rome to showe my book to the holy fader, the pope, and telle to hym mervayles whoch Y hadde y-seye in diverse contrees, so that he, with his wise consayl wolde examine hit with diverse peple that beth in Rome. For ther beth in Rome evermore men dwellynge of diverse nacions of the worlde. And a litel tyme after, when he and his conseil hadde examined hit al thorgh, he sayde me for certayn that all was soath that was therynne. For he sayde he hadde a book uppon Latyn that conteyned that and moch more, after which book the *mappa mundi* ys y-maked, which book he shewed to me. And therfore the holi fader, the pope, hath ratefied and confermed my book in alle poyntes.

2840

2845

And Y praye to alle these that redith this book other hureth hit y-rad, that they wolde pray for me, and Y shal pray for hem. And alle thes that saith for me a *Pater Noster* and an *Ave*, that God forgif me my synnes, Y make hem partyners and graunt hem part of alle my good pilgremage and other good dedes that Y have do and y-wrought and do sithe to my lifis eynde. And Y pray to God, of wham all graces cometh, that He wole alle tho that redith other hureth this book that beth Cristen men fulfille of His grace, and save hem bothe body and soule, and brynge hem | to His joy that ever shall last: He that is in the Trynyté Fader, Son, and Holy Goost, that lyvethe and regneth, God withoute ende. Amen.

2850

2855
Pynson

2832 hyre, hear. **2839 conseyve**, conceive. **2845 soath**, true. **2846 uppon**, written in. **2846–47 *mappa mundi***, world map. **2849 hureth hit y-rad**, hear it read.

# EXPLANATORY NOTES

As exhaustive notes to the *Book* are available both in Warner's Egerton edition and in Seymour's recent Defective edition (though without the support of a bibliography), no effort has been made here to research each source comprehensively or to parse each individual instance of note. Rather, these notes seek to provide sufficient supporting material to aid in close reading of the text, to direct readers' attention to significant issues in scholarship on the *Book*, and to offer suggestions for further reading on areas of potential interest. While many errors of fact and inconsistencies within the text are here noted, no effort has been made to consistently note every instance in which the *Book's* information is skewed or erroneous.

In addition to the notes, we have supplied a detailed glossary of proper names indexed to the text (see pp. 153–76) as well as an overview of the major sources that underlie the *Book* as we have it (see the Appendix, pp. 135–42).

Biblical references are to the Douay-Rheims version. References to the "*Book*" are general, whereas references to particular manuscripts and versions of the *Book* are so noted.

ABBREVIATIONS: **B**: *The Bodley Version of Mandeville's Travels*, ed. Seymour (1963); **D**: *The Defective Version of Mandeville's Travels*, ed. Seymour (2002); **K**: *The Book of John Mandeville*, ed. Kohanski (2002); **S**: *Mandeville's Travels*, ed. Seymour (1967); **R**: London, British Library MS Royal 17 C xxxviii; **W**: *The Buke of John Maundeuill*, ed. Warner (1889).

1–9   This preface, written in the third person and seemingly compiled from infor-
       mation found elsewhere in the text (see the Appendix) is not found in other
       versions of the *Book*. The real identity of the traveler "Sir John Mandeville," if
       indeed such a person existed, has been the subject of long-standing debate.
       (For an overview of the authorship controversy, see K, pp. xxiii–xxviii;
       Seymour, *Sir John Mandeville*, pp. 5–24; and Higgins, *Writing East*, pp. 8–13.)
       While "Mandeville's" identity as an English knight from St. Albans who traveled
       through the Holy Land and the Far East in the early to mid-1300s was long
       accepted as a nucleus of fact, even these basic assumptions are no longer
       considered valid. Seymour states categorically that "(a) *Mandeville's Travels* was
       written on the continent in French, by an unknown hand, c. 1357" and "(b) The
       author was probably not an Englishman, and the existence of 'Sir John
       Mandeville' is completely fictitious" (B, p. 176 n147/13). It is now generally
       supposed that the earliest versions of the *Book* were in French, rather than
       English.
            Whether the author of the *Book* ever in fact traveled has also been a long-
       standing source of debate. From the classic comment that the author probably

never traveled "farther than the nearest library," to Giles Milton's recent assertion of the real travel experience of the author based upon a modern
excursionin the footsteps of Mandeville, opinions vary widely. What is clear is
that much of the *Book* is based on other written sources, many of which have
been traced (see the Appendix for sources for the *Book*).

Even if one accepts "John Mandeville" as a real person and a world
traveler, the dates of travel and of composition of the *Book* remain problematic.
In many of the Insular French texts, the excursion date is given as 1322 and the
book is reported as having been written "after 34 years," i.e., in 1356. Most
Continental texts, however, claim it was written in 1357. In the English
Defective tradition, the date of "Mandeville's" departure ranges from 1300 to
1366 — tending to cluster in the 1320s and 1330s (British Library MS Arundel
140 no. 1's date of 1366 is clearly a scribal error, as the date "1332" is crossed
out and "1366" substituted, apparently as a result of confusion over whether the
date of departure or composition is being given). As Seymour notes, "Jean le
Long's translations, which the author used, were completed in 1351, and the
earliest dated manuscript was written in 1371" (B, p. 175n147/5). He concludes,
"A study of the scribal tradition suggests a date c. 1357," a sensible estimate.

19   *I am kyng of Jewes.* John 19:19–21.

23   *vertu of thynges is in the myddel.* Aristotle (*Nicomachean Ethics* 2.6) and Cicero ("On
Duties" 1.25), among others, speak of the virtue of the middle way. In a clever
semantic shift, the narrator turns Aristotle's idea that every virtue exists as a
mean between vices to his own ends, as proof for Jerusalem's geographical
location as the "mean point" of greatest holiness in a world of sin.

It should be noted, however, that in order for Jerusalem to occupy the
"middle of the world," the world would have to be flat: an idea firmly contra-
dicted by the narrator later in the text.

48   *conquere here ryght heritage.* Warner suggests that the narrator's criticism of great
lords' interest in "disinheriting their neighbors" rather than taking up the
noble cause of crusading in the Holy Land may be a comment upon Edward
III's wars with France, and more specifically the Battle of Poitiers, fought in
1356 (W, p. 157n2.14). Crusading zeal was much diminished in the *Mandeville*-
author's time, the last crusade having embarked for the Holy Land in 1270 and
ended in failure.

72   The Cotton Version declares here that its text was translated from Latin into
French and then from French into English. Most authorities, however, now
believe that the *Book* was originally written in French (see note to lines 1–9).

82–91 Hungary expanded its holdings significantly in the mid-1300s, with the annex-
ation of Bulgaria lasting into the late 1360s. Thus the inclusion of Bulgaria as
a Hungarian territory in this passage is sometimes thought significant to the
dating of the text. Arpad Steiner's "Date of Composition" is devoted to this
brief passage, arguing that it attests to a date of composition between 1365 and
1371. While the *Mandeville*-author appears to derive his route through Hungary
to Constantinople from Albert of Aix's early twelfth-century history of the First

Crusade, Hungary's holdings in the passage clearly reflect a much later time period. Slavonia (*Savoyze*) andCumania (*Comayne*) were not annexed until 1180 and 1233, respectively (see W, p. 157n4.2).

98–106   In his Bodley text, Seymour takes this passage as partial proof that the *Mandeville*-author worked exclusively from sources: "The huge bronze statue of Justinian, erected in 543, originally held in the left hand a gilt orb, the *appil of gold*, surmounted by a cross. This cross was blown down in 1317 and restored in 1325. The legend recorded here, in an account otherwise derived from William of Boldensele, probably stems from this accident. The confusion of the cross and the orb, said to equal a fifteen-gallon jar in size, proves that the author was not writing from personal observation" (B, p. 150n7/1). In the more recent edition of the Defective Version, however, Seymour accedes to the belief that the orb itself had fallen, thus rendering the source-question open once again (D, p. 138n6/31). The fourteenth-century Byzantine scholar Nicephorus Gregoras reports the absence of the cross from 1317 to 1325. William of Boldensele, the *Book*'s main source for this section, reports the orb with cross in the hand of the statue.

Fazy ("Jehan de Mandeville," p. 44) reflects that the period in which the cross/orb was missing was just around the time that the *Mandeville*-author might have been in Constantinople, but by the time his chief source, William of Boldensele, arrived in 1333 it would have been restored. Thus the *Mandeville*-author's account of its absence may be a firsthand observation, unless culled directly from Gregoras.

98   *Seynt Sophie*. "Hagia Sopia" is, in the case of the renowned church, properly translated not as "Saint Sophia," but as "Holy Wisdom." The Hagia Sophia is dedicated not to the saint, but to the Holy Wisdom of God.

110–15   The Monastery of Stavrovouni (literally "Cross Mountain") in Cyprus is dedicated to the Holy Cross. According to tradition, it was founded by St. Helena (see Indexed Glossary: "Eline"), who visited the island with the True Cross after finding it in Jerusalem. The Cross vanished during her stay, but for three nights a bright light was seen on the mountaintop. Investigating, Helena and her companions found the Cross floating above the ground: an event that was interpreted as a sign that a monastery should be constructed there. Thus the hill and the monastery both came to be known as "Stavrovouni."

Cypriot tradition states that Helena left a fragment of the Cross in the keeping of the monks at Stavrovouni. By the 1300s it was generally believed, as here, to be a fragment of the cross of Dismas rather than of Christ. See also the explanatory notes to lines 152 and 653–57 .

Warner offers several local variations on the story of the Cross' coming to Stavrovouni as well as an account of the disposition of the sponge, reed, and other holy relics (W, pp. 158–59nn5.5, 5.7). Varying accounts of the movements of the most sacred relics (the sponge and reed, the spear, pieces of the Cross and the crosses of the two thieves, the crown of thorns, etc.) abound, sometimes out of honest confusion but all too often, as the narrator here goes on to lament, because the claim of possessing a holy relic so often translates to tourism, prestige, and wealth.

113   *Dismas . . . was honged.* See Luke 23:32–43.

116–17 *In . . . oliva.* "The Cross was made of palm, cedar, cypress, and olive." The idea of the Cross as composed of numerous different woods is probably based on a type from Isaias: "The glory of Libanus shall come to thee, the fir tree, and the box tree, and the pine tree together, to beautify the place of my sanctuary" (60:13). Warner (W, p. 159n5.10, 6.6) offers a lengthy overview of the tradition and its permutations, noting the *Book*'s apparent debt to the version found in Jacobus of Voragine's *Golden Legend* (1.278).

Warner notes that the following story "of Seth's visit to Paradise . . . is found in the second part of the apocryphal Gospel of Nicodemus, stopping short, however, at the angel's refusal of the oil of mercy," and that the story exists in numerous versions, the most popular of which has Seth emerging with "grains" to place on his father's tongue, as here. Commonly Seth emerges with three grains, in accordance with the three-wood type of Isaias 60:13 as well as other early accounts of the Cross as being of three, not four, woods: cypress, pine, and cedar. The *Book* here gives Seth four grains, presumably to accord with the four-wood model found in Jacobus.

152   *doughter of a kyng.* Helena's father is elsewhere identified as the legendary King Coel of Britain ("Old King Cole"). The story of her discovery of the True Cross is subject to question, but has long been considered historically true by much of the Catholic world. See also the explanatory notes to lines 110–15 and 653–57.

157–61 The King's Chapel here is Sainte-Chapelle, "founded by St. Louis in 1246 as a reliquary for the holy relics redeemed by him from the Venetian merchants (not the Jews) to whom Baldwin II had pawned them" (D, p. 139n9/17). That the Venetian pawnbrokers should be transformed by the text into Jews is unsurprising, not only because the Jews were so strongly associated with money-lending throughout the Middle Ages, but also because the *Book* shows a marked tendency to represent the Jews as dangerous to and subversive of Christianity. Their depiction here as infidel purveyors of the holy relics of Christendom is well in keeping with this motif.

165   The *risshes of the see* described here are more commonly referred to in the texts as "jonques of the see," prompting Seymour's identification of them with *juncus glaucus*, the bog-rush (D, p. 139n9/21). Seymour goes on to observe, rightly, that "the exhibits at Sainte-Chapelle were medieval forgeries" and that "The Crown of Thorns reported in the gospels is now believed to have been made of the spines of the date palm (*phoenix dactylifera*) . . . the only suitable flora then available in Jerusalem."

The *Book*'s story of the four successive crownings of Christ (with albespina, barberry, briar rose, and finally the "jonques of the see") may reflect a medieval effort to encompass conflicting theories about the Crown of Thorns as well as to allow for a wider range of the thorn-relics on display to be regarded as genuine, much as stories of the separation and distribution of the True Cross to protect it from the infidel helped validate the claims of the many places claiming to own a segment of it.

166–67   *Y have a poynt therof.* The narrator's claim to possess a thorn from Christ's crown is an example of his linking his own life to the narrative, a truth-claim model found often in the course of the *Book*.

175–76   *And therfor hath the albespyne many vertues.* Warner notes that the protective properties of the albespina are referenced as far back as Ovid and thus long predate the coming of Christ (W, p. 160n6.26).

188   *Hayl, kyng of Jewes.* Matthew 27:29; Mark 15:18; John 19:13.

196   *[Y]drions* probably stems from Greek *anydros* (anhydrous; free of water vapor). Both Pliny and Isidore of Seville describe "enhydros" as a kind of agate that expels water.

210–13   The report of reverence for Aristotle's tomb, including the detail that proximity to the tomb was believed to provide a person with insight into the truth of matters, is also noted in the widely circulated tradition of sentential materials rooted in the Arabic *Mokhtâr el-Hikam*, translated into Spanish as *Bocados de Oro*, which was in turn translated into Latin as *Liber Philosophorum Moralium Antiquorum*, the source for Guillaume de Tignonville's French translation, *Dits Moraulx*. It appears in Middle English, for example, in *Dicts and Sayings of the Philosophers*, as part of the background for Aristotle (ed. Sutton, 13.56–70 [pp. 65–66]).

216–19   In most versions of the story the peak of Athos is said to cast the marketplace of Myrina on the isle of Lemnos into shadow. Pliny the Elder reports the phenomenon in his *Natural History* (Book 4, chapter 2) as does Solinus, who goes on to relate that Athos towers above the precipitation line and that as a result the ash at its peak never washes away (chapter 20).

223   *emperouris paleis.* Neither the palace of Boukoleon nor the Hippodrome adjoining it is noted by the *Book*'s main source of information about Constantinople, William of Boldensele. Such details, not traceable to available sources, have convinced some scholars of the authenticity of at least part of the *Book* as the firsthand account of a traveler. Those supporting the idea of the *Mandeville*-author as a traveler to at least some degree notably include Bennett (*Rediscovery of Sir John Mandeville*) and Moseley (*Travels*). For an overview of arguments pro and con, see Kohanski, "Uncharted Territory," pp. 64–68.

228–34   The story of the engraving found in the grave of the wise man, asserting his proto-Christian faith, was commonly attached to the mythic figure Hermes Trismegistos. Here, Hermes is conflated with Hermogenes of Tarsus, the Greek rhetorician of the late second century AD. The *Book*'s direct source for the story is unclear, but Oliverus Scholasticus refers to "certain heathen gentiles" who "had the Holy Sprit on their lips, but not in their heart, and prophesied plainly about Christ" (*Capture of Damietta*, p. 50), and Roger Bacon notes that Trismegistos' views on the creative nature of God accord with those of St. John the Evangelist despite the fact that the former "lived near the time of Moses and Joshua"

(*Moral Philosophy*, pt. 1, p. 646). Other analogues are found in Jacobus of Voragine's *Golden Legend* (2:376) and elsewhere.

238–39   *the Pope John the Twelfthe sende lettres.* In other manuscripts of the *Book*, these letters are generally attributed to Pope John XXII, who held the office from 1316 to 1334. The reference here to "John the Twelfthe," who was pope from 955 to 964, probably results from an error in transcribing the Roman numeral. The papal power "to bind and to assoil" is a reference to the Roman Catholic belief that Christ gave power to the popes as successors to St. Peter, the first pope, both to damn and to forgive.

248   *greet covetise.* John XXII was roundly criticized after his death for his efforts to assert dominion over the Greek Church. Although the emperor Andronicus III did firmly reject the pope's assumption of power, this return message with its reference to John's "great covetousness" was a widely circulated fake.

249–74   Many of the practices attributed to the Greek Church in this passage are re- versed or unfounded. For example, the reference to the Greeks as "anointing no sick man before his death" suggests that the Greeks practice the sacrament of unction only on the deathbed. In fact, however, Greek practice diverged from Roman in that the Greeks offered frequent unction for the sick, and the Romans only "extreme" (deathbed) unction. The accusation that the Greek Church sanctions fornication is, of course, absurd, and hardly accords with the harsh moralism of the following statement: that if one marries more than once, one's children are bastards. The prohibition of second marriages held only for clergy. Lay people were, however, discouraged from marrying more than three times (a prohibition the Wife of Bath would doubtless have challenged).

250   *Maundé.* The Maunde was the ceremony of washing the feet of the poor on Holy Thursday, also known as Maundy Thursday (Dies Mandati). The sacra- ment of sour or wheaten bread is in token of the church's ministry to the poor, in accordance with Christ's new mandate to "love one another" (see John 13:34). That the Greek Church considered the bread consecrated on Maundy Thurs- day especially holy, as the passage goes on to suggest, was considered an error of their belief by the Roman Church.

284   *mastik.* Resinous gum which has been produced on the Greek island of Scios for centuries. The Genoese in the Middle Ages held a profitable monopoly on the island's mastic, which was marketed as a medicine. It was (and is) also chewed recreationally, like chewing gum, especially in the Middle East. The book later reports tables and stairs made of "mastyk" at lines 2450 and 2454.

292–93   *Turkes haldeth Turkey.* By the time the *Book* was written, the Hospitallers had in fact retaken parts of Asia Minor, notably the city of Smyrna (Izmir) which they held from 1344 to 1402. The *Mandeville*-author follows Boldensele, whose account was written in 1336, before the capture of Smyrna.

293–98   The story of St. John having commissioned his own tomb and lain down in it while still alive, as well as the report that when opened the tomb was found to contain only manna (lines 290–91), dates back as far as the sixth century, where it is found in pseudo-Abdias' *Apocryphal Acts of the Apostles*. The *Book* probably takes the story from Jacobus of Voragine's *Golden Legend*. In any case, the idea that nothing but manna is to be found in the tomb clearly conflicts with the idea that St. John remains in his tomb alive, his stirrings causing the earth above him to shift.

301   *iles of Grece*. The "isle of Greece," i.e., Crete, was never given to the Genoese ("Jonays," line 302). Rather, after the fall of Constantinople to the Latins in 1204, it was sold to the Venetians. The *Book* has a tendency to confound the Venetians with others; see, for example, lines 157–61 (and the corresponding explanatory note), where they are misidentified as Jews.

302   Both *Cofos* and *Lango* appear to refer to the Greek isle of Cos, with which the story of Hippocrates' daughter is generally associated. Warner suggests that the story may owe a debt to the role of the serpent in the cult of Asculepius, prominent on the island (W, p. 163n12.16), or to Hippocrates' son Draco. Although most of the surrounding material derives from William of Boldensele, the *Book*'s source for this story — which does not appear in Boldensele, but survives elsewhere in many forms — is unknown. Common speculation is that it was transmitted through a crusader history, as were many such tales.

344   *Seynt Poule in his pistle*. The text makes a leap here, common in the Middle Ages, from "Collos," the archaic name for Rhodes, to St. Paul's letter to the Colossians. According to Catholic tradition, however, the Colossians were the people of Colossae, east of Ephesus in Asia Minor, not the people of Rhodes. The Hospitallers held the island of Rhodes from 1309 to 1523, when it was captured by the Turks.

346–48   It is not entirely clear whether the *Book* refers here to the grapes themselves, on the vine, or to the wine. Cypriot wine (later known as "Commanderia") was highly valued in the Middle Ages, and there are numerous reports of its changing color over time, although accounts disagree as to whether it becomes darker or lighter with age.

350–58   Believed to stem ultimately from the classical story of the beheaded Gorgon, this story was apparently current in the Middle East during the time of the Crusades. Variants are recorded by Walter Map, among others. Warner (W, p. 164–65n14.6) offers several variations of the story.

368   *castel of Amors*. According to tradition, the "castle of Love" is so called because it occupies the site of a former temple of Eros. The site is famous, too, as the fourth-century hermitage of St. Hilarion. Although Hilarion was buried at the site, his chief biographer, St. Jerome, reports that his body was later removed to his birthplace in Palestine.

377–81   Tyre (Sûr), one of the key ports of the Holy Land, was under Christian control from 1124 to 1291. It was recaptured in 1291 by the Saracens and subsequently razed.

383   *bossh many*. The text here seems to be unique in noting that *bossh* may be found on the shoreline. Other manuscripts (e.g., D, p. 18; K, p. 12; S, p. 20) are unanimous in reading instead "rubies." The sense for *bossh*, according to the

OED, could be either "forests" or "merchant ships," with the latter fitting especially well in the present context of a port haven where supplies can be procured.

385   *well of gardeyns.* The "Fons Hortorum" is the Fountainhead or Ras el 'Ain, which supplied ancient Tyre with water by means of a series of cisterns and a now-ruined aqueduct. It is here associated with the well of the Canticle of Canticles 4:15.

387–88   *I-blessid be . . . souke.* Luke 11:27.

394–95   *she fundide the cité of Cartage.* Our manuscript here reads "he fundide" (see textual note to line 394), which would seem to suggest Aeneas as the founder of Carthage. "He" here is likely a scribal misreading of "heo" (she), the term that prevails in the Defective Version generally. The case for the female pronoun is strengthened by the fact that Dido is generally considered the founder of Carthage (compare *Aeneid* 1.480–522).

395–96   The narrator here conflates Agenor, who was Dido's father and the king of Tyre, with Achilles, the Greek hero of the Trojan War.

400–01   The apocryphal ascription of Jaffa's founding to Noah's son Japhet is widespread, hinging on a false etymology derived from the similarity of names. Here the story is drawn from William of Boldensele, the *Book*'s chief source on the Holy Land. Lines 2018–27 relate the story of the world being divided among the three sons of Noah after the flood, with Shem taking Africa, Ham Asia, and Japhet Europe. The ports of the Middle East may well have been considered part of Europe by crusade-minded Europeans.

Ham and Shem are here transposed, as was common in the Middle Ages. For discussion of Ham's reported role as ruler of Asia, see the explanatory note to lines 2018–48.

406–07   The *mile* in the Middle Ages was not a standardized measure, different areas having standard miles of varying lengths. The *Book* generally takes "miles of Lumbardy" as its measure of distance, but distance measures in the book are so notoriously skewed that they are of little practical value. Seymour references a passage in Warner's Insular Version (58.33) that equates Lumbard miles with "the miles of our country," i.e., England (D, p. 142n19/21); he goes on to equate these miles with the continental league, or half of a "great league." The "great league" seemingly refers to the "leagues" or "great miles" of France and Germany, which were equal to two English miles (see W, p. 162n11.13).

423   The *Gravely See*, discussed at greater length at lines 2423–27, was said to be a great sea of sand, complete with waves and fish, in the land of Prester John. The reference is almost certainly to one of the great eastern deserts, but owing to the uncertain geography of the *Book* nearly any desert from Turkmenistan's Karakum to Mongolia's Gobi may underlie the reference. Seymour (D, p. 166n115/16) identifies it with the Takla Makan desert, on the old Silk Road through the Persian empire.

The Foss of Memnon (line 415), described here as a *swolwyng* ("gulf") of that sea, had long been famous for its vitreous nature. The idea that any metal put into the Foss would become glass is, however, obviously an exaggeration.

443   *thre children*. Chapter 1 of the Book of Daniel repeatedly refers to Daniel and
       his three companions as "children," most notably as "children of Israel" (1:3)
       and "children in whom there was no blemish" (1:4). But in the account of the
       fiery furnace, it is made clear that they are grown men, whom Nebuchadnezzar
       has "set over the works of the province of Babylon" (3:12), and children only
       in the symbolic sense, as "children of God." The popular belief that they were
       small children may stem in part from the medieval Europeans' prediliction for
       stories of infant piety, such as the tale told by Chaucer's Prioress.

446   This *strong castel* is Saladin's fortress of Al Kalah, erected in 1166.

457–58 *And many . . . Mount Moyses*. The apparent discontinuity of the text here is the
       result of the "Egypt Gap," a lengthy lacuna in the *Book*'s description of Egypt
       that is shared by most manuscripts in English, causing them to be dubbed
       "Defective." Versions that do contain the Egypt material usually include the
       following topics: how the sultans of Babylon came to power; the powers and
       prerogatives of the sultans (including their armies, their many wives, and their
       concubines); a contrast between the sultan's Babylon (Cairo) and Babylon the
       Great on the Euphrates River, where the Tower of Babylon stood; an account
       of the environs of Cairo and the yearly flooding of the Nile; the geography and
       people of Egypt; the story of the Temple of the Phoenix in Heliopolis, with a
       discussion of the phoenix as a symbol of Christ; the mice, slave markets, and
       ingenious incubators of Egypt; crops such as bananas, melons, figs, and balm,
       and their Christian associations; the Saracen practice of selling false balm to
       unsuspecting pilgrims; the pyramids as "Joseph's granaries"; the Egyptian
       alphabet; pilgrimage routes from Western Europe to Cairo; the way from Cairo
       to Mount Sinai; the church, miracles, and relics of St. Katherine on Mount
       Sinai; and the holy places associated with Moses on Mount Sinai.
           The two texts in English that preserve the Egypt material are the Cotton
       and Egerton manuscripts. Modern editions that include the Egypt material are
       Moseley's Penguin translation of the Egerton Version (*Travels*) and Seymour's
       two Oxford editions of the Cotton Version (*Mandeville's Travels*, 1967 in Middle
       English; 1968 in Modern English).
           Our manuscript, Royal 17C, is notable for the smooth transition it makes
       over the Egypt Gap. Whereas most Defective manuscripts join the edges of the
       gap in an unclear sentence beginning in Egypt and ending at the Mount of St.
       Katherine, Royal 17C bridges the gap less awkwardly, beginning a new sentence
       to make the transition to the Mount of St. Katherine. The non sequitur persists,
       of course, but in a far less obvious form (see K, pp. xl–xli).

503   *Cariatharba*. *Kirjath arba* in fact means "City of the Four," a reference to the Tal-
       mudic assertion that four of the Patriarchs, including Adam, are buried there.
       The text's assertion at lines 496–97 that David, Abraham, and Jacob are buried
       there with their wives Eve, Sara, and Rebecca is clearly garbled. Commonly
       those who accompany Adam are Abraham, Isaac, and Jacob, and their wives
       Eve, Sara, Rebecca, and Rachel. Royal 17C's substitution of David for Adam
       may simply be an error, or may reflect the fairly common medieval belief that
       Adam was not, in fact, buried in Hebron, despite the assertion of Joshua 14:15:

"The name of Hebron before was called Cariath-Arbe: Adam the greatest among the Enacims was laid there."

The name *Cariatharba* properly refers to Hebron itself, although the text here uses it interchangeably with the "Spelunca Duplex," the Double Cave in which the sepulchers of the Patriarchs are said to lie. The tomb was off-limits to both Christians and Jews, but several reports from travelers of the period suggest that Jews could sometimes buy access, while Christians were utterly prohibited.

505   *as Holy Writ sayth: Tres vidit et unum adoravit*. The Latin, contrary to the implication of the text, is not biblical but liturgical, being the antiphon for vespers on Quinquagesima Sunday. The basis for the line is, however, found in Genesis 18:2–3.

511–13   Warner notes: "according to rabbinical authority he sinned in the tenth hour after creation and was expelled from Paradise in the twelfth. So too the curious thirteenth century catechism of science known as *Sydrac and Boctus* (quoting the later English Metrical Version):

> And in Paradyse they wore
> Seuen howers and no more.
> The thyrde hower after his makyng
> Gaue Adam name to all thyng:
> The syxth hower ete his wyfe
> The appull that made all the stryfe:
> The seuenth hower Adam dyd of yt ete,
> And was chasyd and streyth out bete.
> (*The History of Kyng Boccus and Sydracke . . . translatyd by Hugo of Caumpeden out of Frenche into Englysche*, about 1510).

A Mahometan legend, on the contrary, declares that he lived no less than five hundred years in Paradise before tasting the forbidden fruit" (W, pp. 175–76n34.21). (See Book 1, lines 2251–58 of the Lansdowne manuscript in Burton's edition of *Sidrak and Bokkus*.)

517   *cambil*. Many travelers, including Burchard of Mt. Sion and Odoric of Pordenone, speak of a kind of red earth that is dug and eaten in the area. The name *cambil* is found in none of the *Book*'s usual sources, however, and seems to link the *Book*'s substance to the native *kinbil*, a reddish powder that derives from a shrub found in Arabia and the East. It has a long history in Arabic medicine, generally as a treatment for skin conditions. The *Book*'s account is unusual both in naming it and in refraining from identifying it as dirt, as most other travelers of the period do.

526–33   Accounts of prophecies surrounding the "Dry Tree" were widespread in the Middle Ages, as were accounts of its healing powers. As Seymour notes, "The prophecy alluded to derives ultimately from the Book of Sirach, and for a time was thought to relate to the Emperor Frederic II (d. 1230). Although the miraculous properties of the Dry Tree are well attested (e.g. in Vincent de Beauvais), it is only in *Mandeville's Travels* that they include a preservative against *the fallynge euyl*, i.e. epilepsy; elsewhere this preservative refers to the evils attendant on falling off a horse!" (B, p. 158n47/29). Warner concludes that this error proves the use of a written source, but such a conclusion is not inescapable, based upon the evidence. For more on the Dry Tree, see W, p. 176n35.5.

538   *Lo, we have herd hym in Effrata*. Vulgate Psalm 131:6.

566–69   Scrapings from the porous, white-rock floor of the "Grotto of the Milk" are still used medicinally by women, especially for pregnancy and women's ailments.

575–76   *And his wyckednesse . . . into his owen heed.* Compare 1 Kings 25:39 and 3 Kings 2:44.

587   *she hadde y-bore 12 children*. Rachel had only two children according to the Bible, Jacob's thirteen children being born of four women: his wives Rachel and Leah, along with their respective slave girls, Bilhah and Zilpah. The number twelve here seems to be the result of the fact that Joseph had twelve male offspring among the thirteen (see Genesis 35:22–26).

590   *condiht*. The conduit by which water reaches Jerusalem is said to have been built by Pontius Pilate.

602–04   *a cherche of Mercaritot . . . when he deyde*. This rather confusing passage is attempting to convey that Saint Karitot (the prefix *mer* meaning "saint") was the abbot of a monastery to the south of Jerusalem. The idea of a painting depicting the sorrow of the monks at Mercaritot's death stems from a misreading of Peter Comestor's *Historia Scholastica* (*PL* x.x, ch. 178), which says that the *compaginati* (skeletons) of the monks can still be seen, not the *compincti* (paintings). As the painting never existed and the monastery is reported by Ludolph von Suchem to have been in ruins in the early 1300s, it is clear that the *Mandeville*-author had not traveled to this particular destination.

609   *40*. The manuscript leaves blank the space where the number should be in this sentence. The Defective manuscripts tend to read "40" whereas other versions tend toward "140." Counting from the fall of Jerusalem to Saladin in 1187, 140 is not far off. The reading of "40" in the Defective texts may be justified, however, if one counts from the fall of Acre in 1291. Thus "40" has been preferred here.

623–25   The miracle of the lamp going out on Good Friday and relighting itself on Easter is mentioned by Bernard the Monk, circa 865, and by numerous historians thereafter. Celebration of the miracle continues in Easter week to the present day.

630   *Adamis hed*. Other medieval travelers including the pseudo-Odoric, whose *Liber de Terra Sancta* provided occasional source material for the first part of the *Book*, report having seen the skull of Adam on display in Jerusalem, a detail not found in any version of the *Book*. Contemporary accounts suggest that the skull was a common pilgrimage stop throughout the 1300s; the *Book*'s failure to mention it is therefore somewhat puzzling.

631   *Adam*. Other manuscripts say Abraham.

632–33   *lith Godfray the Boleyn, and Baudewyn.* The tombs of the two prime crusader fig-
          ures, Godfrey and Baldwin, remained in place, although in great disarray, until
          they were destroyed by the Greeks in 1808.

636–37   *God, our kyng . . . myd of the erthe.* Vulgate Psalm 73:12.

640–41   *That thou seist is ground . . . of this feith.* Possibly a reference to Vulgate Psalm
          117:22, in which exegetes understood Christ as being described as "The stone
          which the builders rejected," who has now become "the head of the corner,"
          i.e., the cornerstone of the faith.

644   *40 yer was Y neyghbore to this generacion.* Vulgate Psalm 94:10.

645–51   Seymour calls this equation "absurd" (D, p. 145n30/2) but it may not be wholly
          so. The Roman ten-month calendar in fact contained only 304 days, split into
          ten months of thirty or thirty-one days each, with the remainder of the year taken
          up by a lengthy gap over the winter before the new year began in spring. Thus
          while only 304 days of the year were enumerated by the calendar, the year was
          not only 304 days long. The months of January and February were later intro-
          duced to bring the days of winter into the fold.
                 A calendar that relied on a strict 304 day annual cycle would, of course, be
          spectacularly inaccurate, but if the medieval writer knew only that the old Ro-
          man calendar had enumerated 304 days per year, and did not take the gap into
          account, the calculation would be quite tidy. If Christ was, as is commonly
          argued, 33 years and 3 months old at the time of His death (our text says 32
          years and 3 months) according to the Julian year of 365 days, He would indeed
          have been 40 years old in years of 304 days. The math at least is sound, if not
          the science.

653–57   Tradition states that Helena traveled from Constantinople to Jerusalem to seek
          the True Cross and found all three crosses together c. 326 AD. Although Helena
          is credited here with the "assaying" of the crosses — touching each to a dying
          woman and recognizing the True Cross in the one that restores her to health
          — that credit is more generally given to St. Makarios, bishop of Jerusalem. The
          Church of the Holy Sepulcher was, according to Church tradition, built by
          Helena to house the Cross. (This tradition obviously conflicts with that of the
          Cross' transport to Stavrovouni; see the explanatory note to lines 110–15.)
                 Helena is also said to have left a trail of servants on the mountaintops
          between Constantinople and Jerusalem, relaying the news of her success in-
          stantly by a chain of signal fires, a plan reminiscent of Clytaemnestra's in the
          Oresteia. This story of the fire on the mountains may also be connected with the
          legend of Stavrovouni.

660   *the emperour of Constantynople* is clearly an error for "the emperor Constantine."

677–79   *Woman, byhold thy sone . . . . byhold thy moder.* John 19:26–27.

689   *Gilden Gate that may noght be opned.* According to tradition, the southeastern gate
          into the city of Jerusalem was opened only twice a year during the Christian occu-
          pation of the Holy Land: on Palm Sunday, in remembrance of Christ's entry into
          the city, and on the feast day of the Exaltation of the Cross ("Holy Cross Day").

695   *Nostre Dame de Vatyns*. The Church of St. Mary, Latin, was the first church in Jerusalem to follow the Latin rite. A group of merchants from Amalfi, granted the site by the Caliph in the early eleventh century, built a monastery to help house pilgrims. The Hospital of St. John, from which the Order of Hospitallers sprung, was an offshoot of that monastery. St. Mary Le Grande, built in the early twelfth century, was an abbey of nuns to help house female pilgrims, who were often unwelcome in monastic lodgings.

697 ff.   For an exhaustive account of the legends, source material, and history surrounding the *Templum Domini*, see W, pp. 180 ff.

702–03   *Y hadde letters . . . synet*. The *Mandeville*-author seems desirous of impressing the reader with the special favor he receives from the Sultan in the form of the seal — superior to the mere signet — which allows him free passage in the Holy Land. William of Boldensele speaks of having a letter from the Sultan, but it is not sufficient to gain him entry to the temple. That such entry may not have been so very restricted, however, is suggested by Symon Simeonis (possibly the more direct source of this passage), who describes in some detail his acquisition of the Sultan's special sign which allows him and a bevy of companions "to proceed without tribute to the Sepulchre of the Lord, and to visit all the oratories and other holy places without payment of any tax" (*Itinerarium*, p. 97). Like Sir John, Symon describes the deep veneration done to the seal everywhere he takes it, but he also notes that the common method of gaining such favors is "to anoint the hands of [the Sultan's dragomen] generously with the oil of florins and to offer them very handsome gifts" (*Itinerarium*, p. 99). Thus the seal is less a sign of extravagant favor than the result of extravagant bureaucratic payoffs.

709–10   Charlemagne's fictional expedition to the Holy Land forms part of the Charlemagne legend. Several commentators, however, recount the actual presence of the ostensible foreskin of Christ as a holy relic in medieval France. Seymour (D, p. 145n32/31) cites Peter Comestor, William of Tripoli, and Vincent of Beauvais as sources for the historical existence of the relic. At one point, at least six French churches claimed to possess it.

717   *solde of hem*. Emperor Titus took Jerusalem in 70 AD. St. Ambrose relates the story of his selling Jewish prisoners, a detail found in the many popular accounts of Jerusalem's destruction. The selling of the Jews is a key structural point, for instance, of the Middle English *Siege of Jerusalem*, ed. Livingston, lines 1319–20 (see also pp. 35–36).

719–26   As other versions of the *Book* make clear, it is Julian ("the Apostate") who had previously been Christian but had forsaken his faith, not the Jews in the story. Similarly, it is Hadrian rather than the Jews who, though not a Christian, "loved Christian men more than any other men, save men of his own faith." The earthquake that destroyed the Temple is a matter of historical record.

743–44   *I saw water comyng out of the Temple*. Ezechiel 47:1.

758   *byfore*. Other versions make explicit that these were part of the Jewish worship before Christ.

761   *Forsothe . . . y wist hit noght.* Genesis 28:16.

765   *He.* Other versions specify that this is Christ.

772   *when he dyde sle Urye.* The story of David's murder of Uriah is told in 2 Kings 11–12.

779   *Templers.* The Knights Templar were founded in 1119.

785   *probatica piscina.* The pool of Bethesda, in John 5:2.

789–90   *Take thy bed and go.* Matthew 9:2.

825   *Pees to yow.* John 20:19, 21, 26.

827   *My Lord, my God.* John 20:28.

841   *I have synwed, disseyved ryghtfull blood.* Matthew 27:4

860   *Fader, if hit may be, do let this Passion go fro me.* Luke 22:42.

866   *yit semeth ther . . . in the stoon.* While Boldensele offers the story of the left foot-print, a matching right footprint was kept as a holy relic at Westminster Abbey for centuries. Seymour takes the *Mandeville*-author's failure to note the existence of this English relic, which was well-known in his time, as further evidence that the *Book* was not originally English in composition (D, p. 146n40/9).

870–71   *Blessed be tho . . . kyngdome of Hevene.* Matthew 5:3.

875–76   Saint Julian is the patron saint of hospitality.

892–93   *He that taketh the prophete . . . he shal take mede of a prophete.* Matthew 10:41.

897   *Say that thes stones ben maked bred.* Luke 4:3.

901   *Jhesu, David sone, have mercy on me.* Matthew 9:27.

905–09   This passage is clearly based in the high salinity of the Dead Sea, which causes things to float with near-miraculous ease. This bit of information becomes garbled in a variety of ways in transmission however. The most accurate sense of the passage is perhaps preserved by the Cotton and Egerton texts, which tell us that, while the Dead Sea supports no indigenous life, it also will receive no living thing into it: when criminals are thrown in to drown, they simply float. Egerton goes on to tell us, however, that dead things (such as ships) cannot enter it without sinking at once (*Travels*, ed. Moseley, p. 89). Cotton mirrors our text here and asserts, following Peter Comestor, that iron floats on the surface, and feathers sink. (S, p. 77). In both cases the sea's special quality is given a magical cast.

In the Pynson text, the essential detail that men do not in fact sink and drown in the Dead Sea has been lost. The passage instead reports: "no man nor beast that has life that is therein may live, and that has been proved many times for they cast therein men that are deemed to death" (K, p. 29; translation ours).

Our text's simple assertion that "no kind of beast may live therein, and that has been assayed many times," is of uncertain meaning: does it suggest only the absence of indigenous life, or the idea also that the water kills all living things that enter it?

That the emperor Vespasian did throw criminals into the Dead Sea to test its powers of flotation is attested by Josephus in *De Bello Judaico*, from which this account of the Dead Sea is largely derived, probably through an intermediate source.

910–12　Due to an apparent eyeskip, the middle of the anecdote of the apples of Sodom has here been omitted. The Pynson text's account is typical: "And there grow trees of fair color that bear fruit and seem ripe, but when a man breaks them or cuts into them he finds nothing in them but coals of ashes, in tokening that through vengeance of God these cities were burnt with fire of hell" (K, p. 29; our translation). Warner identifies the fruit with the Colocynth (W, p. 186n50.4).

941–42　*Her is My Sone . . . herith Hym*. Matthew 3:17.

978　*Byhold the Lombe of God*. John 1:29.

1001–02　*Now shal ye have the figures . . .* What follows in the manuscript (on fol. 27r) are two lines of supposed Hebrew letter forms intended to correspond with the letter names provided in lines 1000–01, themselves associated with the Latin alphabet (see textual note to these lines).

This manuscript of the *Book* preserves only two alphabets: the Hebrew here and the Saracen at lines 1373–74. Among the many variants of the *Book*, however, as many as nine different alphabets can be found, most of them garbled and corrupted to varying degrees, if not entirely fanciful. Letts, in his useful overview of the alphabets (*Sir John Mandeville*, pp. 151–60), delineates them thus:

> Greek: presents no problems
> Egyptian: based on Coptic
> Hebrew: genuine but corrupt, except in [MS] Paris 4515
> Saracen: based on Runic
> Persian & Chaldean: doublets based on Nestorian
> Tartar-Russ: a "ghost," manufactured from Saracen and Cathayan
> Cathayan & Pentexoire: doublets. No source has been discovered, probably invented. (p. 160)

Moseley follows Letts in pointing out both that the author borrowed the alphabets from the best sources available and that he incorporated them as a form of truth-claim, an "additional means of convincing his readers of the seriousness of his material" (*Travels*, p. 191), in conscious imitation of the style of other contemporary travel writers. Moseley's further note, however, that "unlike us, [his original readers] would have had only a slight chance of checking them," suggests a somewhat nefarious intent to trick (*Travels*, p. 191), whereas Letts credits the author with more benevolent aims: a desire to "be of use to travellers" and to "increase the atmosphere of wonder and mystery which surrounds the whole book" (p. 152).

1009–10　*Of Babyloyn shal a colver come out . . . worlde*. Although the source of this quotation is unknown, the Latin "columba" (dove) is generally taken to be an error for "coluber" (serpent), the reading that appears in many other versions of the *Book*. Seymour speculates that "the prophecy . . . is perhaps based on Genesis 49:17 and Comestor's gloss ([*PL* 198] col. 1454) on Daniel 6" (D, p. 147n46/7).

1012–13   *Wo be to thee Corysaym . . . Bethsayda.* Matthew 11:21–23, Luke 10:13–15. "Woe be to thee Capharnaum" is inadvertently left out of the translation in the Royal 17C manuscript.

1021   *Hayl be thow . . . God is with thee.* Luke 1:28.

1032–34   *Jhesu autem transiens . . . et cetera.* Luke 4:30: "But he [Jesus], passing through the midst of them, went his way." The fuller text of the last two quotations stems from Exodus 15:16 and is given in some other versions. It translates: "Let fear and dread fall on them in the greatness of thy arm: let them become unmoveable as a stone, until thy people, O Lord, pass by: until this thy people pass by, which thou hast possessed."

1038–42   Mount Tabor has been accounted the place of Christ's Transfiguration since at least the fourth century (though Mount Hermon has also vied for the honor). By the late sixth century three churches had been built on Mount Tabor, one for each tabernacle ordained by Christ.

1041–42   *Hit is good to be her, make we 3 tabernacles.* Matthew 17:4.

1055–56   *Thou of litel feith, whi hast thou doute?* Matthew 14:31.

1057–59   The location of Christ's "table" in this passage is more usually associated with the miracle of the loaves and fishes. Tradition attaches Christ's feeding of the five thousand faithful to a plateau near Mt. Tiberias.

1059   *And ther they knew Hym in brekyng of breed.* Luke 24:35.

1067   *they ben called Jacobynes . . . converted hem.* The Jacobites were actually named for the sixth-century Byzantine monk Jacobus Baradeus, whom they followed. As this passage relates, the Jacobites rejected the practice of auricular confession. The Georgians (lines 1093–96) were followers of St. George, as here reported. The "belted Christians" (line 1097) are sometimes identified with the Coptic sect. Nestorianism (*Nideus*, line 1098) was, of course, the most widespread form of Christianity in Asia and the Middle East. Heng notes that the representation of these variant forms of Christianity is "Remarkable. . . . Rather than vilify and excoriate what would be classified in Europe as deviatory heresies by the norms of late-medieval Latin Christianity, the *Travels* offers variation from the Latin Christian norm as a potential source of pleasure, when the careful location of contrast and distinction, in dogma and practice, is managed" (*Empire of Magic*, p. 252). In this way the deviant forms of Christianity make up a part of the *Book*'s "exotica" (*Empire of Magic*, p. 245).

1070–76   *Lord, y-shryve me to Thee . . . herte.* Compare Vulgate Psalm 110:1. *My trespas Y have maked knowen to Thee.* Vulgate Psalm 31:5. *Thou art my God . . . to Thee.* Compare Vulgate Psalm 117:28. *Forwhy a mannes thoght . . . to Thee.* Compare Vulgate Psalm 93:11. Most of these passages do not in fact include any direct reference to confession, and so they do not function well as explication for the Jacobites' position against shriving oneself to a priest.

1118   *an ymage of Our Lady.* Warner quotes Oliphant: "The picture is supposed to have been painted by St. Luke, and it is popularly believed by those who reverence it to consist half of stone and half of flesh; but nobody cares to verify this statement, as to look upon her image-portrait is said to produce instantaneous death" (W, p. 191n61.5).

1160   *he shall go . . . Synople.* Seymour calls the inclusion of Pulverall and Synople on the route to Jerusalem "nonsense" (D, p. 149 n52/27), and indeed their location on the Black Sea does place them out of the common way for travelers from Europe to Palestine. Their inclusion here stems from Albert of Aix, the *Book*'s chief source in this section, who mentions them as fallback positions for Christian soldiers driven back by the Saracens in the First Crusade.

1173   *Reed See.* This is apparently an error for "Greet See," a term often used for the Mediterranean (as here) as well as for the Black Sea and the Ocean. See Indexed Glossary: "Greet See."

1216   *skleys.* In other versions *skleys* clearly refers to sleds, not food.

1219   *Kerra, Kerra!* Seymour suggests Persian *khar* ("trouble") in preference to the more obvious reading of Arabic *karrah* ("Attack!") (D, p. 150n55/27).

1230   *Mesap* and *Arne* stem from Arabic *mashaf* ("book") and *horme* ("holy").

1248–53 The story of Tabina (more commonly "Takyna") apparently stems from a misunderstanding of the Arabic word *taki* in the Koran's description of the Annunciation. Warner attributes the error in the *Book* to William of Tripoli, who "renders Arab. *Taki* (God-fearing) by 'Si tu es *Taquius*,' adding as a 'glosa Saracenorum,' the explanation that this imaginary being was an enchanter, etc. The Englishman Rob. Redinensis, who translated the Korán into Latin for Peter, Abbott of Cluny, in 1143, was better informed" (W, p. 192n66.xv) and avoided the error.

1256   *Have no drede, Marie.* Compare Luke 1:30, where the angel Gabriel says this to Mary at the Annunciation.

1263   *Missus est angelus Gabriel.* Luke 1:26: "The angel Gabriel was sent."

1263–65 *fasteth . . . wyves.* A reference to the Muslim holy month of Ramadan.

1267–68 *And they seith . . . on the Cros.* The sense of this passage is that the Saracens believe the Jews lie in claiming to have crucified Christ. Chapter 15 of both the Cotton and Egerton Versions goes on to detail the supposed Saracen belief that Jesus was never crucified, but rather was assumed directly into Heaven, leaving Judas Iscariot to be crucified in his stead. Thus, they say, the righteousness of God is upheld, which would be marred if He allowed the innocent to be punished.

         The following passage, with its certainty of the Saracens' willingness to convert to the true faith, is on a "wishful-thinking" model common in medieval European engagements of the Islamic world.

1290–91 *The letter sleeth and the gost maketh quyke.* 2 Corinthians 3:6.

1300–18 This passage, commonly referred to as the "Sultan's speech," may be modeled on a passage in Caesarius of Heisterbach's *Dialogue on Miracles* in which a monk is subjected to the harangue of a disgruntled emir who sees clearly into the common faults of the Christian world (Book 4, ch. 15). The exchanges between

Alexander and Dindimus, king of the Brahmins, are also pertinent here, though Dindimus denounces the faults of Alexander's modern world rather than referring specifically to Christianity, as Alexander is a pagan. For these exchanges, see Kratz's translation of *Historia de Preliis* (*Romances of Alexander*, pp. 55–65). Lines 2590–2620 offer a shorter version of the Alexander/Dindimus letters. See also the explanatory note to lines 2573–2637. In all of these texts, the author sees fit to criticize aspects of his own society, but must place these critiques in the mouth of a character from a radically different culture, one untouched by the corrupt society who, perhaps, sees clearly where others do not.

The Saracens' tacit acceptance of Christianity as the true faith is a common feature of medieval European depictions of the Muslim world. Most texts of the *Book*, in fact, record the Sultan as saying that *his* people know well by *their own* prophecies that Christians will prevail in the Middle East, once they learn to live more Christian lives and thus secure the aid of God.

Like the myth of the Christian Emperor Prester John in the East — with whose aid the Holy Land could be converted and annexed for Christianity forever — this belief that the Saracens both accepted and awaited their inevitable defeat in anticipation of a more perfectly Christian world helped fuel the hopes of a Europe eager to extend its religious sovereignty.

1371–77   See explanatory note to lines 1001–02, where Letts attributes this "Saracen" alphabet to a Runic root. Warner claims for it "strong affinities with the Slavonic alphabet known as the Glagolitic," correctly remarking that it is "certainly not, as Mand. would have it, that of 'the Sarzenes' or Arabic" (W, p. 194n71.18). The narrator's reference to the thorn and yogh of the English alphabet has been perceived by some, including Warner, as a possible indication of the author's nationality.

1373–74   *now shal Y telle the figures . . . .* As earlier (see explanatory note to lines 1001–02), the scribe copies out on fol. 34r three lines of what are meant to be a foreign alphabet, in this case, Saracen.

1395–1402   The sense of this passage is somewhat clearer in other versions. The Pynson text tells us that Athanasius "was accused to the pope at Rome, that he was a heretic. And the pope sent for him and put him into prison and while he was in that same prison he made this psalm [the Athanasian Creed] and sent it unto the pope and said that if he was a heretic, then that was heresy, for that was his troth and his belief. And when the pope saw that, he said therein was all our faith" (K, p. 46; our translation). Athanasius was bishop of Alexandria until his death c. 373 AD.

Several inaccuracies in the *Book's* report are imported from Odoric. Athanasius did return to his bishopric in his lifetime, and the Athanasius buried in Trebizond is a tenth-century saint of the same name. While the details of Athanasius' conflict with the Church heirarchy are essentially factual, the Athanasian Creed is now commonly believed to have been written by St. Ambrose.

1403–05   Hayton (*Lytell Cronycle*, ed. Burger, book 1, p. 17) reports how Alexius Comnenus made himself emperor of Trebizond in 1204, at the breakup of the Byzantine Empire.

1406–32   The *Book's* source for the story of the Castle of the Sparrowhawk is not known. Jean de Arras' French romance *Melusine* is an analogue, but was compiled between 1387 and 1393, certainly later than the *Book*. It includes only the story of the king of Armenia, not the account of the poor man who seeks wealth and happiness.

    Many texts of the *Book* also include a third protagonist, a knight of the Temple, who "asked for to have always his purse full of money of gold. And the lady granted him his asking, but she said that he asked destruction for his order. And so it befell afterward" (B, pp. 81–83; our translation), an intriguing footnote to the Templars' fall from power. Warner (W, p. 194n73.17) provides a useful overview of the Sparrowhawk episode.

    Seymour (D, p. 151n65/16) identifies the castle with Kizkalesi, built to protect the Lesser Armenian port of Korikos in 1151. Hayton, one of the *Book's* chief sources, was lord of Korikos in the late 1200s.

1467   *he was called Jobab*. See Indexed Glossary ("Job") for the conflation of Job with Jobab.

1469   *manna*. Warner identifies the manna referred to here as most likely the product of *Alhagi camelorum*, a leguminous plant (W, p. 196n76.7).

1476–92   Bovenschen (*Die Quellen*, p. 77) gives a comprehensive account of sources on the Amazons available to the *Mandeville*-author. He perceives this account as a compilation from many different sources. Seymour (D, p. 152n68/17) believes the account of class distinctions among the Amazons, marked by which breast is burned, is original to the *Book*.

1501–03   Learned speculation abounds as to the root of the story of the Sciapods. John of Marignolli in 1338 attributed the story to the use of parasols in hot climates, which were then "converted" by "poets" into feet (*Cathay*, ed. Yule, 3.256). Seymour cites Odoric's reference to "*unam pedem faxiolorum*, apparently an aromatic basil venerated by Hindus," as well as suggesting a mutated gene causing foot deformity among African tribesmen (D, pp. 152–53n69/13).

1505–08   The usual division of India by European geographers was into Greater and Lesser, a pattern generally followed in the *Book*. Although the boundaries of medieval Europe's conception of "India" are extremely broad (see Indexed Glossary: "Ynde"), Greater India generally corresponds to the Indian subcontinent, while Lesser India refers to the more Mideastern area from southern Arabia to the subcontinent proper. Seymour (B, p. 163n84/21) associates the third "India" mentioned here with Tibet, although a third "India," roughly corresponding to Ethiopia, is now commonly linked to the story of Prester John, the fabled "Emperor of India." It would, of course, hardly be northern and cold, but the *Book's* placement of a reference to the third India in such close proximity to a discourse on Ethiopia is suggestive.

1513   *a mas*. The manuscript here reads "Amas." Apparently either the scribe or his exemplar has mistaken it for a country.

1569–86   The difference between simulacrum and idol is somewhat confused here. The distinction that appears to underlie the passage is one between simulacra as fanciful images, such as three-headed beasts, and idols as images of natural creatures, such as Hercules. The transposition of the examples (Hercules as simulacrum, the ox-man as idol) thus clouds the issue. This confusion is found generally throughout the Defective texts.

The Cotton text sets out a clearer distinction as well as reversing the definitions:

> For simulacres be images made after likeness of men or of women or of the sun or of the moon or of any beast or of any kindly [natural] thing. And idols is an image made of lewd will of man that man may not find among kindly things, as an image that hath four heads, one of man, another of an horse or of an ox or of some other beast that no man hath seen after kindly description. (S, p. 127).

Thus its examples of Hercules as simulacrum and ox-man as idol are placed in the proper context.

1586–87   *And they do worship . . . ferst on the morwe*. Other versions include more details about this worship. The Cotton text, for example, explains that because meetings with particular animals are considered auspicious, especially first thing in the morning, the people make images of them and place them where they will see them. The text then goes on to deplore the fact that even some Christians hold this superstition, despite having sound doctrine to guide them better. The pagans also believe in augury and ornithomancy, but the text suggests they would be better served by a belief in Christianity (S, ch. 18).

1597   *For Y have dronke of that well*. The narrator's claim to have drunk from the Fountain of Youth is one of the more striking in a long line of attempts to assert his authenticity as a world traveler and firsthand authority on the marvels of the Eastern world. His account of having traveled through the Vale Perilous in the company of a pair of monks (lines 2510–23) is believed by most scholars to be an effort to insert himself into the actual experience of Friar Odoric of Pordenone, who reports his own traversal of the Vale in his *Itinerarium*. The narrator's pained admission that he was not able to visit the Garden of Eden, although he has passed by it (lines 2705–06), is a striking negative example of the same phenomenon, clearly intended to enhance the narrator's role as the truthful guide.

1609   *gaule gaule*. Odoric, from whom the report of this anointing stems, does not record the substance. Since ox gall was widely used in medicines, painting, and cleansing, it seems likely that the substance would be gall, rather than dung.

1618   *they brenne hym*. The sense here seems to be that the dead man is to be spared the indignity of being devoured by worms and his body disposed of in the more sanctified, ritualized manner of cremation.

1620   *they brenne her with hym*. For comparison of textual variations in this account of the practice of suttee, see K, pp. xxxi–xxxiii. The report of the practice derives from Odoric, and is found again at lines 1831–33, in Calonache.

1629   *Be thow noght of wanhope, but trywe*. John 20:27. It is interesting that the *Mande-ville*-author chooses to translate *incredulus* as *wanhope* (despair), as if disbelief in God is not merely disbelief but a kind of depression as well. Compare *Ayenbite of Inwit* (ed. Gradon), section 29/12, and Chaucer's Parson's Tale, X[I]693.

1633   *Seynt Thomas hande*. While the account of St. Thomas' shrine is largely derived from Odoric, he does not mention the miraculous hand of judgment. Versions of the story were widely circulated in the Middle Ages, however, and the story may well have been adapted here from the *Letter of Prester John*.

1650 ff. Many texts of the *Book* here contain a subtle indictment of the impiety of Christians as compared with the religious fervor of the Juggernaut's worshipers. The Pynson text remarks that "a man shall find few Christian men that will suffer so much penance for Our Lord's sake as they do for their idol" (K, p. 55; our translation). The Cotton text is even more pointed: "And, shortly to seye you, thei suffren so grete peynes and so harde martyrdomes for loue of here ydole that a Cristene man, I trowe, durst not taken vpon him the tenthe part the peyne for loue of oure lord Jhesu Crist" (S, p. 129).

        The narrator's tolerance for the practices and beliefs of other (non-Judaic) religions and his willingness to view their fervor as a corrective to Christian apathy have long been a subject for discussion in scholarship on the *Book*. His admiration for the faith and commitment of the Easterners as well as the Saracens is well documented, although he of course maintains his belief in Christianity as the only true faith.

1677–78 *wexeth and be multeplied and fulfyll the erthe*. Genesis 9:1 and 9:7.

1687–1778 This lengthy passage on the roundness of the world is interpolated at the point where, in Odoric's account of his journey east, he reflects that he can no longer see the North Star because of the curvature of the earth. The interpolation, which cuts the narrator's discourse on the "Isle of Lamory" into two parts, is found only in a small number of English manuscripts of the *Book* and is missing from K. Drawing heavily on Sacrobosco's *De sphaera*, the narrator seemingly intends to show that the earth is a sphere. He claims to have traveled far enough to be able to prove the curvature of the earth through astronomical measurements, which show the pole stars at varying heights depending upon one's latitude. The narrator's mathematical reckonings are quite distorted. It is unclear how he has determined that he has seen 95 degrees and nigh half a minute of the firmament or why, if that were the case, another 80.5 degrees would render him master of "all the firmament" (lines 1707–08). One hundred seventy-five degrees and half a minute would be shy of "all the firmament," even if one treated the earth as a hemisphere. Still, the ensuing discussion of how those in the south are "foot against foot" with those in the north suggests that the world is to be understood as a complete sphere of 360 degrees, despite the numerical confusion.

        In seeking to establish genealogical relationships among the various manuscripts of the Defective Version of the *Book*, Seymour initially used the interpolation of this lengthy discourse on the roundness of the world as the mark of a subgroup, the "A-texts" ("English Manuscripts," p. 169). In his edition of the

Defective Version, however, he has restructured his subgroupings, and the rotundity of the world passage is barely noted. He remarks of the Royal 17C manuscript, "It has four of the five characteristic features of subgroup 2 . . . but includes the account of the rotundity of the world; with this exception it avoids all the features of subgroup 1" (D, p. xxi). (Subgroup 2 were formerly the "B-texts," but subgroup 1 does not correspond to the previous A-texts. Unfortunately, Seymour makes no reference to his previous structure in outlining the newer one, and so the reasons for this realignment remain unclear.) This new approach tends to gloss over the fact that this lengthy passage on the roundness of the world is found in only a very limited number of English manuscripts, and that its inclusion in Royal 17C suggests the manuscript represents the conflation of more than one copy-text.

1688–90   *Transmontane . . . Anteryke.* Transmontayne is the northern Pole Star, balanced in the text by the southern Pole Star, Anteryke. While there is no true southern Pole Star (the closest modern claimant, Sigma Octantis, is far too dim to serve mariners in any useful capacity) the text may refer to the star Canopus, one of the brightest stars in the sky, which is not visible in the more northern latitudes. Canopus is mentioned in the text at line 2679, but not as the Pole Star.

1724–26   *for and a man . . . no shadowe.* The time "when the night and the day are alike long" refers, of course, to the vernal and autumnal equinoxes. At noon on the equinox, a spear held upright at the equator should make no shadow, a point made by Eratosthenes. Jerusalem resides, however, along the thirty-second parallel and so in practice the experiment would not work. The belief that it would is based on the common medieval conception of Jerusalem as "the middle of the world" (see explanatory note to line 23).

1727–28   *God hath y-wrought hele in the myddel of the erthe.* Vulgate Psalm 73:12.

1737–39   *dryvynge beestys . . . how that might be.* Words used for driving and calling beasts, such as "gee," "haw," "sooey," and "gawayeh," are idiosyncratic, and unlikely to be duplicated by other cultures or learned by those who study a language. Thus it is surprising to hear them in what the traveler takes to be a foreign land.

1751   *Have no drede that Y have the erthe honged of noght.* Compare Job 26:7.

1757–58   The narrator's previous assertion, "I say . . . he was y-come into his owen marches" (lines 1739–40), as well as his assertion of his own sense of the earth's circumference here, are characteristic of the *Book's* assumption of authority on matters of geographical calculation and may act as another form of truth-claim on the part of the narrator, who clearly wishes to speak with the authority of one who has seen for himself. Ironically, the passage is borrowed from Brunetto Latini, who similarly offers to emend the calculation he has at hand "after [his] little wit" (see D, p. 156n81/20). For comparison of the following passage — the reckoning of the earth's circumference — with those found in other texts of the *Book,* see K, pp. 36–37.

1759–71   The image is of two concentric circles, the smaller representing the earth and the larger the firmament. Dividing the figure into 360 degrees, as the passage goes on to suggest, provides two arcs corresponding to each degree: the larger representing the size of one degree of the firmament and the smaller representing the corresponding one degree of the earth's circumference. Thus, if one knows the size of the larger arc and the size ratio of the two concentric circles, one can calculate the size of the smaller arc. Once this is known, simply multiplying by 360 degrees will neatly render the earth's circumference.

The calculation itself is confused here by the fact that, rather than supplying the necessary information — the length of one degree of the firmament and the size ratio of firmament to earth — the scribe apparently adds up the 360 degrees represented by each sphere, thus coming up with the number 720. Multiplying 720 by 360 provides no useful information as neither is a measure of distance, nor does the product come near the stated 21,005 miles.

The plan for the calculation comes from Eratosthenes through Vincent of Beauvais. Eratosthenes equates one degree with 700 stadia (furlongs) and thus is able to carry the calculation through as our text is not. See Vincent of Beauvais, *Speculum Naturale* VI.13, col. 377.

1771–78   The effort to determine the world's "height" implies a commitment to some form of hemispheric model, at least for the purposes of the calculation. This view is bolstered by the text's insistence that those areas of the world too far east and west of the center cannot be considered. While such a caveat would seem at first glance to render accurate computation hopeless, it may be that the objective is to establish an equatorial baseline from which to calculate the height of the top half of the spherical earth.

1775   *clymates*. *MED* (1a) explains that a "climate" is "the region of the earth dominated by a particular planet."

1787   *maces*. The spice known as mace is the rind of the nutmeg.

1794–95   *Gret Cane of Catay*. Khan was the title of the rulers of the Mongol Empire. The Great Khan figures largely in the latter chapters of the *Book*, wherein his empire and its customs will be discussed at length.

1800   *meele*. *MED* (n.1a) cites this line to mean "dried sap ground into meal or flour."

1804   *tryacle*. Here the term implies an antidote. See *MED* n.a.

1855   *houndes hedes*. The cynocephali (men with dogs' heads) are reported in the Andaman Islands by Marco Polo (*Travels*, ed. Latham, Book 3, chapter 18). Seymour (D, p. 157n85/23) suggests that "the myth is perhaps linked to the larger lemur indris of Madagascar, but the common baboon in southern Africa also have dog-like heads." For two illustrations, see Williams, *Deformed Discourse*, p. 139. Friedman points out the connections in medieval thinking between cynocephali and Muslims (*Monstrous Races*, pp. 67–69), emphasizing their oft-cited civilized behavior and thus potential for conversion. Possibly the most famous cynocephalus in medieval culture is St. Christopher, whose head changed from canine to human after his conversion. See Friedman, pp. 72–74.

1860–61   *in maner of pater-noster of aumbre*. I.e., "in the same way that we make rosaries out of amber beads." The passage in Cotton reads: "And he hath abouten his nekke

ccc. perles oryent, gode and grete and knotted as Pater Nostres here of amber"
(S, p. 144).

1888   *men that haveth noon heed.* The Blemmyae make frequent appearances in
medieval travel- and wonder-narratives. See Friedman, *Monstrous Races*, pp.
145–46, on Alexander's encounters with the Blemmyae. For an excellent illustration, see Friedman, p. 139, plate 40a. See also Williams, *Deformed Discourse*,
pp. 134–35.

1890   *men that haveth a plat visage.* Seymour (D, p. 157n86/14) associates the flat-faces
with lepers.

1924   *begoun.* Probably a reference to *bagni*, the Persian word for beer.

1944   *pegmans.* For a comprehensive overview of medieval accounts of the pygmies,
see W, pp. 203–04n103.11.

1965   *vynes.* Apparently a doubling of "ryvers." Pynson (K, p. 62) has "ryvers and vyn-
ers" but omits the idea that fish and wildfowl are to be found in both. Seymour,
in his Cotton translation, inexplicably refers to both as "vivers" in which fowl of
all descriptions are to be found (*Mandeville's Travels* [1968], p. 164).

1969–73 Odoric describes the red skins; they are sometimes identified as the hide of the
red panda or "catbear," known for its muskiness. Vincent of Beauvais, however,
notes the common folk-belief that panthers attracted their prey with the
sweetness of their breath. The *Book* may here be conflating the two.

1983–84 *a contrefeit of a mannes foot uppon her hedes.* Seymour identifies this headdress
with the *gu-gu* or *ku-ku*, a cloth tail of sorts that hung from the hats of high-
ranking Tartar wives (B, p. 170n127/16; D, p. 160n93/6).

2009   *myne felawes and Y were soudeours with hym.* Odoric's three years as a missionary
in Kaán-balik (Beijing), the Great Khan's capital city, are here transformed by
the narrator into his own sixteen-month stint as a mercenary in the Great
Khan's army. For the narrator's ongoing program of co-opting the experience
of Friar Odoric as his own, see also the explanatory note to line 1597.

2018–48 The story of how the title "Khan" stems from Noah's son "Cham" is presented
here as fact, but the narrator then goes on to assert that the title is not "Cham"
but "Cana," stemming from "Changyse" (Genghis), the first of the great Khans.
The intent is apparently to supplant the first, perhaps more usual, etymology
of the title with the second.
In Genesis it is Ham who takes primacy over Egypt while Shem takes Asia;
however, the transposition that enables the association of the Khan with Ham
on etymological grounds was common. In fact, the word *khán* is Mongolian for
"lord." Henry Yule, however, points out a distinction in the Mongolian tongue
between *khán* (lord) and *kaán*, the title reserved for the Great Khan (cited in W,
p. 205n109.xxiv), which apparently derives from *Khákán*, "Khan of Khans."

2037   *a knyght all white.* Seymour (D, pp. 160–61n95/18) offers a bibliography on the
white knight, who apparently represents the shaman Tab-Tengri. In legend, Tab-
Tengri rides to consult the sky-god (Tengri) before the election of the Khan.

Mongolian worship of Tengri as the "one God" may underlie many medieval accounts of the essential Christianity of the Mongols. The Khan is later reported venerating the Cross (lines 2179–83), and the custom of giving him gifts is traced back to a biblical precedent (lines 2185–87) as if he were himself Christian.

2049   *Isacan*. From Mongolian *yasa kaán*: the Code of the Great Khan, set down by Genghis Khan in 1225. For a useful discussion of the code, see Ayalon, "Great Yasa."

2083   *so wan he the lond of Cathay*. Seymour (D, p. 161n97/9) speculates that these details may refer to the first in the long series of campaigns by which Genghis Khan rose to rule Cathay: the conquest of the Karakhitai in 1209.

2089   *grettest Cane*. The first "Great Khan" was Genghis Khan (c. 1162–1227). The son who succeeded him as Great Khan was Ogodai, who ruled from 1229 to 1241. The *Book*'s spelling, "Chicoto" (line 2087), may point to an erroneous belief that Genghis's third son, Chagatay, had succeeded him. Chagatay and Ogodai are often conflated.

The Prussian and Russian campaigns were largely the work of Ogodai's nephew (Genghis' grandson) Batu. Batu established the Blue Horde, which became the cornerstone of the more famous Golden Horde, the Kipchak Khanate, centered on the Volga. The conquest of all Europe from this base was narrowly averted by internal problems in the Mongol Empire, which forced the westward-moving Mongols back toward the heart of the empire at a critical juncture, whence they never returned in force. For further information on the Khanates see Juvaini, *Genghis Khan*; Boyle, *Mongol World Empire*; Saunders, *History of the Mongol Conquests*; and Chambers, *Devil's Horsemen*.

2090–2098 While these inscriptions may derive in part from actual letters sent by the Khans to the popes, the ideas of the Great Khan employing a "great seal" and a "privy seal" and invoking what appears to be the Christian God are clearly interpolations. Seymour calls Hayton's claim that a bishop in his party baptized the Great Khan Mongke in 1254 "very doubtful" (D, p. 161n98/10).

2100 ff.   Warner's note (W, p. 207n114.xxv) is extremely useful on the matter of the feasts of the Mongol year. While Odoric (the *Book*'s source here) says there are four great feasts, he delineates only two: the Great Khan's birthday and what he calls "festum Circumcisionis," the feast of the Circumcision. Since circumcision was entirely unknown among the Mongols, it seems likely that Odoric means not a celebration of the Khan's circumcision day, but rather the New Year; the Feast of the Circumcision in the Catholic calendar is January first. Marco Polo describes both the Great Khan's birthday and the New Year as significant celebrations in the Mongol world, but he places the New Year celebration more accurately in February, when the Chinese New Year begins.

2116–17   *astrelabers . . . coles brennyng*. Some text is clearly missing from this passage, as an astrolabe is not a device that can be said to be full of sand or burning coals. The error is pervasive in the Defective Version and is probably due to an eyeskip. The Cotton text reads: "And every of them have before them astrolabes of gold, *some spheres, some the brainpan of a dead man, some vessels of gold* full of coals burning" (Seymour, *Mandeville's Travels* [1968], p. 179, our italics). A scribe, looking back and forth to his copy-text, might easily skip from one "gold" to the next, deleting the text between.

2145–46   *he tretith more with Cristen men than with Sarasyns*. In the context of the *Mandeville*-author's acclaimed respect for other religions, it is interesting to note that this reference to the Khan's preference for Christians is apparently original to the *Book*.

2161–69   The Khan's opulent car of *lignum aloes* (Jinko-wood — line 2163) might provide the ruler with greater privacy but certainly not with greater secrecy as to his movements — the meaning most often inferred from *privé mayne* (line 2162). Most texts agree that he rides upon "no horse" rather than "an horse," unless he desires secrecy. The glorious car is thus his more usual mode of transportation. It seems likely, too, that it would be drawn by the elephants and horses, rather than carrying them within it.

2177   *Veni creator spiritus*. "Come, creating spirit"; beginning of a hymn sung on the feast of Pentecost.

2187   *No man come in my sight voyde*. Exodus 23:15.

2225   *toun*. Probably an error for "tent," the reading given by the Pynson and most other texts. The passage goes on to specify that the Khan is buried with his home for the next world.
           The Cotton text includes a passage suggesting that the Khan's burial is kept secret from the common people, allowing the lords to claim that he has been divinely transported to Heaven (Seymour, *Mandeville's Travels* [1968], p. 195), thus rendering it doubly unlikely that he would be placed in state in the middle of the town. Moseley (*Travels*, p. 160) notes that he has imported the same passage into his predominantly Egerton edition "from MS Royal 20 B. X.," but due to the movement and renaming of manuscripts, it is now unclear to what manuscript he refers.

2268–69   The legend that Alexander the Great had fortified the pass of Derbend was widely accepted in the Middle Ages, and is referenced by such authors as Marco Polo, Benjamin of Tudela, and William of Rubruck. According to the tenth-century Arabic traveler Abu Al Mas'udi, however, Derbend was fortified by the Persians in the sixth century to protect against incursions by the Alans, Turks, and other invaders from the north (see W, p. 211n126.10).

2293   *Perce*. The Pynson, Egerton, and Cotton Versions all make clear that Armenia, not Persia, is the land under discussion. In Pynson, Armenia "begins at Persia and lasts westward to Turkey in length" (K, p. 72; our translation).

2306–07   *that contré is covered al with derknes*. There are many medieval tales of lands of darkness, which are generally explained as melding observation of the arctic night with biblical interest in the "valley of the shadow of death." The *Book*'s source, Hayton, claims to have witnessed this land of darkness with his own eyes in the realm of Georgia; the *Book* translates it to Abkhazia. In either case, the long arctic night is an unlikely explanation given the local lattitude. Warner speculates that "no doubt there was some natural phenomenon in the neighborhood which favoured, if it did not originate, the legend" (W, p. 212 n128.6). Seymour suggests "a seasonal fog" (D, p. 164n109/2).

The area around the Garden of Eden is also described as a land of darkness "where no man may see on day ne on nyght" at line 2698.

2322–23   *Of Our Lorde this is y-do, and that is mervayl in our eyen.* Vulgate Psalm 117:23.

2328   *vuryk and rychasse.* The phrase is of uncertain meaning, and comparison with other texts of the *Book* reveals little since our manuscript takes a unique turn in adding this clause to the description of Turkey. The word *vuryk* is of particular issue since it does not appear to occur anywhere else in Middle English. For our gloss of the term as "wealth," we have relied on context and the assumption that it functions in tautology with *rychasse*, a French spelling of the word for "riches," cited in the *MED* (*richesse*).

2342–47   The narrator here draws on the story of the "barnacle goose," an animal introduced to bestiary lore in 1187 by Geraldus Cambrensis. Barnacle geese were said to grow off pine beams floating in the water, attached by their beaks and taking nourishment from both the wood and the sea. T. H. White theorizes that the story arose in response to the generally "wingy" look of several species of shellfish (especially mussels) and the fact that some species of geese were never seen to nest (*Bestiary*, pp. 267–68). The vegetable lamb, also known as the borametz, has its most extensive study in Henry Lee's *Vegetable Lamb*. See also Williams, *Deformed Discourse*, pp. 208–10, and especially Bennett, *Rediscovery of Sir John Mandeville*, p. 219, where an illustration from the *Livre des merveilles* (Paris, Bibliothèque Nationale Française 2810, fol. 120v) depicts a distinctively Islamic character bearing the open piece of fruit, miniature lamb within, to Christian travelers. The travelers are holding a branch full of barnacle geese.

2370   *And then shal these Jewes speke Ebreu.* I.e., in the time of the Antichrist, when the tribes of Gog and Magog will break free of their prison and set out to wreak havoc on the earth. The narrator suggests that all the world's Jews are simply biding their time, waiting to aid and abet this final assault on Christendom. The *Book's* hostility toward Judaism is especially marked in the context of its greater tolerance for Islam and Nestorianism. For a compelling investigation of the *Book's* attitude toward the Jews, see Braude, "Mandeville's Jews among Others."

2392 ff.   Belief in the existence of Prester John, the powerful ruler of a vast Nestorian Christian empire to the east, was a major bolster to European confidence in the inevitability of Christian victory over Islam. If ever the two mighty realms of Christendom could be brought to act together to win the Holy Land, victory seemed certain. This may account for the persistence of the myth, even after numerous travelers had failed to find any proof of its veracity.

Both William of Rubruck and Odoric identify Prester John with the Khan of the Keraits, and admit that he is not as generally imagined by Europeans. The apocryphal *Letter of Prester John* (c. 1165), however, asserts the existence of a structured and vital Christian community under Prester John in the East. Seymour notes that while the Keraits had become nominal Nestorians in the early eleventh century, "all the accounts of the friars (Carpini, Rubruck, Odoric) stress the degeneration of their practice and belief to levels of barbarism" (D, p. 166n115/9). For further information, see Atiya, *History of Eastern Christianity*; Moffett, *History of Christianity in Asia*; and Dunlop, "Karaits of Eastern Asia." See also explanatory note to lines 1300–18.

2401   *for hit is longer way.* India is of course closer to Europe by sea than China, and closer to Europe than the Khan's capital city by any possible route. The medieval European conception of "Inde," however, does not correspond well with the modern boundaries of India. The *Book* associates "Inde" variously with northern, eastern, and western Asia, and even with east Africa. Prester John was variously credited with being emperor of India and of Ethiopia, titles which may have been felt to be synonymous at the time. See Indexed Glossary: "Ynde."

2423   *Gravel See.* See explanatory note to line 423.

2430   *hit is maner of ire.* The description of the fruit as "iron" probably results from a confusion of "faerie" with "fer" (iron). Thus fey fruit becomes iron fruit.

2468–70   *The patriarke of Seynt Thomas . . . alle the kynges.* The sense in most other manuscripts is that the patriarch of St. Thomas is analogous to the pope, while the archbishop, bishop, and abbot in that land are all kings. This text's grammatical structure suggests that such a reading is not intended here, but the reading that is offered is somewhat nonsensical.

2473–91   The Paradise of the Assassins was a false heaven, constructed by Catholonabeus (Hassan i Sabbah, also known as "The Old Man of the Mountain") to induce men to undertake political murders on his behalf. Using a combination of drugs (whence the common name of the Assassins: *Hashishi'yun*) and promises of eternal reward in this garden of delights, he lured many men to kill and die in his service before he was hunted down and his "Paradise" destroyed in the mid-thirteenth century. Warner (W, p. 216n137.6) offers a thorough discussion of the cult of the Assassins and the various branches of the sect. Pinto, in her recent *Mandeville's Travels*, offers comparative passages on the Assassin's Paradise from the *Book*, Marco Polo, Odoric of Pordenone, and Ibn Khalikan (pp. 60–64).

2491   *I shal gyve yow londe flowying mylke and hony.* Leviticus 20:24.

2512   *2 freres menoures of Lumbardye.* The narrator's assertion that he entered the Valley Perilous in the company of these friars is generally taken as an attempt to insert himself into the experience of Friar Odoric of Pordenone, who reports on his journey through the Valley in the *Book's* chief source for this section. As with other truth-claim passages in the text, the narrator is presented as having firsthand experience he apparently lacks. While much of the account is borrowed from Odoric, the *Book* adds such further details as the presence of a hell-mouth and the deaths of four of the narrator's companions.
            Both Warner (W, pp. 216–17n138.xxxi) and Seymour (D, pp. 167–68n 120/15) devote considerable energy to attempting to fix the location of the Valley.

2531   *stones in her eyen.* The story of women with stones in their eyes apparently refers to the Bithyae of Scythia, reported by Vincent of Beauvais (*Speculum Historiale*

IV.15). Vincent, however, describes them as having *pupillas geminas* (double pupils), a description the *Mandeville*-author appears to have misinterpreted as *pupillas gemmas* (gemstone pupils) (see D, p. 168n122/14–17).

2533–45   Many pagan religions incorporate some form of ritual sexual contact between women and strangers, either before or after marriage. As Seymour notes, however, the *Mandeville*-author has apparently conflated two accounts that occur side by side in Vincent of Beauvais to create his somewhat bizarre explanation for the employment of the *gadlybyriens*: one of a culture in which male guests at a wedding are encouraged to have sex with the bride, and the other of a group of "snake-eating troglodytes" (D, p.168n122/22).

2561   *gyrsaunt*. While the narrator originally suggests the giraffe is a bird, he does go on to describe it in terms more applicable: as being like a horse or a deer but with substantially more neck.

2569–70   *lonhorauns . . . tontys*. MED has no citations for either of these terms; however, the "Anddontrucion" of the Middle English *Prose Life of Alexander* (ed. Westlake, p. 71) is a similar beast, presumably a rhinoceros.

2573–2637   The text offers a dual account of the Brahmins and their philosophy of simplicity and peace, first describing them as inhabitants of a *gret ile and plenteuous* (line 2573), and then repeating the account of them as a second people, the inhabitants of Synople (line 2605). Seymour, in attempting to establish genealogical relationships among the Defective manuscripts, initially used this dual account of the Brahmins as the distinctive mark of a whole subgroup of manuscripts, the "B-Texts" of the *Book* (see "English Manuscripts," p. 169). That the manuscript edited here contains both this double account and the long discussion of the world's rotundity (the mark of an "A-text" in Seymour's early structure; see explanatory note to lines 1687–1778) marks this manuscript as an anomaly among texts of the Defective Version. It is generally listed as "Independently derived" in hand-lists of the English manuscripts of the *Book*. See Seymour, *Sir John Mandeville*, p. 44, and K, p. 96.

     The narrator's assertions that the Brahmins and Synoplians please God despite being non-Christians and that we cannot know of whom God approves are apparently original to the *Book* and are frequently commented upon as exemplary of the narrator's great tolerance for people of other faiths. It is notable, however, that his tolerance is more pronounced toward those he has never seen, such as the Brahmins. The *Book* does not tolerate Judaism, nor, despite the narrator's personal admiration for the conduct of the Sultan and his people, does it fully tolerate Islam. Indeed, most texts including this one begin with an exhortation to the men of Christendom "to conquere oure ryght heritage [the Holy Land] and chace away the myssetrewantes" (lines 42–43).

2628   *I shal put to hem my lawes manyfold*. Hosea 8:12.

2629–30   *I have other sheep that beth noght of this foold*. John 10:16.

2635   *Calle thow noght thilke thingis unclene which God hath clensed*. Acts 10:15.

2643   *peple ben all in fetheris*. The feathered men apparently result from a confusion of the French *toutz pelluz* (all rough) with *toutz pennez* (all feathers). The reading *toutz pelluz* is found in the Continental Version of the *Book* (see D, pp. 169–70n127/14).

2663   *Witsoneday*. Pentecost, the seventh Sunday after Easter. The feast of Whitsunday commemorates the descent of the Holy Spirit on the apostles and is often preferred as a time for baptism of converts and ordination of priests.

2665–69 This explanation of the title "Prester John" is apparently original to the *Book*.

2671   *as men of Grece doth*. I.e., in the form used by the Greek Orthodox Church.

2674   *wordes which Goddes body is makid with*. I. e., the Consecration of the Eucharist.

2681–95 Seymour claims a basis in fact for the story of the gold-digging ants: "In the Karakoram mountains between India and Pakistan marmots (*Arctomys Hima-layanas*, called 'mountain ants' in Persian) burrow to a depth of three feet to a gold-bearing stratum of sand and throw up the spoil, which the local Minaro people still refine" (D, p. 171n129/21). While a marmot is actually a groundhog-like rodent, hearing the story at second hand one might easily take these "mountain ants" for ants in fact.

2685–2769 Seymour ("English Manuscripts," p. 183) describes the Royal 17C manuscript as bound in "3 + 1–7⁸, 8⁴ (wants 1,4)." R is missing a folio here, the first leaf of the final signature. Text from *men of the countré* (line 2685) to *And than the prestys and the religyous cutte* (lines 2768–69) is supplied from the Pynson Version (K, pp. 88–91). While the two texts generally accord fairly well, it seems likely, given the length of the interpolated passage, that Royal 17C's treatment of the material would have been somewhat abbreviated by comparison.

          The manuscript also misses the last few lines, which would have been on the missing fourth leaf of the eighth quire. These have also been supplied from K. See the explanatory note to lines 2856–57.

2700–04 While the narrator here and at lines 2737–41 firmly asserts the roundness of the earth — a point he has made at length previously in the text (at lines 1687–1778) — the idea of the east as "at the beginning of the earth" accords more clearly with a flat-earth model. The narrator may here be conflating an old source with newer ideas.

          While the passage leaves the matter of the eastern dawn's relation to English midnight slightly unclear, most other texts of the *Book* are somewhat clearer on this point. Cotton's rendering is typical: "But that is not that east that we clepe our east on this half where the sun riseth to us. For when the sun is east in those parts toward Paradise Terrestre, it is then midnight in our parts on this half for the roundness of the earth" (Seymour, *Mandeville's Travels* [1968], p. 234). Thus the place where "we" see the sun rising is not as far east as the Garden of Eden, for when the sun rises over Eden, "we" are still in utter darkness.

2705–06 *Of Paradyse can I nat speke . . . and that angoreth me*. The narrator's admission that he did not go to the Garden of Eden is generally taken as a canny variation on the truth-claim motif. While Eden was popularly believed to be located in this region, to claim to have actually visited the place would have strained credulity to the breaking point. Since it was commonly believed that Eden was unapproachable due to factors such as its great height and the raging torrent of rivers issuing from it (noted by such luminaries as Vincent of Beauvais, Isidore of Seville, and Peter Comestor), the narrator's presentation of himself as the traveler who must reluctantly concede that the popular opinion is correct makes an effective claim for his veracity.

2782   *And of the skulle . . . make a coppe.* The people of "Ryboth" (Tibet) preserved the practice of using human skulls as drinking vessels for religious ceremonies until well into the twentieth century.

2808   *And alle eyndes of the erthe shal drede Hym.* Vulgate Psalm 65:4.

2809   *All people shal serve to Hym.* Vulgate Psalm 71:11.

2810–11   This non-Trinitarian view of God may be reflective of Nestorian Christianity in the Far East. The following account of the worship of idols and simulacra, however, with the natives' insistence that "Cristen men haveth images of Our Lady and of other" (lines 2817–18), suggests a predominantly non-Christian faith, presumably the worship of Tengri, by whose grace virtue is instilled in such statues. The worship of Tengri as "the one God" is at least monotheistic and may have inspired the *Book*'s optimism regarding the closeness of Eastern religion to European Christianity.

2818–21   The narrator here defends the Catholic practice of incorporating statuary into worship, insisting that this does not constitute idolatry because worshipers venerate not the statue itself but the holy figure it represents. The narrator does, however, admit to worshiping the saints, a practice at which extreme Protestant thinkers would soon take umbrage.

2824–25   Chaco *and* Calo. From the Greek *kakos* (bad) and *kalos* (good). Seymour (D, p. 172n134.24) notes that Plato's term "cachodemon" (evil spirit) was in lively use by encyclopedists such as Vincent of Beauvais.

2834–37   As so often happens in the course of medieval manuscript transmission, the numbers have here become somewhat corrupt. The narrator asserts that he embarked on his travels in 1332 and wrote the book in 1366. Thus he has written the book in the thirty-fourth year after his departure, not the twenty-fourth as the text asserts. In the Pynson edition the narrator says he left on his travels in 1332, and has "compiled this book and written it the year of our lord 1366 at 33 years [*sic*] after my departing from my country" (K, p. 92; our translation). The Egerton text is nearly identical, although its numbers agree to a thirty-four-year span of time. The Cotton text records a departure in 1322, followed by the writing of the book in 1356, thirty-four years later; in this it accords with many Continental texts of the *Book*.

    The narrator's assertion that he has left much unsaid so that the next traveler may have something unheard-of to report is one of his friendlier truth-claims.

2838–48   This passage, commonly referred to as the "papal interpolation," is found in all the complete English texts of the *Book* with the exception of the two English manuscripts of the Bodley Version (Bodleian Library MSS Rawlinson D 99 and eMusaeo 116) and also in a single Latin text (Durham University MS Cosin V. iii. 7). It is thus generally considered to have been added into the *Book* sometime after it was first translated into English. Such assertions of papal sanction were a common form of truth-claim in the Middle Ages.

Seymour argues persuasively (B, p. 174n146/7) that the interpolation "could hardly have occurred much before 1400," as lingering memory of the Babylonian captivity, the papacy at Avignon from 1309–77, would have rendered the inaccuracy of the author's claim to have met with the pope in Rome in 1356 immediately apparent.

Efforts to use the interpolation to help date the English versions of the *Book* have met with limited success. For further reference, see Higgins (*Writing East*, pp. 254–60), May ("Dating the English Translation"), Moseley ("Sir John Mandeville's Visit"), and Thomas ("Date of *Mandeville's Travels*).

2852   *part of alle my good pilgremage*. While at least one scholar (*Mandeville's Travels*, ed. Hamelius) has perceived the book as having hidden Lollard leanings despite its early date and uncertain early connection with England, Seymour makes the excellent point that this passage is decidedly non-Lollard in its views: "The traditional disposing of *part of alle myn pilgrymage* was one of many contemporary customs associated with the pilgrim which were censured by the Lollards" (B, p. 175n147/13). One might compare Margery Kempe, another traveler frequently accused of Lollardy but never convicted, and her insistence on parceling out the grace accrued in her travels.

2856–57   The final leaf (4th leaf, 8th quire) is missing from the manuscript, as is a large section from earlier in the eighth quire (see explanatory note to lines 2685–2769). The final lines have therefore been imported from the Pynson edition (K, p. 93), which parallels this passage very closely.

 # Textual Notes

ABBREVIATIONS: see Explanatory Notes.

Obvious corrections of scribal errors and apparent omissions have been made in the text and are recorded without comment below. We have consulted Seymour's EETS critical edition of the Defective version and Kohanski's edition of Pynson's first print of Defective.

2	*worlde*. R: *wordle*. Further examples of this spelling will be silently amended to *worlde*, which form also often occurs in the manuscript.
4	*mervailles*. R: *mervaille*. Crossed final double *l*s in all words are read as abbreviations and silently expanded only when necessary.
17	*was*. So K, D. R omits.
21	*as the*. R: *and*. K, D: *as for the*.
38	*that*. So K, D. R: *he*.
41	*which*. R: *whenne*. K, D: *for the whiche*.
46	*lordes*. So K. R: *londes*. D: *lordis*.
77	*principal*. R: *pricipal*. K: *pryncypall*. D: *principale*.
78	*man*. R: inserted above the line.
82	*lorde*. So K. R: *londe*. D: *lord*.
84	*Rosse*. So K, D. R: *Rome*.
86	*lond of*. R: inserted above the line.
	men₂. So K, D. R: *me*.
100	*to holde*. R: inserted above the line.
110	*to*. So D. R, K omit.
137	*they₁*. R: *the*; hereafter *the* in the manuscript for *they* will be silently emended.
143	*he*. So K, D. R omits.
145	*angel*. R: *angle*. K: *aungell*. D: *aungel*.
184	*with*. So D. R omits. K: *of one*.
200	*Bouch*. R: *boüch*. K, D: *bouche*.
208	*which*. So D. R: *which was*. K: *whyche*.
214	*hyghe*. R: *hyhe*. K: *hygh*. D: *grete*.
215	*is*. R: *his*. K, D: *it is*.
227	*the*. So K, D. R omits.
241	*playn*. R: *playn playn*.
244	*subdiectos*. R: *subdiiectos*. K, D: *subiectos*.
252	*unctioun*. R: *unccoun*. D: *vnccioun*. K is missing the section that corresponds with lines 250–90.
254	*shal have ne joye*. R: omits *ne*. D: *schul noþer haue ioiȝe*.

280	*ageyn.* R: *geyn.* D: *aȝen.*
283	*George.* So D. R: *Gorge.*
320	*and she.* R omits *she.* K, D: *þat.*
335	*saw.* R: *was saw.* K: *sawe.* D: *sauȝ.*
347	*beth₂.* So D. R omits. K: *ar.*
357	*that.* R: *the.* K: *they whyche.* D: *þe whiche.*
372	*erthe.* R: followed by inkblot.
394	*she.* R: *he.* K: *that.* D: *heo.*
396	*Didon.* R: *Dido.* K: *Dydon.* D: *Sidon.*
398–99	*he shall go fro Cypre by see to port Jaffe, for that is the next haven to Jerusalem.* R omits due to eyeskip. Supplied from K, p. 13. D: *he schal go fro Cypre to port Iaff by see, for þat is þe nexte hauene to Ierusalem.*
437	*And.* So K, D. R: *In.*
454	*of₂.* R: inserted above the line.
459	*no.* So K, D. R: *no no.*
461	*hit₁.* R: *his.* K, D: *it.*
473	*is.* So K, D. R omits.
488	*he.* So K, D. R: *they.*
509	*for.* R: *for Idum*; the word *Idum*, which confuses the sense, is not found in K or D.
515	*kyn.* So K, D. R: *kyng.*
549	*rosers.* So K. R: *roses.* D: *roseris.*
597	*of₂.* So D. R omits. K is missing the section that corresponds to lines 593–637.
609	*40.* So D. R: blank space; some Defective manuscripts have *40*; other versions have *140*. See D, p. 177n28/22, and our explanatory note to line 609.
613	*toun.* R: *toun ~~wat~~.*
620	*forfyde.* R: *forsyde.* D: *payned.*
634	*y-wryte.* R: *y-wryte ~~this~~.*
636	*That is to say thus.* R omits. D: *þat is to say.*
638	*rasis.* So D. R, K: *basis.*
645	*But.* R: *But ~~Ɵ~~.*
658	*a.* R: *a ~~va~~.*
688	*without.* So K. R: *with.* D: *wiþoute.*
715	*brenne.* R: *brenne ~~that cite~~.*
748	*yerd.* R: *yerd ~~with the which~~.*
776	*Templum.* R: *templum ~~dominium~~.*
795	*his.* So K. R: *is.* D: *þe.*
807	*that.* So K, D. R omits.
841	*That is to say.* So K, D. R omits, but supplied to parallel other quotations.
857–95	Corresponding section is missing in K.
873	*an asse.* R: blank space. Supplied from D, p. 40.20.
884	*is a chirche.* R omits. Supplied from D, p. 41.2.
886	*hit.* R: *his.* D: *it.*
894	*is.* So D. R omits.
897	*in the which.* R omits *which.* K: *where.* D: *whare.*

904	*that is y-called.* R omits *is.* K, D: *that men call.*
939	*Job.* So K. R: *Joph.* D: *Ioab.*
942	*Y am.* R: *Y ~~have~~ am.*
971	*is.* So K, D. R omits.
988	*noght.* R: *ner.* K: *nat.* D: *nouȝt.*
996	*hedes.* So K. R, D omit.
1000–01	*alpha . . . loïcirs.* R: In the interlinear space above each word-for-a-letter, the "corresponding" Latin letters have been written by what might be a second scribe. We have attempted to replicate the appearance of this in our text. See explanatory note to lines 1001–02.
1058–59	*fractione.* So K, D. R: *fraccione.*
1079	*scelera.* So K, D. R: *celera.*
1089	*men.* So K, D. R omits.
1091	*convenable.* R: *cognable.* K, D: *covenable.*
1111	*And Seynt Poul was a fisician.* R omits. Supplied from D, p. 50. K: *and that holy man saynt Poule was a phesycyen.*
1142	*Port.* So K, D. R: *Por.*
1161	*go.* R: inserted above the line.
1164	*the Lay.* So K, D. R: *delay.*
1231	*as.* So K, D. R: *and.*
1240	*they.* So K. R omits. D: *þei.*
	Virgyne. So D. R omits. K: *virgyn.*
1248	*sorceryes.* R: *sesaryse,* corrected to *sesaryie.* K: *sorcery.* D: *sorsery.*
1261	*sight.* So D. R: *light.* K: *syght.*
1268	*noght on.* R: an illegible word has been canceled between *noght* and *on.*
1269	*so.* So K. R: *so so.* D omits.
1274	*and in the.* R: *and in the and in the.*
1302	*on.* So K, D. R omits.
1327	*turned.* R: *turnd.* K: *tourned.* D: *yturned.*
1329	*hit.* R: *hit hit.*
1362	*drynketh$_2$.* R: *drynkeþ ~~wyn~~.*
1369	*party.* So K, D. R: *partly.*
1371–74	See textual note to lines 1000–01.
1376	*two.* So K. R: *tw.* D: *twey.*
1377	*men.* R: *me.* K, D omit.
	yogh. R: *youh.* K: *zowx.* D: *ȝoghe.*
1388	*Gret.* R: *greet.* K omits. D: *Grete.*
1393	*Trapasond.* R: *Tapasond.* K, D: *Trapazonde.*
1423	*nynthe.* R: *nythe.* K, D: *ix.*
	degré. R: *de* inserted above the line.
1447	*so.* So K, D. R: *se.*
	dide. So D. R: *dude.* K: *dyd.*
1453	*to.* R: inserted above the line.
1460	*hit.* R: *his,* with a *t* written above. K, D: *it.*
1468	*yer$_1$.* R: inserted above the line.
1482	*lordes.* So K. R: *lordes lordes.* D: *lordis.*
1491	*beth ofte.* R: *beth ~~good we~~ ofte.*

1501	*that hit.* R: *that ~~is~~ hit.*
1508	*ther.* R: *ther ~~is~~.*
1513	*a mas.* So K. R: *Amas.* D: *a masse.* See explanatory note.
1515	*adamaundes.* R: *adaundes.* K: *adamande.* D: *adamaunde.*
1608	*kyng.* R: *and maketh theron a gret blessyng and then the kyng.* Phrase repeated because of eyeskip.
1611	*kyng.* So D. R: *kyng and.* K: *kinge.*
1612	*y-do.* R: *y-do &.*
1674	*they.* So K. R omits. D: *þei.*
1687–1778	Corresponding section missing in K.
1697	*degreez.* So D. R: *the degreez.*
1700	*And.* So D. R: *of.*
1717	*fro.* So D. R: *for.*
1744	*he₂.* So D. R: *he he.*
1760	*another.* R: *another ~~compas~~.*
1775–76	*whiche beth y-clepid clymates. And these cuntreez that Y spake of beth not in these clymates.* R omits; supplied from D, p. 82.
1839	*strangly.* R: *stranly.* K: *worow.* D: *worry.* D (p. 85) cites other versions that read *swolewe.*
1860	*hundred.* R omits. K: *iii.c.* D: *CCC.* The 300 prayers referred to immediately after (line 1862) suggest the word "hundred" has been mistakenly omitted here.
1883	*that₁.* So K, D. R: *the.*
1893	*of.* So K, D. R omits.
1921	*And.* R: *And ~~that~~.*
1934	*soules.* So K, D. R: *soul.*
1935	*soules₁.* So K. R: *soul.* D: *soulis.*
1936	*that.* So K, D. R: *tha.*
1939	*and.* R: *an.* K, D: *and may.*
1971	*as₁.* So K, D. R: *as also.*
1978	*sege.* So K, D. R: *se.*
1992	*emperouris table.* So D. R: *emperour is a table.* K: *emperours table.*
2018	*the.* So K, D. R: *the the.*
2033	*4.* R omits. K: *forth.* D: *ferþe.*
2048	*he.* So K, D. R: *they.*
2078	*ther.* R: *þ*, with *er* curl partially obscured by otiose stroke.
2089	*also.* R: *alos.* K, D omit.
2102	*berynge.* R: *be g.* Letters illegible, supplied from K, p. 66. D omits.
2109	*they₁.* R: *they ~~wel~~.*
2120	*byfore crieth.* R: *byfore ~~hem maketh pees and then tho men~~ crieth.*
2126	*earis.* R: here (on fol. 68r) and at line 2134 (fol. 68v) *earis* has been inserted in a different hand, perhaps over an erasure.
	philosophere. R: *philophere.* K: *phylosopher.* D: *philosofir.*
2134	*earis.* See textual note to line 2126 (*earis*).
2173	*fire.* R: *faire.* K: *fyre.* D: *fyr.*
2240	*Y.* R: *he.* Emended to keep the first person consistent within the Khan's speech.

2250–51	*in Bethleem. In the lond of Corasen.* R: Punctuation of the manuscript overtly makes one phrase of the lines, which makes no sense.
2254	*men of.* So K, D. R: *men.*
2279	*to com fro.* R omits. Supplied from K, p. 72. D: *to come doun fro.*
2294	*Port.* So K, D. R omits.
2299	*and.* So K, D. R omits.
2331	*unto.* R omits. K:(p. 74) reads *fro high Ermony unto the wyldrnes of ynde the lesse* (p. 74). D: *fro highe ermonye unto the wildernesse of ynde the lasse.* In both, *the lasse* clearly refers to *ynde the lasse* rather than *Ermony theLasse*, as our manuscript would suggest. A less extreme emendation, in keeping with the sense of R, has been preferred here.
2428	*playn.* So D. R omits. K: *pleyne.*
2441	*goold.* R: *goold by.*
2461	*children.* So D. R: *ch*, with dots underneath indicating it was to be crossed out. K: *childre.*
2487–88	*and hys welles, and he dyd.* Supplied from K, p. 80; unreadable in R. D: *and his wellis. And he hadde.*
2591	*and.* R: *and and.*
2624	*loveth₁.* R: *loveþ hym.*
2685–2769	*men of the countré . . . the religyous cutte.* R omits (missing folio); text supplied from K, pp. 88–91.
2769	*the flessh.* R: *with the flesh.* We have emended to make the additional material from K grammatical (see textual note to lines 2685–2769).
2771	*flieth.* R: *fleith.* K: *flye.* D: *fleeþ.*
2777	*is.* So K, D. R: *his.*
2805	*haveth.* So D. R: *and haveth.* K: *have.*
2815	*grace.* So K, D. R omits.
2837	*yer.* R: *yer and for as moche.*
2856–57	*to His joy . . . God withoute ende. Amen.* The manuscript lacks this passage which was on a missing final leaf; supplied from K, p. 93.

Both Warner and Bovenschen worked extensively to establish the sources to which *The Book of John Mandeville* owes much of its material. Bovenschen's "Untersuchungen über Johann von Mandeville" and the notes to Warner's *Buke of John Mandeville* continue to provide the most substantial underpinning for our understanding of the *Book*'s use of sources. Although much has been added to our knowledge by the continuing source-study of later scholars, remarkably few of Bovenschen's and Warner's original attributions have been superseded.

The *Book* draws in material from an impressive collection of medieval sources that are still known today. Provided here is an annotated listing of some of the most central sources for our text, along with a secondary listing of sources used less overtly, or less comprehensively, in the *Book* as a whole. Many of the Latin sources were almost certainly used by the author in French translations.

For detailed coverage of the attributions of individual passages, the reader is advised to consult the notes to Warner's Roxburghe Club edition of the Egerton text (W), Seymour's *Defective Version* and *Bodley Version*, and Deluz's *Livre de Jehan de Mandeville* (pp. 428–91), which provides a highly detailed breakdown of the *Book*'s sources in tabular form. To all these scholars and their work we are indebted here.

MAIN SOURCES

ALBERT OF AIX, *HISTORIA HIEROSOLIMITANAE EXPEDITIONIS*

Albert of Aix (now sometimes referred to as Albert of Aachen, based on the belief that he may have been a canon of Aix-la-Chapelle, rather than Aix-en-Provence as previously assumed) is known chiefly as a chronicler of the First Crusade, which began in 1095. His history (c. 1125), though long out of date by the time of the *Book*'s authorship, supplies several of the *Book*'s pilgrimage routes, including the route through Hungary to Constantinople (lines 92–97) and the route to Jerusalem through Asia Minor.

Albert's own work, like the *Book* that borrows from it, is based on reports both written and oral, rather than on firsthand experience.

THE ALEXANDER ROMANCE

The Alexander Romance originated largely in the accounts of Pseudo-Callisthenes and includes, among much else, the history of Alexander's conquests, accounts of Alexander's childhood and of his death, and the famous Letter of Alexander to Aristotle, describing the wonders of the East. While no original version survives, the Alexander material made its way into Latin late in the third century, and was later incorporated into Vincent of Beauvais' *Speculum Majus* as well as being translated into vernacular versions. Notable borrowings from this material in the *Book* include:

- the marvels of Bactria, such as wool-bearing trees and gryphons (lines 2383–91)
- the waxing and waning trees (lines 2428–31)
- the accounts of Alexander's dealings with the Brahmins (lines 2590–2620)

HAYTON THE ARMENIAN, *FLOS HISTORIARUM TERRAE ORIENTIS*

Hayton (variously Haiton, Heyton) was a member of the royal family of Lesser Armenia, and he served the state in various political and military functions before retiring, late in life, to become a monk. His *Flower of Histories of the East* (c. 1300) is in four books: a geographical survey of the East (broadly conceived), a short Muslim military history, an account of the early history of the Mongols and their Khans, and a plan for uniting the Mongols and Christians against the Saracens to retake the Holy Land. Hayton notes that his information comes from three impeccable sources: the Mongols' own histories, the firsthand accounts of his uncle, King Hayton of Lesser Armenia, who spent his reign in close contact with the Great Khanate, and his own experience in the Mongol world.

Hayton's work was a source for the geography of Asia, as well as for history concerning the Egyptians and the Tartars. The *Book*'s sixteenth chapter, "Why He Is Y-cleped the Greyt Cane," stems directly from Hayton, as do numerous small references to the politics of Asia Minor and the description of "Asye the Depe" at lines 2248–78.

JACQUES DE VITRY, *HISTORIA ORIENTALIS SEU HIEROSOLYMITANA*

Jacques de Vitry (c. 1160–1240) served as bishop of Acre in the early 1200s and traveled extensively in Palestine and Egypt. Offered the patriarchate of Jerusalem, he refused it in favor of other duties, but he did write the *Historia* (c. 1218), a firsthand account of the Holy Land as he experienced it. *The Book of John Mandeville* borrows many details about the Holy Land, Islam, and even natural history from Jacques, including:

- the (erroneous) attribution of the founding of Damascus to Eliezer of Damascus (lines 1106–07)
- the reference to the freezing river (lines 1126–27)
- route information from Antioch to Jerusalem (lines 1178–85)
- information on Mohammed and Khadija, and the sects of Islam (lines 1337–48)
- the story of the lodestones (lines 1515–42)

Especially known for his opposition to heresy, Jacques was a keen student of sectarianism within the Church and notably provides much of the *Book*'s information about variant Christian sects (e.g., lines 1063–1100).

JOHN OF PLANO CARPINI, *HISTORIA MONGOLORUM*

John of Plano Carpini was a Franciscan friar who acted as papal emissary to the Great Khan in the wake of the Council of Lyon in 1245. With two other emissaries, he carried a papal letter by way of Moscow and Kiev to the *ordu* of Batu Khan on the Volga River, arriving in 1246, then continued to the court of Kuyuk Khan in Karakorum, returning to

Avignon in 1247 with the Khan's reply. His book, appearing several decades before the more highly-publicized work of Marco Polo, was the first record of the Mongol world available to the European Christian audience. It served as a major source for the *Book*'s accounts of Mongol history, social structure, and culture, probably through the mediation of Vincent of Beauvais (see below). The *Book*'s account of the Tartars (lines 1193–1201) stems from John, apparently by way of Vincent, as does much of the last half of chapter 17, "Aray of the Court of the Gret Chane," and the account of Tibetan funeral rites performed by a son for his dead father (lines 2763–78).

THE LETTER OF PRESTER JOHN

One of many medieval "hoax-letters" — false correspondences from historical or legendary figures — *The Letter of Prester John* was supposedly sent to the Byzantine emperor Manuel c. 1165 by Prester John, emperor of India. Based on the popular myth that the Far East was home to an immensely powerful Christian kingdom and the hope that that kingdom could be pressed into service to assist in the suppression of the Saracens, the letter was apparently fabricated to offer hope to increasingly disheartened crusaders and their governments. The letter describes the glorious empire of Prester John in detail, and *The Book of John Mandeville* mines it for such passages as:

- the story of the Fountain of Youth (lines 1594–1600)
- the title "Archiprotapapon" for the prelate of Polumbum (line 1607)
- the description of Prester John's kingdom (lines 2398–14)
- the Gravel Sea with its unusual fish (lines 2423–27)
- part of the account of the Brahmins (lines 2573–2624)

ODORIC OF PORDENONE, *ITINERARIUS*

Odoric, a Franciscan missionary, traveled to Beijing by a sea route beginning from Padua c. 1318 and returning in 1330. His travels took him through the Persian Gulf and to points all along the coasts of India, Indonesia, and China. In China he traveled extensively inland, and, after spending three years at the Khan's Great Court in Beijing, returned by an overland route which probably included the first European visit to Lhasa, Tibet. Odoric's account is the key source for much of the *Book* from chapter 13, "Dyverseteis of Peple and of Contreis," onward, although by no means confined to that section. Specific borrowings from Odoric include:

- the loathliness of Chaldean women (line 1473)
- the stories of the great heat of India affecting men's testicles (lines 1556–57) and the use of ships without nails (lines 1562–63)
- the account of ox-worship in India (lines 1602–13)
- the account of suttee, as practiced in India (lines 1622–23)
- the descriptions of St. Thomas' shrine (lines 1627–35) and the juggernaut-car (lines 1650–69)
- the account of licentiousness in Lamory (lines 1671–79)
- the story of the self-sacrificing fish (without its Christian interpretation) (lines 1820–27)
- the account of the pygmies (lines 1943–49)
- the description of the Great Khan's hall (lines 1968–73)
- the description of the paradise of the Assassins (lines 2473–91)
- the journey through the Valley Perilous (lines 2492–2500)

- the description of Tibet and its funerary rites (lines 2763–83)
- the account of the long-nailed Mandarin (lines 2792–95)

Evidence suggests that the *Book*'s author made use of this text largely through John le Long's 1351 French translation, rather than in the original Latin. It should also be noted that Odoric himself, though an actual traveler to the Far East, made extensive use of Marco Polo's account of the East in writing his own, so much so that he inadvertently describes his voyage from India toward China backwards, having modeled it on Polo's return trip from China to India.

PSEUDO-ODORIC, *LIBER DE TERRA SANCTA*

This book, attributed inconclusively to Odoric of Pordenone, is described by Yule as "consisting of short chapters, containing a detailed itinerary in Palestine with the distances, etc., and . . . of very little interest. It ends with a chapter on 'Machomet' of a short denunciatory kind" (*Cathay*, p. 18). While the book's style bears little resemblance to Odoric's, and no account survives of his having traveled through Palestine, the book nonetheless supplied the *Mandeville*-author with some of his Palestinian material. The story of the Magi (lines 556–57), as well as the *Book*'s descriptions of the Charnel of Innocents (lines 562–63), the tomb and chair of St. Jerome (lines 563–65), and the church of St. Nicholas (lines 565–69) derive from this source.

VINCENT OF BEAUVAIS, *SPECULUM NATURALE* AND *SPECULUM HISTORIALE*

Although information is scant, it seems likely that the Dominican Friar Vincent (c. 1190–1264) spent most of his adult life in scholarly pursuits at the monastery of Beauvais. His magnum opus, the *Speculum Majus*, is in four parts — the *Naturale*, *Doctrinale*, *Morale*, and *Historiale* — although the *Morale* is sometimes considered to be interpolated.

Referred to by Letts as "Mandeville's great standby" (*Sir John Mandeville*, p. 29), Vincent's encyclopedia underpins much of the *Book*. Indeed, so pervasive is the *Book*'s use of Vincent that it would be impossible to attribute every passage in which its presence might be felt. The *Speculum* cites hundreds of authors, among them Pliny, Jerome, and Isidore of Seville, as well as including long extracts from John of Plano Carpini and extensive bestiary information. Much of the *Book*'s lore on the subjects of natural history, geography, and the monstrous races probably stems from Vincent. Representative examples of the use of Vincent in the *Book* include:

- the undisturbed dust on the slopes of Mts. Athos and Olympus (lines 221–23)
- the story of the establishment of the female Amazon state after the death of Scolopitus (lines 1476–83)
- information about the diamond and its properties (lines 1509–42)
- unusual treatments of the dead and blood-drinking/bestial cultures (lines 1838–50)
- the description of the stone traconyghte (lines 1851–53)
- the fabulous races of the East (lines 1886–1900)
- the stories of "poison women" (lines 2541–45) and women with the evil eye (lines 2530–32)
- part of the account of the Brahmins (lines 2573 ff.)
- the giant ants (lines 2681–95)

WILLIAM OF BOLDENSELE, *ITINERARIUS (DE QUIBUSDAM ULTRAMARINIS PARTIBUS)*

William (Wilhelm) was a German knight who traveled through Palestine on pilgrimage in 1332–33, and wrote his itinerary of the journey in 1336. Much of *The Book of John Mandeville*'s first half, especially information about Constantinople and the Holy Land, stems from William's account. Nicholson and Yule, in the 1911 *Encyclopedia Britannica*, famously remarked that the *Mandeville*-author had "followed its thread, though digressing on every side, and too often eliminating the singular good sense of the German traveler" (p. 562). Representative examples of the *Book*'s use of William include:

- the discourse on the Church of the Holy Sepulchre (lines 616 ff.)
- the descriptions of Nazareth and Mount Tabor (lines 1017–47)

Like Odoric's text, Boldensele was translated from Latin into French by John le Long in 1351, and was most likely used by the *Book*'s author in its French form.

WILLIAM OF RUBRUCK, *ITINERARIUS*

William (Guillame de Rubruquis), a Franciscan friar, served as a missionary to the Tartars in the early 1250s. Leaving Palestine for Tartary in 1251, he visited the court of Mangu Khan (Kuyuk's successor) and returned to Acre in 1255. Despite his extensive descriptions of the Mongols and their culture, his most definitive contribution to the *Book* is the story of the monk who climbs Mount Ararat and finds the ark perfectly preserved there (lines 1440–48). His work is frequently used in the second part of the *Book* as a secondary reference, adding dimension or detail to accounts drawn from Hayton, Odoric, and others.

WILLIAM OF TRIPOLI, *DE STATU SARACENORUM*

The Dominican Friar William, working in Acre in the early 1270s, claimed to have baptized over a thousand Muslims. The Muslims, he said, were easily brought to the true path because of the close similarity between Christianity and Islam. His appreciation of the sincerity of the Saracens' faith, as well as his sense that it approximated Christianity in important ways and would therefore provide a perfect platform for conversion, informs *The Book of John Mandeville* throughout. More specific borrowings from William include:

- the dominions of the Sultan of Babylon (lines 452–57)
- information about the Koran and the prophet Mohammed (lines 571–81)
- ch. 12, "Truthe of Sarasyns," with the exception of the Sultan's monologue (lines 1228–1377)

OTHER SOURCES

The following sources have also contributed materially to *The Book of John Mandeville*. A close analysis of their individual contributions is available in Deluz, *Livre de Jehan de Mandeville*. Her chapter "La 'Librairie' de Mandeville" (pp. 39–72) is also quite useful in tracing the *Book*'s sources.

BEDE, *DE TEMPORIBUS*

An early eighth-century treatise on chronology, including a summation history of the world from Creation to the time of Bede.

BURCHARD OF MOUNT SION, *DESCRIPTIO TERRAE SANCTAE*

A pilgrimage guide to Palestine, c. 1283, with a strong geographical emphasis.

DEFENSOR OF LIGUGÉ, *LIBER SCINTILLARUM*

A collection (c. seventh century) of selected extracts from the works of the Church fathers.

EUGESIPPUS, *TRACTATUS DE DISTANCIIS LOCORUM TERRAE SANCTAE*

A twelfth-century description of the Holy Land.

FLAVIUS JOSEPHUS, *VITA* AND *DE BELLO JUDAICO*

Josephus' autobiography and his firsthand account of the Jewish uprising against the Romans in the first century AD.

GERVASE OF TILBURY, *OTIA IMPERIALIA*

Written for the Holy Roman Emperor Otto IV in the early thirteenth century, the *Otia* is largely an encyclopedic collection of cosmological, geographical, historical, and folkloric information. It also includes commentary from Gervase on scientific, religious, and political matters.

HONORIUS AUGUSTODUNENSIS (HONORIUS OF AUTUN), *ELUCIDARIUM*

A twelfth-century summary of Christian theology in dialogic form. The *Elucidarium* was translated into French in the thirteenth century.

IMAGO MUNDI

A twelfth-century philosophical text on cosmology, chronology, and astronomy attributed to Honorius.

IBN KHALLIKAN, *KITAB WAFAYAT UL AYN*

A late thirteenth-century collection popularly known as *The Obituaries of Eminent Men* or *The Biographical Dictionary*, including a biography of Hassan ibn Sabbah (Catholonabeus), the master of assassins described in the *Book*.

IDRISI (ABU ABDULLAH MOHAMMED IBN AL-SHARIF AL-IDRISI), *GEOGRAPHY*

A twelfth-century atlas and world geography, produced under the auspices of the Sicilian king Roger II Guiscard. Idrisi worked from sources, personal observation, and information supplied by fieldworkers, and is famous for both his critical approach to geography and the meticulous maps that accompany his work.

ISIDORE OF SEVILLE, *ETYMOLOGIAE*

An early seventh-century summa of all available knowledge, both ancient and modern. The importance of the *Etymologiae* as a textbook and reference book throughout the Middle Ages and into the Renaissance can hardly be overstated.

ITER ALEXANDRI AD PARADISUM

A fourth-century account of a journey to Paradise by Alexander the Great, used as a source for parts of the medieval Alexander Romance.

JACOBUS OF VORAGINE, *LEGENDA AUREA*

A late thirteenth-century compilation of saints' lives.

JOHN OF SACROBOSCO, *DE SPHAERA*

An explanation, c. 1230, of spherical geometry on the Ptolemaic model.

JOHN OF WURZBÜRG, *DESCRIPTIO TERRAE SANCTAE*

A pilgrimage guide, c. 1165, to the Holy Land.

LATINI, BRUNETTO, *LI LIVRES DOU TRESORS*

The first vernacular encyclopedia in Italian, from the mid-1200s.

MACROBIUS, *IN SOMNO SCIPIONIS COMMENTARIUS*

Macrobius' fifth-century commentary on Cicero's *Dream of Scipio* also includes detailed material about the spherical nature of the earth and its division into northern and southern hemispheres by an equatorial ocean.

MARTINUS POLONUS (MARTINUS OPPAVIENSIS; MARTIN VON TRAPPAU), *CHRONICON PONTIFICUM ET IMPERATORUM*

A thirteenth-century handbook of popes and emperors composed for Clement IV from sources both historical and legendary.

OROSIUS (PAULUS), *HISTORIARUM ADVERSUM PAGANOS*

A fifth-century history spanning the period from the Creation to 417 AD. Written at the behest of Augustine of Hippo mainly as a refutation to growing anti-Christian sentiment, the *History* depicts world history as Christian history.

PETER COMESTOR, *HISTORIA SCHOLASTICA*

A twelfth-century sacred history of the world, extremely popular in medieval Europe.

RICOLDO DE MONTE CROCE, *LIBER PEREGRINATIONIS* (*ITINERARIUM*)

A late thirteenth-century account of Ricoldo's travels in the Holy Land and in the Near East, the *Liber* also serves as a guide for missionaries.

SOLINUS, *COLLECTANEA RERUM MEMORABILIUM*

A third-century compendium of the marvelous and interesting, the *Collectanea* was one of the most frequently cited books in Europe well into the Middle Ages.

SYDRACH, *LA FONTAINE DE TOUTES SCIENCES*

A dialogic encyclopedia of popular wisdom from the thirteenth century.

THEITMAR, *PEREGRINATIO*

Theitmar, a German pilgrim traveling in the Holy Land in 1217, gives one of the first comprehensive European accounts of the state of the Holy Land after the Saracen takeover.

THEODORICUS, *LIBELLUS DE LOCIS SANCTIS*

A twelfth-century description of the sacred sites of the Holy Land.

WILLIAM OF TYRE, *HISTORIA RERUM IN PARTIBUS TRANSMARINUS GESTARUM*

A twelfth-century work of Holy Land history, so successful that numerous continuators later published Holy Land accounts under William's name. Both William and his continuators are used as sources for the *Book*.

 **BIBLIOGRAPHY**

Ambrose (Pseudo-Hegesippus). *De Excidio Hierosolymitanae*. In *Hegesippus qui dicitur sive Egesippus: De bello Judaico ope codicis Cassellani recognitus*. Ed. Karl Friedrich Weber and Julius Caesar. Marburg: Impensis N. G. Elweti Bibliopolae Academici, 1864. [A fourth-century redaction of Flavius Josephus' *De Bello Judaico*.]

Aristotle. *Nichomachean Ethics*. Trans. Martin Ostwald. Indianapolis: Bobbs-Merrill, 1962.

Atiya, Aziz Suryal. *The Crusade in the Later Middle Ages*. London: Methuen, 1938. Rpt. New York: Kraus, 1965.

———. *A History of Eastern Christianity*. Notre Dame: University of Notre Dame Press, 1968.

Ayalon, David. "The Great Yasa of Chingiz Khan: A Re-examination." Part I. *Studia Islamica* 36 (1972), 8–158.

———. "The Great Yasa of Chingiz Khan: A Re-examination." Part II. *Studia Islamica* 38 (1973), 107–56.

Ayenbite of Inwit. Ed. Pamela Gradon. 2 vols. EETS o.s. 23, 278. London: Oxford University Press, 1965, 1979.

Bacon, Roger. *Metaphysica*. In *Opera hactenus inedita Rogeri Baconi*. Ed. Robert Steele and Ferdinand M. Delorme. Oxford: Clarendon Press, 1909.

———. *Moral Philosophy*. See *Opus Majus of Roger Bacon*.

———. *The Opus Majus of Roger Bacon*. Trans. Robert Belle Burke. Philadelphia: University of Pennsylvania Press, 1928.

Benjamin of Tudela. *The Itinerary of Benjamin of Tudela: Travels in the Middle Ages*. Intro. Michael A. Signer, Marcus Nathan Adler, and A. Asher. Malibu, CA: Joseph Simon, 1983.

Bennett, Josephine Waters. "Chaucer and *Mandeville's Travels*." *Modern Language Notes* 68 (1953), 531–34.

———. *The Rediscovery of Sir John Mandeville*. MLA Monograph Series 19. New York: MLA, 1954.

The Bodley Version of Mandeville's Travels. Ed. M. C. Seymour. EETS o.s. 253. London: Oxford University Press, 1963.

The Book of John Mandeville: An Edition of the Pynson Text with Commentary on the Defective Version. Ed. Tamara Kohanski. Medieval and Renaissance Texts and Studies 231. Tempe: Arizona Center for Medieval and Renaissance Studies, 2001.

Bovenschen, Albert. *Die Quellen für Reisebeschreibung des Johann von Mandeville*. Berlin: W. Pormetter, 1888.

———. "Untersuchungen über Johann von Mandeville und die Quellen seiner Reisebeschreibung." *Zeitschrift der Gesellschaft für Erdkunde*. Berlin: Reimer, 1888.

Boyle, John Andrew. *The Mongol World Empire: 1206–1371*. London: Variorum, 1977.

Braude, Benjamin. "Mandeville's Jews among Others." In *Pilgrims and Travelers to the Holy Land*. Ed. Bryan F. Le Beau and Menachem Mor. Studies in Jewish Civilization 7. Omaha, NE: Creighton University Press, 1996. Pp. 133–58.

The Buke of John Maundeuill, being the travels of Sir John Mandeville, knight, 1322–1356: A hitherto unpublished version, from the unique copy (Egerton MS 1982) in the British Museum. Ed. George F. Warner. Printed for the Roxburghe Club. Westminster: Nichols & Sons, 1889.

Butturff, Douglas R. "Satire in *Mandeville's Travels*." *Annuale Medievale* 13 (1972): 155–64.

Caesarius of Heisterbach. *Dialogue on Miracles*. 2 vols. Trans. H. Von E. Scott and C. C. Swinton Bland. Intro. G. G. Coulton. New York: Harcourt Brace, 1929.

Camargo, Martin. "*The Book of John Mandeville* and the Geography of Identity." In *Marvels, Monsters, and Miracles: Studies in the Medieval and Early Modern Imaginations*. Ed. Timothy S. Jones and David A. Sprunger. Studies in Medieval Culture 42. Kalamazoo, MI: Medieval Institute Publications, 2002. Pp. 67–84.

Cameron, Kenneth Walter. "A Discovery in *John de Mandevilles*." *Speculum* 11 (1936), 351–59.

Campbell, Mary B. *The Witness and the Other World: Exotic European Travel Writing, 400–1600*. Ithaca: Cornell University Press, 1988.

Cathay and the Way Thither. Ed. and trans. Henry Yule. 4 vols. Hakluyt Society, second series 33, 37, 38, 41. London: Hakluyt Society, 1913–16.

Chambers, James. *The Devil's Horsemen: The Mongol Invasion of Europe*. New York: Atheneum, 1985.

Chaucer, Geoffrey. *The Riverside Chaucer*. Third edition. Gen. ed. Larry D. Benson. Boston, MA: Houghton Mifflin, 1987.

Cicero. "On Duties." In *Brutus. On the Nature of the Gods. On Divination. On Duties*. Trans. Hubert M. Poteat. Chicago: University of Chicago Press, 1950. Pp. 463–610.

The Defective Version of Mandeville's Travels. Ed. M. C. Seymour. EETS o.s. 319. Oxford: Oxford University Press, 2002.

Deluz, Christiane. *Le livre de Jehan de Mandeville: Une "géographie" au XIVe siècle*. Louvain-la-Neuve: Institut d'Études Médiévales de l'Université Catholique de Louvain, 1988.

Dicts and Sayings of the Philosophers. Ed. John William Sutton. Kalamazoo, MI: Medieval Institute Publications, 2006.

Dunlop, Douglas. "The Karaits of Eastern Asia." *Bulletin of the School of Oriental and African Studies, University of London* 11 (1943–46), 276–89.

Fazy, Robert. "Jehan de Mandeville: Ses voyages et son séjour discuté en Egypte." *Asiatische Studien/Etudes Asiatiques* 4 (1950), 30–54.

Friedman, John Block. *The Monstrous Races in Medieval Art and Thought*. Cambridge, MA: Harvard University Press, 1981.

Geraldus Cambrensis (Gerald of Wales). *History and Topography of Ireland*. Trans. John O'Meara. New York: Penguin, 1982.

Ginzburg, Carlo. *The Cheese and the Worms: The Cosmos of a Sixteenth-Century Miller*. Trans. John Tedeschi and Anne Tedeschi. Baltimore: Johns Hopkins University Press, 1980.

Grady, Frank. "'Machomete' and *Mandeville's Travels*." In *Medieval Christian Perceptions of Islam: A Book of Essays*. Ed. John Victor Tolan. New York: Garland, 1996. Pp. 271–88.

Greenblatt, Stephen. *Marvelous Possessions: The Wonder of the New World*. Chicago: University of Chicago Press, 1991.

Hanna, Ralph, III. "Mandeville." In *Middle English Prose: A Critical Guide to Major Authors and Genres*. Ed. A. S. G. Edwards. New Brunswick, NJ: Rutgers University Press, 1984. Pp. 121–32.

Haraszti, Zoltan. "The Travels of Sir John Mandeville." *Boston Public Library Quarterly* 2 (1950), 306–16.

Hayton the Armenian. *La Flor des estoires de la terre d'Orient*. Ed. Charles Kohler et al. In *Recueil des Historiens des Croisades: Documents arméniens*. Gen. ed. Edouard Dulaurier. Vol. 2. Paris: Imprimerie Nationale, 1906. Pp. xxiii–cxlii, 111–363. Rpt. Farnborough, England: Gregg International Publishers, 1969.

Heng, Geraldine. *Empire of Magic: Medieval Romance and the Politics of Cultural Fantasy*. New York: Columbia University Press, 2003.

Higgins, Iain. "Imagining Christendom from Jerusalem to Paradise: Asia in Mandeville's Travels." In *Discovering New Worlds: Essays on Medieval Exploration and Imagination*. Ed. Scott D. Westrem. New York: Garland, 1991. Pp. 91–114.

———. *Writing East: The "Travels" of Sir John Mandeville*. Philadelphia: University of Pennsylvania Press, 1997.

———. "Mandeville." In *A Companion to Middle English Prose*. Ed. A. S. G. Edwards. Rochester, NY: D. S. Brewer, 2004. Pp. 99–116.

Horner, Patrick J. "*Mandeville's Travels*: A New Manuscript Extract." *Manuscripta* 24 (1980), 171–75. [Bodleian Library, Digby 88.]

Howard, Donald R. "The World of Mandeville's Travels." *Yearbook of English Studies* 1 (1971), 1–17.

———. *Writers and Pilgrims: Medieval Pilgrimage Narratives and Their Posterity*. Berkeley: University of California Press, 1980.

Jacobus de Voragine. *The Golden Legend*. 2 vols. Trans. William Granger Ryan. Princeton: Princeton University Press, 1993.

Jean d'Arras. *Mélusine: Roman du XIVe siècle*. Ed. Louis Stouff. Geneva: Slatkine Reprints, 1974.

Josephus, Flavius. *The Great Roman-Jewish War: A.D. 66–70 (De Bello Judaico)*. Trans. William Whiston. Rev. D. S. Margoliouth. Ed. and intro. William R. Farmer. New York: Harper, 1960.

Juvaini, Ata-Malik. *Genghis Khan: The History of the World-Conqueror*. Second ed. Trans. J. A. Boyle. Intro. David O. Morgan. Seattle: University of Washington Press, 1997.

Kazhdan, Alexander P., ed. *The Oxford Dictionary of Byzantium*. 3 vols. New York: Oxford University Press, 1991.

Kohanski, Tamarah. "Uncharted Territory: New Perspectives on Mandeville's Travels." Ph.D. Dissertation, University of Connecticut, 1993. *DAI* 55.03A (1993), p. 0560.

———. "Two Manuscripts of *Mandeville's Travels*." *Notes and Queries* n.s. 42 (1995), 269–70.

———. "'What Is a "Travel Book," Anyway?': Generic Criticism and *Mandeville's Travels*." *Literature Interpretation Theory* 7 (1996), 117–30.

Kratz, Dennis, ed. and trans. *The Romances of Alexander*. New York: Garland, 1991.

Lee, Henry. *The Vegetable Lamb of Tartary: a curious fable of the cotton plant, to which is added a sketch of the history of cotton and the cotton trade*. London: Sampson Low, Marston, Searle, and Rivington, 1887.

Letter of Prester John. La lettre du Prêtre Jean: Les versions en ancien français et en ancien occitan. Ed. Martin Gosman. Groningen: Bouma's Boukhuis, 1982.

Letts, Malcolm. "Sir John Mandeville." *Notes and Queries* 191 (1946), 202–04, 275–77.

———. "Sir John Mandeville." *Notes and Queries* 192 (1947), 46–48, 134–36.

———. "Sir John Mandeville." *Notes and Queries* 193 (1948), 52–53.

———. *Sir John Mandeville: The Man and His Book*. London: Batchworth Press, 1949.

A Lytell Cronycle: Richard Pynson's Translation (c. 1520) of La Fleur des histoires de la terre d'Orient (c. 1307). Ed. Glenn Burger. Toronto: University of Toronto Press, 1988.

Mandeville's Travels: Translated from the French of Jean d'Outremeuse. Ed. Paul Hamelius. 2 vols. EETS o.s. 153–54. London: Kegan Paul, Trench, Trübner & Co., 1919–23. Rpt. London: Oxford University Press, 1960–61. [Cotton version.]

Mandeville's Travels. Ed. M. C. Seymour. Oxford: Clarendon Press, 1967. [Cotton version, in Middle English.]

Mandeville's Travels. Ed. M. C. Seymour. London, Oxford University Press, 1968. [Cotton version, in Modern English.]

Mandeville's Travels: Texts and Translations. Ed. Malcolm Letts. 2 vols. Hakluyt Society, second series 101–02. London: Hakluyt Society, 1953. [Modernized Egerton and other versions.]

Map, Walter. *De Nugis Curialium: Courtiers' Trifles*. Ed. and trans. M. R. James. Rev. by Christopher Brooke and Roger Mynors. Oxford: Oxford University Press, 1983.

Mas'udi, Abu al. *The Meadows of Gold: The Abbasids*. Ed. and trans. Paul Lunde and Carolyn Stone. London: Kegan Paul, 1989.

May, David. "Dating the English Translation of *Mandeville's Travels*: The Papal Interpolation." *Notes and Queries* n.s. 34 (1987), 175–78.

———. "*Mandeville's Travels*, Chaucer, and *The House of Fame*." *Notes and Queries* n.s. 34 (1987), 178–82.

McIntosh, Angus, M. L. Samuels, and Michael Benskin. *A Linguistic Atlas of Late Mediaeval English*. 4 vols. Aberdeen: Aberdeen University Press, 1986.

The Metrical Version of Mandeville's Travels. Ed. M. C. Seymour. EETS o.s. 269. London: Oxford University Press, 1973.

Milton, Giles. *The Riddle and the Knight: In Search of John Mandeville, the World's Greatest Traveller*. New York: Farrar, Straus and Giroux, 2001.

Moffett, Samuel Hugh. *A History of Christianity in Asia*. Vol. I: *Beginnings to 1500*. San Francisco: Harper, 1992.

Moseley, C. W. R. D. "Chaucer, Sir John Mandeville, and the Alliterative Revival: A Hypothesis concerning Relationships." *Modern Philology* 72 (1974), 182–84.

———. "The Metamorphoses of Sir John Mandeville." *Yearbook of English Studies* 4 (1974), 5–25.

———. "The Availability of *Mandeville's Travels* in England." *Library*, fifth series 30 (1975), 125–33.

———. "Sir John Mandeville's Visit to the Pope: The Implications of an Interpolation." *Neophilologus* 54 (1970), 77–80.

———, trans. See *Travels of Sir John Mandeville*.

Nicholson, E. B., and Henry Yule. "Mandeville, Jehan de." *Encyclopedia Brittanica*, ninth ed., 1883.

———. "Mandeville, Jehan de." *Encyclopedia Brittanica*, eleventh ed., 1911.

Oliverus Scholasticus (Oliver of Paderborn). *The Capture of Damietta [Historia Damiatina]*: Trans. J. J. Gavigan. Philadelphia: University of Pennsylvania Press, 1948. Rpt. New York: AMS Press, 1980.

Parkes, Malcolm Beckwith. "The Influence of the Concepts of *Ordinatio* and *Compilatio* on the Development of the Book." In *Medieval Learning and Literature: Essays Presented to Richard William Hunt*. Ed. J. J. G. Alexander and M. T. Gibson. Oxford: Clarendon Press, 1976. Pp. 115–41.

Phillips, J.R.S. "The Quest for Sir John Mandeville." In *The Culture of Christendom: Essays in Medieval History in Commemoration of Denis L. T. Bethell*. Ed. Marc Anthony Meyer. London: Hambeldon Press, 1993. Pp. 243–55.

Pinto, Ana. *Mandeville's Travels: A Rihla in Disguise*. Madrid: Editorial Complutense, 2005.

Pliny the Elder. *Natural History: With an English Translation in Ten Volumes*. Trans. H. Rackham. Cambridge, MA: Harvard University Press, 1947.

Polo, Marco. *The Travels of Marco Polo*. Trans. and intro. Ronald Latham. Harmondsworth, NY: Penguin, 1958.

The Prose Life of Alexander from the Thornton MS. Ed. J. S. Westlake. EETS o.s. 143. London: Kegan Paul, Trench, Trübner & Co., 1913.

Sacrobosco, John of. *The Sphere of Sacrobosco and Its Commentators*. Ed. and trans. Lynn Thorndike. Chicago: University of Chicago Press, 1949.

Saunders, John J. *The History of the Mongol Conquests*. Philadelphia: University of Pennsylvania Press, 1971. Rpt. 2001.

Seymour, M. C. "A Medieval Redactor at Work." *Notes and Queries* 206 (1961), 169–71.

———. "The Origin of the Egerton Version of *Mandeville's Travels*." *Medium Aevum* 30 (1961), 159–69.

———. "Secundum Iohannem Maundvyle." *English Studies in Africa* 4 (1961), 148–58. [Bodleian Library, MS Ashmole 751]

———. "The Early English Editions of *Mandeville's Travels*." *Library*, fifth series 19 (1964), 202–07.

———. "The Scribal Tradition of *Mandeville's Travels*: The Insular Version." *Scriptorium* 18 (1964), 34–48.

———. "The English Epitome of *Mandeville's Travels*." *Anglia* 84 (1966), 27–58. [British Library, MS Additional 37049.]

———. "The English Manuscripts of *Mandeville's Travels*." *Edinburgh Bibliographic Society Transactions* 4 (1966), 169–210.

———, ed. "Mandeville and Marco Polo: A Stanzaic Fragment." *AUMLA: Journal of the Australasian Universities Language and Literature Association* 21 (1964), 39–52. [Bodleian Library, MS eMusaeo 160.]

———. *Sir John Mandeville*. Authors of the Middle Ages 1. Aldershot: Variorum, 1993.

Sidrak and Bokkus. Ed. T. L. Burton. EETS o.s. 311–12. Oxford: Oxford University Press, 1998.

Siege of Jerusalem. Ed. Michael Livingston. Kalamazoo, MI: Medieval Institute Publications, 2004.

Solinus, Caius Julius. *The Excellent and Pleasant Worke: Collecteana Rerum Memorabilium*. Trans. Arthur Golding (1587). Gainesville: Scholars' Facsimiles and Reprints, 1955.

Steiner, Arpad. "The Date of Composition of *Mandeville's Travels*." *Speculum* 9 (1934), 144–47.

Symon Simeonis. *Itinerarium Symonis Semeonis ab Hibernia ad Terram Sanctam*. Ed. Mario Esposito. Dublin: Dublin Institute for Advanced Studies, 1960.

Thomas, J. D. "The Date of *Mandeville's Travels*." *Modern Language Notes* 72 (1957), 165–69.

The Travels of Sir John Mandeville. Trans. C. W. R. D. Moseley. New York: Penguin, 1983. [Egerton version, translation.]

Tzanaki, Rosemary. *Mandeville's Medieval Audiences: A Study on the Reception of the Book of Sir John Mandeville (1371–1550)*. Burlington, VT: Ashgate, 2003.

Vincent of Beauvais. *Speculum Historiale*. Douai, 1624. In *Speculum quadruplex sive Speculum maius: naturale/doctrinale/morale/historiale* 4. Graz: Akademische Druck und Verlagsanstalt, 1964–65.

———. *Speculum Naturale*. In *Speculum quadruplex sive Speculum maius: naturale/doctrinale/morale/historiale* 4. Graz: Akademische Druck und Verlagsanstalt, 1964–65.

Virgil. *Aeneid*. Trans. Allen Mandelbaum. New York: Bantam, 1981.

Westrem, Scott. "Two Routes to Pleasant Instruction in Late-Fourteenth-Century Literature." In *The Work of Dissimilitude: Essays from the Sixth Citadel Conference on Medieval and Renaissance Literature*. Ed. David G. Allen and Robert A. White. Newark: University of Delaware Press, 1992. Pp. 67–80.

White, T. H. *The Bestiary: A Book of Beasts*. New York: Putnam, 1960.

William of Rubruck. "The Journal of Friar William de Rubruquis." In *The Travels of Sir John Mandeville*. Ed. A. W. Pollard. London: Macmillan, 1905. Pp. 261–325.

Williams, David. *Deformed Discourse*. Montreal: McGill-Queen's University Press, 1996.

Zacher, Christian. *Curiosity and Pilgrimage: The Literature of Discovery in Fourteenth-Century England*. Baltimore: Johns Hopkins University Press, 1976.

———. "*Mandeville's Travels*." In *A Manual of the Writings in Middle English*. Ed. Albert E. Hartung. Vol. 7. XIX: Travel and Geographical Writing. New Haven: Connecticut Academy of Arts and Sciences, 1986. Pp. 2239–41, 2452–57.

🌿 Glossary

Words are glossed in the text the first two or three times; after that they are listed here. A word is not in the glossary if all examples in the text have been glossed.

about *around; nearby*
adamaund *lodestone*
afor(e) *before*
after *according to*
again/agayn/ageyn/agen *against; before; opposite; again*
als/as *as; as well as; such as*
aray *array; condition*
asay *test*
asemblé *a gathering*
asoundre *asunder*
aughte *ought*
auter/autre *altar*

bad(e) *ordered*
bate *dispute*
beest/beist *beast*
beth *is; are*
bidde/bad *requested*
bien *are*
bigge *buy*
bore *born*
bren(ne) *burn*
bro(o)d(e) *broad*
brugge *bridge*
but if *unless*
but only *except*
byyonde *beyond*

catel(l) *possessions*
chalenge *claim*
chese *chose*
chose *chosen*
cleped *called*

comyn *common*
crie *cry; be announced*

dede *deed;* see also **dey(e)**
deel *part*
de(e)r *injure*
defaute *fault; lack*
departeth *separate(s)*
der/dare see **de(e)r**
deserite *disinhert*
dey(e)/deyghe *die;* **dede** *died; dead*
y-dight/y-dyght *adorned; constructed*
dire *dearly*
diverse *different*
divise *tell*
do *do; make; put*
dyamaund *diamond*

eddre *adder; snake*
(e)elde *age*
elles *else; otherwise*
eyen *eyes*
eynde *end*
eyre *air; heir*

falle *fall; happen*
faste *firmly*
fele *many*
ferst(e) *first*
flom *river*
for *because of*
forme fader *ancestor*
f(o)undede *founded*
fro *from*

149

ful *full; very*
fundede see **f(o)undede**

gat *got; begot*
geve *give*
good *good; goods*
y-grave *buried*
gres/grecis *steps*
gret *great; large*

haven *harbor*
heel/hele *health; salvation*
hele *heal*
hem *them*
her(e) *her(s); herself; their(s); here; hair*
hey(ghe) *high*
hiderward *hither*
hit *it*
y-holde *held; considered; controlled*
holdeth *control(s); hold(s)*
hull *hill*
hure *her*
hym *him; himself; it; itself*

ile *island*
in *in; on*
into *into; until*

journey *day's journey*

kynde *kind; nature; tribe*

y-lad *led; guided*
lasteth/lastith *extend(s)*
let /leet/leyt *let; caused [something to be done]*
licknys/licknes *likeness*
longeth *belong(s)*
lynage *family; tribe*
lyveth *live(s); believe(s)*

maner *kinds of; manner*
marcheth *extend(s)*
mervail(l) *marvel*
mortais *mortice*
most *most; largest; greatest*
mysdowers *evildoers*

myssetrewantes *misbelievers*

n(e)y(e)/neygh *near; nearly*
noght *not; nothing*

of *of; by; from; off; to*
on *on; in; one*
oo *one*
oon *one*
opynli *publicly*
or *or; before*
ost *host*
other *other; or*

parteth *divide(s)*
party *part*
passe *cross; pass*
paynem/paynym *pagan(s)*
pece *piece*
playn *plain*
plenerly *fully*
plenté *abundance; adundantly*
prest *priest*
preve *prove; test*
pylour *pillar*

quyke *alive; living*

reed *red; reed*
repreves *insults*
right(e) *right; true; truly; very; direct*
ro(o)ch(e) *rock*

say *say; saw*
se *see*
see *see; sea*
seist see **se**
semeth *seems to be*
sey(e) *say; saw, seen*
seyn *say; seen*
shappes *shapes*
shewed *showed*
sike *sick*
simulacres *images*
sith(e)(n) *after; since*
sle *slay;* **slow** *slew*
slow *slow;* see also **sle**

soche *such*
somtyme *formerly*
soudan *sultan*
spechis *languages*
stage *tier*
stedes *places*
stonke *stunk*
suffre *allow; endure; suffer*
syth *since*

table board *tablet*
then(ne) *thence; then*
thider/theder *thither; to there*
thilke *these same; those; this*
tho *then; those; they*
thorgh *through.*
thow(e) *although; thou*
title *inscription*
tockne *symbol; sign;* **in tockne** *as a symbol, sign*
tockn(e)yng(e) *a sign; significance;* **in tockn(e)yng(e)** *as a sign of; signifying*
tour *tower*
translate *transport*
trespas *sin*
trowe *believe*
trywe *faithful; true*
tumbe *tomb*

vale *valley*
vertu *virtue; power*

viage *voyage*
visage *face*
vitayles *food*

waies see **weyes**
werre *war*
wex(e) *grow; become*
weyes *routes*
wham *whom*
whe(e)r(e) *where*
whyder *where*
wist(e) *knew*
with *with; by*
wode *wood*
wolde past tense of **wole**
wole *will; wish; want*
woned *accustomed [to]; once*
wo(o)t see **wyte**
worlde *world*
worship *worship; honor*
wroth *angry*
wyte *know;* **wo(o)t** *knew*

Y *I*
y- marker of past tense or past participle
yede *went*
yit/yyt *yet; still*
ynow *enough*
yvel *evil*

Biblical references in this glossary are not exhaustive: rather they are meant to offer a starting point for those who wish to seek further information. All biblical references are to the Douay-Rheims version.

Similar spellings are occasionally grouped to save excessive cross referencing. In such cases, the first in the group may not be the first alphabetically, but will be the first encountered in the text. Textual references are by line number in this edition.

Aaron, 748. Aaron the Levite, brother of Moses (Exodus).

Abcare (Akas), 2276, 2302, 2304. Abkhazia, region in northwest Georgia on the Black Sea.

Abdenago, 445. Abednago, originally called Azariah, one of those cast into the fiery furnace by King Nebuchadnezzar (Daniel 1–3).

Abdom, 974. The prophet Obadiah (Abdias).

Abel, 491, 1109. Abel, son of Adam; slain by his brother Cain in the first murder (Genesis 4).

Abraham (Habraham), 486, 496, 504, 506, 519, 521, 899, 924, 1107, 1285, 1345. Abraham the patriarch (Genesis 11–25).

Abyor, hylle, 2301. Mount Elbruz, in the Caucasus Mountains between the Black and Caspian Seas.

Acheldemak (Field of Blood), 843. Aceldema, the Field of Blood, purchased with the money given to Judas for his betrayal of Christ (Matthew 27:3–10; Acts 1:18–19).

Aches, 216. Mount Athos, on the Acte peninsula in northeast Greece.

Achilles, 395. Achilles, the Greek hero of the Trojan War. The text confuses him with Agenor, Dido's father and ruler of Tyre.

Ackaron (Akkaron, Arne, Mesap), 1229, 1230, 1242, 1257, 1277, 1282, 1330. The Koran, holy book of Muslims.

Acon (Vacres), 405–08, 413, 423, 1181. Acre (formerly Ptolemais), port city north of Haifa.

Adam, 26, 137–47, 491, 507–13, 515, 630, 631, 1673, 1676, 2699. Adam, the first man (Genesis 1–3).

Admonye, Litel. See **Hermony the Lasse**

Adrian, 723, 726. Hadrian, emperor of Rome, 117–38 AD.

Affe. See **Jaffa**

Affrik, 395, 2024. Africa.

Affynpayn, 95. The city of Philippopolis (Plovdiv), on the Maritsa River in Bulgaria.

Agar, 1345. Hagar, the Egyptian servant who became the mother of Ishmael by Abraham (Genesis 16).

Agariens, 1347. Descendants of Hagar, the servant of Abraham and Sarah (Genesis 16).

Airach, hille (Thane), 1435. Mount Ararat, in Armenia. Possibly from the Persian *kuh-i-nuh*, Mountain of Noah.

Akas. See **Abcare**

Akkaron. See **Ackaron**

Alape (Alappe, Anolpe), 438, 456, 663. The city of Aleppo, in northern Syria.

Albane, ryver, 1171. The Abana River, in Lebanon.

Albanye, 1907–08. Alternative name for the province of Manzi in southern China. The application of the name Albanye to this region is not elsewhere attested. See also **Mancy**

Aldema, 914. The city of Admah, on the Red Sea.

Alfeigh, 81. Probably Silesia, a region of east central Europe, in the upper Oder River valley.

Alisaundre (Barkent, Port de Feare), 2268–69, 2273, 2294. The city of Derbend, on the west coast of the Caspian Sea, named for its mountain pass (Persian *dar-band*: narrow passage). Derbend is mythically associated with Alexander the Great; the pass of Derbend, between the Caspian Sea and the Caucasus Mountains, was known as Alexander's Iron Gate, hence *port du fer*.

Alisaundre, King (Alysaundre), 208, 1494, 1566, 2268, 2355, 2376, 2590, 2607, 2613, 2620, 2649. Alexander the Great.

Allfetida, Lake of, Another name for the Dead Sea. See also **Dede See**

Almayn (Almayne), 79, 89, 191, 1191–92, 1697. Germany.

Alysaundre, 1495. The city of Alexandria Margiane (Merv, Mary) in southern Turkestan (later Turkmeniya).

Alysaundre, Kyng. See **Alisaundre, King**

Amazayn (Amasoyn, Amasoyne), 64,

1476, 1493. Amazonia, the land of the Amazons, believed to be near Scythia.

Amonites, 1348. The Ammonites, an ancient Semitic people descended from Lot (Genesis 19:30–38).

Amors, castel of, 368. Deudamour (Dieu d'Amour), Frankish name for the Castle of St. Hilarion in northern Cyprus.

Amyas, 987. The city of Amiens, France.

Anania. See **Cidrac**

Andrew, Seynt, 1006. St. Andrew the Apostle, brother of Simon (called Peter) (Matthew 10:2).

Animote, 729. Most texts cite the name "Helyam," a corruption of Aelia. Animote here appears to stem from the Latin, suggesting "the city of Life."

Anna, 958. Hannah, mother of the prophet Samuel (1 Kings 1).

Anne, 181. Annas, the high priest at Jerusalem when Christ was arrested (John 18:19–24).

Anne, Seynt, 192, 781. St. Anne, mother of the Virgin Mary.

Anolpe. See **Alape**

Antecrist, 1007, 1010, 2367, 2375. Antichrist, a destroyer who, it is foretold, will fill the world with wickedness before Christ defeats him forever at the Second Coming (1 John 2:18, 22; 1 John 4:3; 2 John 1:7).

Anteryke, 1690, 1700–1701. Reported as the southern pole star, probably from Latin *anterus* (in front) or Latin/Greek *anti* (against).

Apocalips, 286. The Apocalypse, or Revelation to John; the last book of the Bible.

Arabie (Arabye, Araby), 63, 105, 456,597, 662, 903, 1331, 1334,

1344, 1350, 1383, 1511, 2561, 2661. Arabia.

Arabynes, 470. The Arabians.

Archades, playn of, 1173. The plain of Archades, near Damascus.

Archa Noe, 1435. Noah's Ark, in which Noah and his family escaped the Great Flood (see Genesis 6–9).

Archiprotapaton, 1606–07. Reported title of the prelate of Polumbum (Quilon) on the Malabar coast of India. Probably from the Nestorian title *Archiprotopapas*, mentioned in *The Letter of Prester John*, the *Book*'s source for the foregoing account of the Fountain of Youth.

Architriclyne, 1015. From the Greek *architriklinios*, the chief steward of the wedding feast at Cana (John 2:8).

Argete, 2678. Pliny's Argyre, a mythical island in the Great Sea Ocean.

Aristotle, 209. The Greek philosopher Aristotle.

Arke of God (Ark of God), 745, 746, 959. The Ark of the Covenant, in which the stone tablets of the Ten Commandments were stored. See also **Beleth**

Arne. See **Ackaron**

Artoys, 1170. The city of Artah, near Antiochia Pisidiae (Greater Antioch, Yalvac) in Asia Minor.

Artyron, 1434. The city of Erzerum, in eastern Turkey.

Arynona, 204. The Greek isle of Paros.

Ascalon, 428, 595, 601. The city of Askalon, in south Palestine.

Ascolonyte, Herod of Askalon. See **Herodes**

Ascopardes, 470. An Arab tribe, possibly the Sudanese.

Asie the Lasse, 103–04, 292. Asia Minor.

Assary, 2716. The ancient empire of Assyria, in western Asia extending along the Tigris River.

Assirienes, 606. The Assyrians.

Assumpcioun, 880. The Assumption, or taking up into Heaven, of the Virgin Mary.

Assye (Asy), 662, 2023. Asia.

Asye the Depe, 2248. Deepest Asia.

Athillok, 435. The Syrian Desert (*Et-tîh*).

Athos, Mount, 205. Mount Athanasi, on the Greek isle of Lemnos. The true Mount Athos is referred to as **Aches**.

Attonas (Atthonas), 1395. St. Athanasius, bishop of Alexandria, c. 325–73. See explanatory note to lines 1395–1402.

Aunteoch, 1174, 1178. The city of Antioch (Antakya), on the Syrian coast.

Aunteoch the Betre, 1165. The city of Antiochia Pisidiae (Yalvac), in Asia Minor.

Austyn, Seynt, 1078. St. Augustine, bishop of Hippo from 396 to 430.

Azaria. See **Abdenago**

Babyloyn (Babiloyne, Babiloyn, Babyloyne, Cayr), (1) 430, 439, 1133–34, 1379, 2192. A medieval name for Cairo, based on the city's proximity to the ruined town of Baba al 'yun, in Egypt. The story of Nebuchadnezzar conflates Cairo with Babylon in Mesopotamia. (2) 1008–09. The kingdom of Babylon, in Mesopotamia.

Bakarie (Bacarie), 2383, 2392. Probably Bactria (Afghanistan), but possibly the city of Bokhara in southern Turkestan (later Uzbekistan). See also **Battria**

Balthasar, 557. One of the Magi, who visited the baby Jesus with gifts (Matthew 2:1–12).

Barbara, Seynt, 441. St. Barbara, virgin martyr from Heliopolis in Egypt (sometimes believed to be from Nicodemia in Asia Minor).

Barbaryns, 607. The generic "barbarians" is probably meant here.

Barkent. See **Alisaundre**

Barron. See **Coffrace**

Battria, 2288. The city of Bokhara in southern Turkestan (later Uzbekistan). See also **Bakarie**

Baudewyn, 632, 952. Baldwin I, king of Jerusalem (1100–18), and brother of Godfrey of Bouillon.

Bedlem. See **Bethleem**

Bedoyns (Bydoynes), 449, 470. Bedouins; nomadic desert Arabs. From the Arabic *bidwan*, desert dwellers.

Beleth, (1) 438. The city of Bilbeis, north of Cairo, possibly conflated in the text with Ba'albek, east of Beirut, on the site of the ancient city of Heliopolis. **(2)** 745. Moriah (Bethel), where stood the Ark of the Covenant, in which the stone tablets of the Ten Commandments were stored, also called **Morarche**.

Belgrave, 92. The city of Belgrade, Serbia.

Belyan, Mount, 2076, 2078, 2079. Probably a conflation of the Baldjuna Desert, east of Lake Baikal (considered the northern boundary of Cathay) and the Altai Mountains (sometimes called the Belgian Mountains).

Beme, 1698. Bohemia.

Benet, Seynt, 674. St. Benedict of Nursia (c. 480–547), originator of the Benedictine Rule.

Benjamyn, (1) 586. The son of Jacob and Rachel (Genesis 35:16–18). **(2)** 961. The Portion of Benjamin, where the tribe of Benjamin dwelt.

Bernard, Seynt, 369. Probably an error for St. Barnabas, as no St. Bernard is associated with Cyprus.

Bersabe (Bersabee), 485, 601, 1061. The city of Beersheba, west of the Dead Sea. Not, as several versions of the *Book* claim, named for Bathsheba, wife of Uriah; its name in Arabic means "well of the oath."

Beruch (Brenche), 396, 1128. The city of Beirut, Lebanon. "Brenche" probably stems from a misreading of Beruch.

Besfage, 872. The village of Bethphage, on the Mount of Olives near Jerusalem.

Bessamoran, 96. Byzantium (Constantinople, Istanbul). See also **Constantynople**

Bethleem (Bethlem, Bedlem, Effrata), 534, 535, 537, 538, 560, 570, 582, 602, 2250. Bethlehem.

Bethsayda (Bethsaida), 1006, 1011. The town of Bethsaida, northeast of the Sea of Galilee.

Bethtony (Bethany, Betonye, Betanye), (1) 11, 873, 894. Bethany, in Judea. **(2)** 195. The ancient country of Bithynia in Asia Minor, bordering on the Black Sea.

Bible (Byble), 564, 995, 1077, 2812. The Bible, holy book of Christians.

Blood, Field of. See **Acheldemak**

Bomk. See **Polomee**

Bouch of Constantynople (Brace de Seynt Gorge), 200, 201, 283. The "Mouth of Constantinople" or the "Arm of St. George," both identified with the Hellespont, but almost certainly the Bosporus. Confusion between the Bosporus and the Hellespont is common in crusader texts. See also **Hellesponte**

Braban, 1696. Brabant, an old western European duchy in the Netherlands/Belgium area.

Brace de Seynt Gorge. See **Bouch of Constantynople**

Bradremple, 95. The city of Adrianople, on the Thracian peninsula not far from Constantinople.

Bragme (Feith, ile of), 2580. The land of the Brahmins, orthodox Hindus.

Brenche. See **Beruch**

Brike, 2326. Phrygia, in central Asia Minor.

Bruges. See **Bulgarie**

Bugers, 84. Bulgarians.

Bulgarie (Bruges), 83, 92. Bulgaria.

Burgoyne, 1139–40. Burgundy, in eastern France.

Bydoynes. See **Bedoyns**

Cadom, 1959. The great court of the Mongols, near Beijing.

Caffere, 412. The town of Shefa 'Amr, east of Haifa, often identified as the birthplace of Sts. John and James.

Caim (Caym), 492, 1108. Cain, son of Adam and Eve, who slew his brother Abel (Genesis 4).

Calabre, 407. The region of Calabria, in southern Italy.

Calamye, 126. The city of Mailapur (Madras) in southeast India, which has long claimed itself the final resting place of St. Thomas.

Calastre, 204. The Greek isle of Thera (Santorini).

Calcas, 204. The Greek isle of Carki.

Caldee (Caldé, Galdé), 1351, 1383, 1391, 1472, 1496, 2297, 2332, 2342. Chaldea, region of southwest Asia on the Persian Gulf and the Euphrates River.

Calofe, 493. Caleb, an Israelite scout (Numbers 14:6).

Calonache, 1818. Apparently the land of Zampa visited by Odoric of Pordenone; the southern part of Vietnam.

Calvarie, 150, 626, 652. Mount Calvary (Golgotha), where Christ was crucified.

Camelat, 2154. Beijing; from Mongolian *kaán-baligh*, city of the Great Khan. Most texts of the *Book* place the city in the south, as a place for the Khan to winter in comfort.

Cana, (1) 1564, 1588. The district of Thána, along the Bombay coast of India. **(2)** See **Cane, Gret**

Canane, 388. Canaan, an ancient region roughly corresponding to later Palestine.

Cananee, womman, 1014. The Canaanite woman, a model of faith in Matthew 15:21–28. The text here conflates Cana, in Galilee, with Canaan, an ancient region roughly corresponding to later Palestine.

Cananeus, 606. The Canaanites.

Canaphat. See **Egipt**

Canapos, 2676. The star Canopus, in the constellation Carina, not visible north of 37 degrees latitude.

Cane, (1) 1013. The city of Cana, in Galilee. The text here conflates Cana with Canaan, an ancient region roughly corresponding to later Palestine. **(2)** Great Khan; see **Cane, Gret (3)** 2089. Khan, title of Mongol rulers. Lesser Khanates were held beneath the auspices of the Great Khan.

Cane, Gret (Chane, Gret), 1193, 1794–97, 1867, 1921, 1943, 1961, 1967, 2018, 2038, 2047, 2062–85, 2089, 2086–2098, 2100, 2155, 2170, 2190, 2195, 2224–44, 2283, 2303, 2339, 2399, 2400–01, 2415–16, 2464, 2751, 2752, 2755,

Elisaundre, 1395. Alexandria, Egypt.

Eliseus, 974. The prophet Elisha.

Elizabeth, 847. St. Elizabeth, mother of John the Baptist.

Elye, 959. The prophet Eli.

Emaux, 1185. The town of Emmaus (Imwas), between Jaffa and Jerusalem.

Emaux, castel of (Chynay, castle of), 849, 1153. The crusader castle of Emmaus (Imwas), between Jaffa and Jerusalem.

Engelond. See **Ingelond**

Englyssh, 1376. The English language.

Enyas, 394. The Trojan hero Aeneas.

Ephesome, 288, 298. Ephesus, city near the Aegean coast of Asia Minor.

Ermes, (1) 1555. Probably the city of Ormuz (see **2**), although the isle of Ormuz is not far away. **(2)** 2409. The city of Ormuz, on the Strait of Ormuz in southern Iran, at the outlet of the Persian Gulf. **(3)** 234, 2411. The legendary wise man, Hermes Trismegistus (who was not, in fact, the founder of Ormuz, as lines 2407–08 suggest), also sometimes called Hermogenes. See explanatory note to lines 228–34.

Ermon, Mount, 1048. Mount Hermon, inland between Tyre and Damascus.

Ermonye (Ermony, Gret; Ermonye, Heye). See **Hermony the More**

Ermonye the Lasse (Ermonye, Lytel). See **Hermony the Lasse**

Ernax, valeys of, 1165. Possibly the town of Ormanx, in Asia Minor.

Ethel, ryver of, 2262. The Volga River; from Turkish *idil*, river.

Ethiope (Ethiop), 64, 664, 1496, 1501, 1505, 2333, 2335, 2715. Ethiopia.

Eufrates, 1384, 1386, 2330, 2717, 2727. The Euphrates River.

Eurace, 2033. A Tartar tribe. Hayton the Armenian calls them "Cunat."

Europe, 2024. Europe.

Eustace, Seynt, 1172. St. Eustace, who helped spread Christianity through southern and central Europe.

Eve, 497, 507, 1673, 1676, 2699. Eve, the first woman (Genesis 1–3).

Famagost, 362, 368, 1144. The city of Famagusta, Cyprus.

Fariseis, 840. The Pharisees, a Jewish sect.

Fasser. See **Ferne, rever of**

Faxton, 204. The Greek isle of Naxos.

Feith, ile of. See **Bragme**

Ferne, cité of, 1174. Possibly the city of Ilgun, in Asia Minor.

Ferne, rever of (Fasser), 1170. The biblical River Pharphar, flowing from Mount Hermon past Damascus. Its placement here, apparently in Asia Minor, is problematic and may result from a conflation with the "cité of Ferne." See also **Ferne, cité of**

Field of Blood. See **Acheldemak**

Fimes. See **Phenes**

Fison, ryver of. See **Fyson, rever of**

Flagme, 1183. Unclear. Perhaps a port town between Acre and Haifa.

Flandres, 1190. Flanders.

Florach, castel, 1169. Castle Florach, on the south coast of Asia Minor.

Floridous (Floryshid, Feyld), 542–43. The Flowering Field.

Fons Jacob. See **Jacobis Well**

Fraunce (France), 158, 160, 951, 1139, 1189. France.

Frenshe (Frenssh), 951, 1325. The French language.

Fyson, rever of (Physon), 2289, 2720. The Oxus River, between the Aral Sea and the Hindu Kush.

Gabon, 961. Probably the town of Gibeon, in the Portion of Benjamin, north of Jerusalem.

Alexander trapping the Jewish tribes in the impassable hills.

Gomor, 914. The city of Gomorrah in ancient Palestine, destroyed by God for its iniquity (Genesis 19).

Gorge, 2300, 2303. Georgia, in the Caucasus region, on the east coast of the Black Sea.

Grasten, 1208. Possibly a corruption of Dorestena, the ancient name for the province of Silistria in eastern Europe.

Gravely See (Gravel See), 423, 2423. The legend of the Gravelly Sea probably arises from the shifting sands of the desert. See explanatory note to line 423.

Grece, iles of, 301. Greek islands.

Grecis (Grece), 90, 97, 103, 105, 203, 235, 557, 1130, 1141, 1156, 2190, 2313, 2668, 2821. Greece.

Greet Brytayne, 153. Great Britain.

Greet See (Gret See), **(1)** The Mediterranean Sea. See **Metterane, see. (2)** The Black Sea. See **Maure, Oxean. (3)** The Great Sea Ocean. See **Occian**

Gregore, Seynt, 1078, 1081. Pope Gregory I (c. 590–604).

Gregyssh, 2282. Greek.

Grekes (Grecis, Grekis), 135, 606, 1096. The Greeks.

Greu (Gru), 120, 230, 634, 638. The Greek language.

Griff, 1141. The Greek isle of Corfu.

Gyron, ryver. See **Nyle, flode of**

Habraham. See **Abraham**

Hamson, 2306. The district of Hamschen, near the Black Sea.

Hay, 947. The town of Ai, just north of Jerusalem.

Helias. See **Elias**

Hellesponte, 200. The Hellespont (Dardanelles) is a strait in northwest Turkey. The strait referred to here, however, is almost certainly the Bosporus. Confusion between the two is common in crusader texts. See also **Bouch of Constantynople**

Hely. See **Elias**

Hercules, 1574. The demigod Hercules, son of Zeus and Alcmena.

Hermogenes. See **Ermes**

Hermony the Lasse (Litel Admonye; Damacyn the Lesse; Ermonye the Lasse; Ermonye, Lytel), 63, 662, 1406, 2297, 2331, 2717. "Little Armenia," in Cilicia, in southern Asia Minor.

Hermony the More (Damacyn the More; Ermony; Ermonye, Gret; Ermonye, Heye), 63, 662, 1414, 1426, 1433, 2289, 2295, 2302, 2325, 2331, 2716–17. Armenia.

Herodes (Ascolonyte), 441, 791–805, 807. Herod the Great, king of Judea from 37 BC to 4 AD. For Christ's trial before Herod, see Luke 23:6–16. For the slaughter of the innocents and the flight into Egypt, see Matthew 2.

Herodes Agrippa, 808. King Herod Agrippa of Judea, who ordered St. James, the brother of John, beheaded circa 44 AD (Acts 12:2). The more famous Herod Agrippa, nearly converted by Paul in Acts 26, is his son.

Herodes Antipa, 808. Herod Antipas, Roman tetrarch of Galilee, 4 BC to 39 AD, who had John the Baptist imprisoned and killed (Matthew 14:1–12; Mark 6:17–29).

Hillari, Seynt, 367. St. Hilarion (c. 302–372), considered the founder of monastic life in Palestine. Though he died in Cyprus, his body was returned to Palestine.

Hillary, Seynt, 1082. St. Hilary of Poitiers (d. 368), best known for his vigorous and long-standing opposition to Arianism.

Holy Croys, hille of the, 112, 364. The monastery of Stavrovouni in Cyprus, named for the piece of the Cross of Christ said to be preserved there. See explanatory note to lines 110–15.

Holy of Halwes (Sancta Sanctorum), 738. The innermost part of the Temple, where only the high priest might enter, and even he only once a year, on the Day of Atonement.

Holy Sepulcre, Cherche of the. See **Sepulcre, Cherche of the**

Holy Writ (Holy Wrytte), 384, 505, 574, 742, 891, 962, 1011, 1058, 1287. The Bible.

Hospitalers, 342, 693. The religious military order of Knights Hospitallers, established in Jerusalem in the twelfth century.

Hungré (Hungrie, Hungry), 80–87. Hungary.

Idonye. See **Ydoyne**

Incarnacion, 1243. God's incarnation into human form, as the baby Jesus.

Inde (Indee). See **Ynde**

Inde the Lasse. See **Ynde the Lasse**

Inde the More. See **Ynde the Moore**

Ingelond (Engelond), 1, 6, 58, 78, 152, 1139, 1717, 1772. England.

Innocentis, Charnel of the, 562–63. A tomb in Bethlehem, in which the bodies of the infants from Herod's slaughter (Matthew 2:16) are said to be interred.

Irlond, 79. Ireland.

Ismael, 927. Ishmael, son of Abraham and the servant Hagar (Genesis 16).

Israel, (1) 488, 749, 762, 889, 944, 973. The land or generations of Israel. **(2)** Jacob the Patriarch, whose name is changed to Israel (Genesis 32:28 and 35:10). See **Jacob**

Jacob (Israel), 496, 586, 759, 761, 967. Jacob the Patriarch (Genesis 25–50).

Jacobis Well, 990. Jacob's Well in Sychar, Samaria (John 4:6).

Jacobynes, 1067. The Jacobites, actually followers of the sixth-century Byzantine monk Jacobus Baradeus. See explanatory note to line 1067.

Jaffa (Affe, Jaffe, Japhe, Japhet, Jafphe, Jasphe), 399–403, 428, 601, 1147, 1149, 1185, 2631. The city of Jaffa (Joppa, Tel Aviv-Yafo), an important port of entry for pilgrims to Jerusalem, supposedly founded by Japhet, one of the three sons of Noah. See also **Japhet**

Jaffe. See **Jaffa**

Jame, Seynt, 413, 808–09, 813, 1039, 1067. St. James the Great, Apostle, son of Zebedee and brother of St. John. Conflated in line 1067 with Jacob Baradeus, originator of the Jacobites.

Japhe. See **Jaffa**

Japhet, (1) 401, 2019–24. Japhet, son of Noah (Genesis 9). (2) The city of Jaffa. See **Jaffa**

Jaspar, 556. One of the Magi, who visited the baby Jesus with gifts (Matthew 2:1–12).

Jasphe. See **Jaffa**

Java, 1784. The Indonesian island of Java.

Jebus. See **Jebusalem**

Jebusalem (Solome), 592. The account of the melding of the names, "Jebus" and "Solome" to form "Jebusalem" stems from the writings of St. Jerome, but is not widely accepted.

Jerico, 600, 886, 899, 901. The city of Jericho, northwest of the Dead Sea.

Jerom, Seynt, 564. St. Jerome, who made a new Latin translation of the

Bible in the fourth century at the request of Pope Damasus.

Jerusalem, 32, 69, 71, 104, 193, 377, 398–400, 405, 429, 431–32, 454, 467, 484, 487–88, 495, 514, 583, 588, 589–955, 956, 966, 989, 1019, 1104–05, 1135, 1148, 1154, 1181, 1184–85, 1186–87, 1189, 1209, 1717, 1721–22, 1723, 1728–30, 2661. Jerusalem.

Jerusalem, Temple of (Salomon, Temple of), 713–19. Solomon's Temple (3 Kings 5–9).

Jew (Jewe, Jewes), 19–20, 24, 109, 121, 132, 149, 160, 172, 186, 188, 501, 529, 605, 655, 700, 714, 716, 719, 721, 724, 746–47, 765, 840, 925, 968, 993, 997–98, 999, 1029, 1266, 1267, 1271, 1292, 1435, 2352–59, 2365–73, 2376–82. A Jew or the Jews.

Jhesu Crist (Our Lord), 13, 55, 60,109–35, 147, 155, 157, 171–75, 180–88, 230–33, 248, 250, 266, 516, 900–01, 1023–26, 1029–47, 1053–54, 1243–46, 1257–58, 1260, 1267–68, 1294, 1310. Jesus Christ.

Job (Jobab), 1462–63, 1467–69, 1472. Jobab, king of Idumea (Edom), south of Judea (Genesis 36:33). Jobab is here conflated with Job, who is tested by the devil in the Book of Job but then restored by God for his faith. See also **Jope**

Job, Temple, 939. The tomb of Job.

Jobab. See **Job**

John Crisostom (John Crisostome), 193, 811. St. John Chrysostom, patriarch of Constantinople.

John the Baptist (John the Baptiste; John Baptist, Seynt), 768, 808, 973–74, 981, 987, 1067–68. John the Baptist, son of Elizabeth and Zechariah (Luke 1–3; John 1–3).

John the Twelfthe, Pope, 238–39. The reference is almost certainly a misreading for Pope John XXII,

who administered the Church from 1316 to 1334. John XII was pope from 955 to 964.

John the Evaungelist, Seynt, 286–87, 289–91, 293, 692, 830, 1039. St. John the Evangelist, writer of the Gospel of John.

John, Seynt, (1) See **John the Evaungelist, Seynt** (2) See **John the Baptist, Seynt**

Jonas, 392. The prophet Jonah (Jonas) is linked in Catholic tradition with the widow's son who was raised from the dead by the prophet Elijah (3 Kings 17). The tradition is mentioned by St. Jerome and others, but is without biblical basis.

Jonays, 302. The Genoese.

Jope, 2623, 2626. Job the Patriarch, whose faith God tested and approved.

Jordan, Flom, 894, 901, 930–31, 936, 939, 944–46, 1060, 1182. The Jordan River, in northeast Palestine.

Josaphat, Kyng, 861. Jehoshaphat, king of Judah (2 Paralipomenon [Chronicles] 17–20).

Josaphat, Vale, 687, 815, 837, 853, 865, 1046. The Vale of Jehoshaphat, between Jerusalem and the Mount of Olives, to the east.

Joseph, **(1)** 442, 585, 966, 970. Joseph the Patriarch, son of Jacob (Genesis 37–50). **(2)** 1019. Joseph, husband of the Virgin Mary.

Joseph of Barmathia, 668. Joseph of Arimathea, who took the body of Christ for burial (John 19:38–42). He is also credited in popular myth with having carried the Holy Grail to the British Isles.

Josias, 1107. Apparently a corruption of "Isaac," the son of Abraham's old age (Genesis 17).

Josue, 493, 887, 947. Joshua, son of Nun, Israelite scout (Numbers 14:6)

distances are by no means accurate. See explanatory note to lines 406–07.

Loth, 519, 916, 918, 922, 1346. Lot, who escaped the destruction of Sodom and Gomorrah, where his wife was turned to a pillar of salt. His daughters later slept with him in his drunkenness, and the children thus begotten became ancestors of the Moabite and Ammonite tribes (Genesis 19). The text's assertion that Lot was Abraham's brother is incorrect, as Lot was Abraham's nephew, the son of his brother Aran (Genesis 11:27).

Luke, Seynt, 194, 1112. St. Luke the Evangelist, writer of the Gospel of Luke and the Acts of the Apostles.

Lyban, hille of. See **Liban, Mount**

Lybie (Libie), 64, 1703. Libya.

Lybye the Heye, 2335. "Upper Libya" or Pentapolis, whose capital was the city of Apollonia (Susa).

Mabaron, 1625. The coastal region of Coromandel, in southeast India on the Bay of Bengal.

Macamet (Macamete, Machamete) 572, 1231, 1271, 1277, 1286, 1331, 1336, 1337, 1340, 1344, 1349, 1352, 1355, 1367–68. The prophet Mohammed.

Macidone (Macedone, Macydoyn), 208, 214, 215, 1512. Macedonia, on the Balkan peninsula.

Madyn, Mount, 1154. Mount Modin (Mount Latron), near Jerusalem.

Makaryn, castel of, 975. The Jewish fortress of Machareus, on the Dead Sea.

Mambre, Mount, 520. The Mount of Mamre, north of Hebron.

Mambre, Vale of, 490, 948. The Vale of Mamre (Ramel el Khalil), north of Hebron. See also **Ebron**

Mancy, 1902, 1924, 1941, 2010. The province of Manzi, in southern China. See also **Albanye**

Marcha, 299, 301. Probably the city of Myra, on the Lycian coast in Asia Minor, but Seymour has lately suggested Monemvasia, an island off the Peloponnese, whence Malmsey was exported (D, p. 140n15/7).

Marie Cleophe, 695. Mary Cleophas (John 19:25), mother of Sts. Simon, James the Less, and Jude, and grandmother of the Apostles St. James the Greater and St. John.

Marie Maudeleyn (Marie Magdelene, Mari Maudeleyn, Mary Maudelyn), 673, 877, 883. Mary Magdalen, follower of Christ.

Marie, Virgyn (Mari, Virgyn; Marye, Virgyne), 14, 230–31, 1240, 1250, 1256. The Virgin Mary, mother of Christ.

Maritane, 2334, 2335. Mauretania.

Marrok, (1) 1157. The city of Marash, in south-central Turkey. **(2)** 1387. Morocco.

Marrok, Port. See **Murrok, Port**

Marrok, rever, 93. The Maritsa River, in Bulgaria.

Mary, Maria, Marie. See **Marie, Virgyn**

Massydoyns, 606. The Macedonians.

Maubek, castel, 1180. The Muslim stronghold at Ba'albek, east of Beirut.

Maundé (Maundy), 250, 823. The Maunde, on Maundy Thursday (the Thursday before Easter), is a remembrance of the poor.

Maundevile, John (Maundevyle), 1, 58, 2833. Sir John Mandeville, our erstwhile narrator.

Maure (Greet See, Oxean), 1387–88, 1554, 2265. The Black Sea, once believed to be an arm of the Great Sea Ocean. From Latin *mare maurum* ("Moorish Sea").

Jerusalem in Samaria. Although the text seems to make of it a separate city, the name refers to the same place as Sychem and Sykar.

Neflond (Nyvelond), 85, 1207. Livonia, a central European region bordering on the Black Sea.

Nessabor, 2291. The city of Nishapúr, in northeast Persia.

Newbow, 87. The city of Wieselburg (Moszon), Hungary, on the Leytha, northeast of Odenburg (Sopron), and therefore clearly not on the way to Belgrade. Newbow corresponds with Albert of Aix's "praesidium Meseburch" and William of Tyre's "Meeszburg." Seymour glosses his "Neiseburg" in his Cotton edition of 1967 as "Odenburg (now Wieselburg) in Hungary" (p. 300), but the two are separate cities.

Nicholas, Seynt, 283, 565. St. Nicholas, fourth-century bishop of Myra.

Nichosie, 361. The city of Nicosia, in Cyprus.

Nideus, 1098. The Nestorian Christians, who separated from Byzantine Christianity after 431 AD.

Noe, 130, 401, 403, 630, 920, 1435, 1438, 1440, 2019, 2020, 2708. Noah, who survived the great flood by building an ark (Genesis 5–9).

Norway (Northway), 79, 1772. Norway.

Nostre Dame de Sarmany, 1114–15. The church of Our Lady of Saidenaya, north of Jerusalem.

Nubye the Heye, 2336–37. "Upper Nubia," the part of the Sudanese Nile Valley from the second cataract south to Khartoum.

Nubye the Lowe, 2336–37. "Lower Nubia," the part of the Nile Valley south of Aswan, between the first and second cataracts of the Nile.

Nubyse (Nubye), 2334. Nubia, in the Nile Valley.

Nyke, 281, 282, 1162. The ancient Byzantine city of Nicaea (later Iznik) in northwest Turkey.

Nyle, flode of (Nylus, ryver Gyron), 1385, 2715, 2724. The Nile River.

Nylus, ryver. See **Nyle, flode**

Nyse, 2397, 2462. The city of Nisa (Neyseh), in southern Persia.

Nyvelond. See **Neflond**

Occian (Greet See, Oxean), 1554, 1901, 2265. The "O" of the "T-in-O" maps, the Great Sea Ocean believed to surround all three known landmasses (Europe, Africa, and Asia).

Olde Testament (Oolde Lawe, Olde Lawe), 128, 269, 578–79, 2186. The Old Testament of the Bible.

Olimpus, 215, 217. Mount Olympus, in northeast Greece.

Olyvete, Mount (Olivete), 862, 884. The Mount of Olives, a low mountain range east of Jerusalem.

Oolde Lawe, Olde Lawe. See **Olde Testament**

Orda. See **Sarochize**

Orrel, 2677. Pliny's Chryse, a mythical island in the Great Sea Ocean.

Oxean, (1) See **Occian. (2)** The Black Sea. See **Maure**

Palastine (Palastyn, Palestyne), 579, 594–95, 1385, 2661. Palestine.

Palme Sonday, 690, 873. The Sunday before Easter, celebrated to commemorate Jesus' entry into Jerusalem.

Panonye, 80. The Roman province of Pannonia, in southwest Europe.

Paradis (Paradise, Paradys, Paradyse), (1) See **Paradys Terrestre. (2)** 291, 1233, 1234, 2489, 2776. Heaven. **(3)** 2485, 2487. The false paradise of the Assassins. See **Catholonabeus**

Vulgate Psalms 67:32 and 71:10) that one of the wise men was from Ethiopia.

Sabaoth, 954. The town of Shobeck, fifty miles southeast of the Dead Sea.

Sabaste. See **Samay**

Sabissatel, 1434. Probably Mount Sabissa Collasassius, near Erzerum in northwest Turkey.

Salamasse (Patro), 1798, 1799. Unclear. Warner notes that "Salamasse" and "Paten" (here Patro) are "the Thalamasyn and Panten (al. Paten) of Od(oric) . . . but what place is meant must be left to conjecture. Col. Yule supposes it to be upon the coast of Borneo, and suggests Banjermasin" (W, p. 201n94.14).

Salomon, 454, 487, 593, 712, 724, 773, 834. King Solomon of Israel (3 Kings 1–11).

Salomon, Temple of. See **Jerusalem, Temple of**

Samaritane, 964. Samaria, a district of ancient Palestine between Galilee and Judea.

Samaritanis, 969, 992. The Samaritans; from Samaria, a district of ancient Palestine between Galilee and Judea.

Samay (Sabaste), 972, 976, 989. The city of Samaria (Sebastia, Sebaste), capital of the province of Samaria in ancient Palestine.

Sampson the fort, 426. Samson the Strong (Judges 13–16).

Samuel, 851, 958, 961. The biblical Samuel, who was responsible for the enthronement of King David of Jerusalem (1 Kings).

Sancta Sanctorum. See **Holy of Holies**

Saphan. See **Cardabago**

Saphen (Sarepte), 391, 393. The city of Sarphen, near Tyre on the Phoenician coast. See also **Sydonis**

Sara, (1) See **Segor. (2)** See **Sarra**.

Saragi, 558. Offered as an alternative name for one of the Magi, who visited the baby Jesus with gifts (Matthew 2:1–12).

Sarchie, 1590. The city of Baroch, in western India north of Surat.

Sardana, 397. The city of Saidenaya, north of Damascus.

Sarepte. See **Saphen**

Sarizynes (Sarizens, Sarasynnes, Sarysynis, Sarysynes, Sarazens, Sarasyns, Sarizyns, Sarasens), 363, 380, 498, 503, 521, 529, 577, 607, 665, 699, 730, 928, 993, 996, 1063, 1214, 1228, 1234, 1269, 1292, 1329, 1346, 1347, 1365, 1427, 1451, 1907, 2145, 2146. The Saracens, broadly used to refer to Muslim Arabs.

Sark, 1124. The crusader castle of Archas (Arqa), near Tripoli.

Sarmasse, 2291, 2292. Unclear. Listed as one of the principal cities of Persia, but no convincing identification offers itself.

Sarochize (Orda), 1204, 2271. The city of Serai (from *serai*, palace) in Cumania, onetime capital of Kypchak (the Golden Horde). Identified with the city of Tsarev, on the Akhtûba branch of the Volga. "Orda" comes from Mongolian *ordu*, camp or court (whence the term "horde"). John of Plano Carpini, probably the *Book*'s source here, visited Batu Khan's ordu at Serai on his way to meet Kuyuk Khan.

Sarra (Sara), 497, 498. Sarah, the wife of Abraham the Patriarch (Genesis 12, 16–17, 20–21).

Satalay, 350. Probably Eski Adalia, the site of ancient Side; but possibly Adalia (Antalya), a port city on the south coast of Asia Minor.

Saturne, 1547–48. The planet Saturn.

Saure, 2326. The ancient district of Isauria, near Pisidia, in Asia Minor.

Saures, 2312. Shapur II, emperor of Persia, c. 309–79.

Savouris, Seynt, 390. St. Savior, a term for Christ. Hence the church of St. Savior is founded upon the rock from which Christ preached.

Savoyze, 83. The region of Slavonia, in eastern Croatia.

Scale de Terreys, 414. The Ladder of Tyre (*Ras en Nakurah*), a steep headland between Acre and Tyre.

Segor (Sara), 915. The city of Segor (Zoar), on the Dead Sea. Lot fled to Segor when Sodom and Gomorrah were destroyed (Genesis 19:20–24).

Sem, 2022, 2026. Shem, son of Noah (Genesis 9:18–27).

Semeth, 2033. A Tartar tribe, perhaps a conflation of Hayton the Armenian's "Tebeth" and "Sonich."

Sepulcre, Cherche of the (Holy Sepulcre), 671, 674, 692, 697, 727. The Church of the Holy Sepulcher in Jerusalem, believed to encompass Calvary, the Holy Sepulcher of Christ, and the well in which St. Helena found the True Cross.

Sermoyns. See **Garras**

Sermoys. See **Meldane**

Sesarye Philippum, 1185. The ancient city of Caesarea Philippi, in northern Palestine.

Seth, 138, 140, 515. Seth, the son of Adam and Eve (Genesis 4–5).

Seynt Albons (Seynt Albones), 2, 59. The town of St. Albans, England.

Seynt Sophie, cherch of. See **Sophie, Seynt**

Siche. See **Zechie**

Silvestre, Seynt, 984. St. Sylvester, credited with converting the emperor Constantine to Christianity.

Sirre. See **Tyre**

Sirrye. See **Syrri**

Skotlond, 78–79, 1717, 1772. Scotland.

Sobeth, 2033. A Tartar tribe, perhaps a conflation of Hayton the Armenian's "Tebeth" and "Sonich."

Soboth, 2411. The port city of Cambay in western India.

Sodom, 914. The city of Sodom in ancient Palestine, destroyed by God for its iniquity (Genesis 19).

Solome, **(1)** 591. See **Jebusalem**. **(2)** 914. The city of Zeboiim, on the Dead Sea.

Solopenuce, 1480. Scolopitus/Colopheus, legendary king of Amazonia before the female takeover.

Somaber, 1780. Part of the Indonesian island of Sumatra.

Sophie, Seynt, 98, 227. The Hagia Sofia in Istanbul, generally considered the most beautiful church in the world. The church is in fact dedicated not to St. Sophia, but to the Holy Wisdom (*Hagia Sophia*) of Christ.

Sophym, 957. Given here as a place-name, a city close to but separate from Ramatha; in fact, Ramatha Sophym is simply another name for Ramatha (Rama) in the Portion of Ephraim. See also **Ramatha**

Sorman Gramang, 2289. The city of Samarkand, east of Bokhara in Turkestan.

Spayne, see of, 1387, 2337. The Spanish Sea.

Spelunke, 502. The double cave in which the Patriarchs and their wives are interred in Hebron (Genesis 23).

Sperver, castel of, 1407. The fabled Castle of the Sparrowhawk.

Spruse (Spruys). See **Pruysse**

Sternes, 94. The city of Sofia, Bulgaria.

Stevene, Seynt, 688, 811. St. Stephen, the first of the Christian martyrs, who was stoned to death for his faith in Christ (Acts 6–7).

691 by Muslims to honor the place from which they believed Mohammed had ascended to Heaven. Crusaders took over the Dome in 1099, renaming it the "Temple of the Lord." It is said to be on the exact spot where the Temple of Herod stood in the time of Christ.

Teres, Vale of. See **Ebron**

Tesbiria, 204. The isle of Lesbos, off the coast of Asia Minor.

Thane. See **Airach, hille**

Theodosy, 982. Theodosius I, Roman emperor 379–95 AD.

Thoimtot, 281. The fortified crusader camp of Civitot, on the Gulf of Nicomedea.

Thomar, 1463. The city of Carmana (later Kerman) in Persia.

Thomas, Seynt, 825, 880, 1626, 1633, 1636, 2469, 2673. St. Thomas the Apostle, also known as "Doubting Thomas," because he would not believe Christ had risen until he had touched His wounds (John 20).

Tibourne. See **Tybourne**

Tire. See **Tyre**

Titus, 713, 746. Titus, Roman emperor 79–81 AD. Son of the emperor Vespasian.

Torkye. See **Turkey**

Torrens Cedron, 853. The Kidron (Cedar) River, in the Vale of Jehoshaphat (3 Kings 2:37).

Trachise (Trachie, Trachye, Tarchie), 90, 207, 210, 215. Thrace, near Macedonia. The reference to the "city of Thrace" is unclear, as no major Thracian city is near Stagira.

Tracota, 1848. Variously identified with Dragoian in Sumatra, Trinkat in the Nicobar Islands, and Tringano on the Malay peninsula. The story, however, goes back to Vincent of Beauvais' account of the Troglodytes of Ethiopia. The similarity of names may account for the relocation.

Transmontane (Transmontayne, Transmontayn), 1688, 1697, 1713. The northern pole star, from the Latin *trans* + *montanus*, beyond the mountain, possibly "beyond the Alps," from the Latin point of view.

Trapasond, 1393, 1403, 1405, 1433. Trebizond (Trabzon); port city in northeast Turkey, on the Black Sea. See also **Port de Pounce, Le**

Triple, 1180. The port city of Tripoli, north of Beirut.

Troye, 202, 394. The city of Troy, on the coast of Asia Minor.

Turcople, 207. Used here as a place-name, probably arising from the Turcopoli, a tribe of mixed Turkish and Greek descent.

Turkes, 292, 344, 607, 1404, 2273. The Turks.

Turkeston, 2273–74, 2285. Turkestan, between Iran and Siberia.

Turkey (Turky, Turkye, Torkye), 62, 281, 293, 662, 1162, 2261. Turkey.

Turmaget, 1493. Terra Marginen (Turmeniya), east of the Caspian Sea.

Turtouse, 1179, 1180. The port town of Tartous, north of Beirut.

Tybourne (Tibourne), 1050, 1057. The city of Tiberias, on the Sea of Galilee.

Tygre (Tygris), 1384, 1385, 2329, 2716, 2725. The Tigris River.

Tyre, Tire, Tyri (Sirre), 378, 379, 386, 389, 395, 404, 1129, 1130, 1146. Tyre (Sûr), port of entry for Syria.

Uber, 2353. The Caucasus Mountains, probably from *ubera aquilonis*, the breasts of the north. See also **Caspyze, hilles of**

Urie, Urye, 487, 772. Uriah the Hittite, husband of Bathsheba. King David killed Uriah in order to take Bathsheba for himself, and was cursed by God (2 Kings 11–12).

Vacres. See **Acon**

Valayr, 2033. A Tartar tribe. Hayton the Armenian calls them "Ialair."

Valeye Enchaunted (Valey of Fendes; Valey Perlous), 2493. A valley fraught with devils, supposedly near the River Physon, in the Aral region. The story of this valley likely draws from the biblical "Valley of the Shadow of Death."

Valone, 1142. Valona (Vlonë), port city on the Strait of Otranto, between the Adriatic and Ionian Seas.

Venyse, 406, 1140, 1157, 1351, 1392, 1555, 1955. Venice, Italy.

Vespasian, 713. Vespasian, Roman emperor, 69–79 AD.

Walys, 78, 1772. Wales.

Wit Soneday (Witsoneday), 828–29, 2263. Also called Pentecost; a feastday on the seventh Sunday after Easter, commemorating the descent of the Holy Spirit on the apostles.

Ydoyne (Idonye), 937, 1467. Idumea (Edom), an ancient country south of Judea.

Ynde (Inde, Indee), 65, 559, 664, 1351, 1391, 1452, 1505, 1512, 1515, 1543, 1544, 1545, 1554, 1716, 1735, 1776, 1902, 2268, 2272, 2286, 2290, 2341, 2393, 2395, 2555, 2714, 2722. India. The medieval concept of "Ynde" does not, however, correspond well with the modern boundaries of India. The *Book* associates "Ynde" variously with northern, eastern, and western Asia, and even with east Africa. On the well-known conflation of India with East Africa, stemming from late antiquity, see Kazhdan, *Oxford Dictionary of Byzantium,* 2:992–93. See also

Pentoxorie

Ynde the Gretter. See **Ynde the Moore**

Ynde the Heye. See **Ynde the Moore**

Ynde the Lasse (Inde the Lasse, Ynde the Lowe), 65, 664, 1507, 2297. The area from Arabia eastward to the Indian subcontinent.

Ynde the Lowe. See **Ynde the Lasse**

Ynde the Moore (Inde the More, Ynde the Gretter, Ynde the Heye), 65, 1505, 1506, 2341. The Indian subcontinent and adjacent lands to the east.

Ynone, Fosse, 415. The Fosse of Memnon near the Belus River, reportedly named for a monument to Memnon that stood nearby.

Youle Eve, 262. Christmas Eve.

Ypocras, 303, 304. The Greek physician Hippocrates.

Yrlond, 1773. Ireland.

Ysaac, 924. Isaac, son of Abraham and his wife Sarah (Genesis 21).

Ysau, 1467. Used erroneously here as a place name; in most texts the passage suggests Jobab was king of Idumea "after King Esau."

Ysmael, 1345. Ishmael, son of Abraham and his servant Hagar (Genesis 16–17)

Ysmaelites, 1346. Members of the tribe of Ishmael, son of Abraham.

Zabatoriye, rever, 1125. Possibly a reference to a spring near Arqa at the convent of Mar Jirjis. The spring is known for its intermittence.

Zacary, 777. The prophet Zacharias, son of Barachius.

Zechie (Siche), 1479, 2355. The ancient kingdom of Scythia, including parts of Europe and Asia north of the Black Sea and east of the Aral Sea.

MIDDLE ENGLISH TEXTS SERIES

The Floure and the Leafe, The Assembly of Ladies, The Isle of Ladies, edited by Derek Pearsall (1990)

Three Middle English Charlemagne Romances, edited by Alan Lupack (1990)

Six Ecclesiastical Satires, edited by James M. Dean (1991)

Heroic Women from the Old Testament in Middle English Verse, edited by Russell A. Peck (1991)

The Canterbury Tales: Fifteenth-Century Continuations and Additions, edited by John M. Bowers (1992)

Gavin Douglas, *The Palis of Honoure*, edited by David Parkinson (1992)

Wynnere and Wastoure and The Parlement of the Thre Ages, edited by Warren Ginsberg (1992)

The Shewings of Julian of Norwich, edited by Georgia Ronan Crampton (1994)

King Arthur's Death: The Middle English Stanzaic Morte Arthur and Alliterative Morte Arthure, edited by Larry D. Benson, revised by Edward E. Foster (1994)

Lancelot of the Laik and Sir Tristrem, edited by Alan Lupack (1994)

Sir Gawain: Eleven Romances and Tales, edited by Thomas Hahn (1995)

The Middle English Breton Lays, edited by Anne Laskaya and Eve Salisbury (1995)

Sir Perceval of Galles and Ywain and Gawain, edited by Mary Flowers Braswell (1995)

Four Middle English Romances: Sir Isumbras, Octavian, Sir Eglamour of Artois, Sir Tryamour, edited by Harriet Hudson (1996; second edition 2006)

The Poems of Laurence Minot 1333–1352, edited by Richard H. Osberg (1996)

Medieval English Political Writings, edited by James M. Dean (1996)

The Book of Margery Kempe, edited by Lynn Staley (1996)

Amis and Amiloun, Robert of Cisyle, and Sir Amadace, edited by Edward E. Foster (1997; second edition 2007)

The Cloud of Unknowing, edited by Patrick J. Gallacher (1997)

Robin Hood and Other Outlaw Tales, edited by Stephen Knight and Thomas Ohlgren (1997; second edition 2000)

The Poems of Robert Henryson, edited by Robert L. Kindrick with assistance of Kristie A. Bixby (1997)

Moral Love Songs and Laments, edited by Susanna Greer Fein (1998)

John Lydgate, *Troy Book Selections*, edited by Robert R. Edwards (1998)

Thomas Usk, *The Testament of Love*, edited by R. Allen Shoaf (1998)

Prose Merlin, edited by John Conlee (1998)

Middle English Marian Lyrics, edited by Karen Saupe (1998)

John Metham, *Amoryus and Cleopes*, edited by Stephen F. Page (1999)

Four Romances of England: King Horn, Havelok the Dane, Bevis of Hampton, Athelston, edited by Ronald B. Herzman, Graham Drake, and Eve Salisbury (1999)

The Assembly of Gods: Le Assemble de Dyeus, or Banquet of Gods and Goddesses, with the Discourse of Reason and Sensuality, edited by Jane Chance (1999)

Thomas Hoccleve, *The Regiment of Princes*, edited by Charles R. Blyth (1999)

John Capgrave, *The Life of Saint Katherine*, edited by Karen A. Winstead (1999)

John Gower, *Confessio Amantis*, Vol. 1, edited by Russell A. Peck; with Latin translations by Andrew Galloway (2000; second edition 2006); Vol. 2 (2003); Vol. 3 (2004)

Richard the Redeless and Mum and the Sothsegger, edited by James M. Dean (2000)

Ancrene Wisse, edited by Robert Hasenfratz (2000)

Walter Hilton, *The Scale of Perfection*, edited by Thomas H. Bestul (2000)

John Lydgate, *The Siege of Thebes*, edited by Robert R. Edwards (2001)

Pearl, edited by Sarah Stanbury (2001)

The Trials and Joys of Marriage, edited by Eve Salisbury (2002)

Middle English Legends of Women Saints, edited by Sherry L. Reames, with assistance of Martha G. Blalock and Wendy R. Larson (2003)

The Wallace: Selections, edited by Anne McKim (2003)

Richard Maidstone, *Concordia (The Reconciliation of Richard II with London)*, edited by David R. Carlson, with a verse translation by A. G. Rigg (2003)

Three Purgatory Poems: The Gast of Gy, Sir Owain, The Vision of Tundale, edited by Edward E. Foster (2004)

William Dunbar, *The Complete Works*, edited by John Conlee (2004)

Chaucerian Dream Visions and Complaints, edited by Dana M. Symons (2004)

Stanzaic Guy of Warwick, edited by Alison Wiggins (2004)

Saints' Lives in Middle English Collections, edited by E. Gordon Whatley, with Anne B. Thompson and Robert K. Upchurch (2004)

Siege of Jerusalem, edited by Michael Livingston (2004)

The Kingis Quair and Other Prison Poems, edited by Linne R. Mooney and Mary-Jo Arn (2005)

Chaucerian Apocrypha: Selections, edited by Kathleen Forni (2005)

John Gower, *The Minor Latin Works*, edited and translated by R. F. Yeager, with *In Praise of Peace*, edited by Michael Livingston (2005)

Sentimental and Humorous Romances: Floris and Blancheflour, Sir Degrevant, The Squire of Low Degree, The Tournament of Tottenham, and The Feast of Tottenham, edited by Erik Kooper (2006)

Dicts and Sayings of the Philosophers, edited by John William Sutton (2006)

Everyman and Its Dutch Original, Elckerlijc, edited by Clifford Davidson, Martin W. Walsh, and Ton J. Broos (2007)

The N-Town Plays, edited by Douglas Sugano, with assistance by Victor I. Scherb (2007)

DOCUMENTS OF PRACTICE SERIES

Love and Marriage in Late Medieval London, selected, translated, and introduced by Shannon McSheffrey (1995)

Sources for the History of Medicine in Late Medieval England, selected, introduced, and translated by Carole Rawcliffe (1995)

A Slice of Life: Selected Documents of Medieval English Peasant Experience, edited, translated, and with an introduction by Edwin Brezette DeWindt (1996)

Regular Life: Monastic, Canonical, and Mendicant Rules, selected and introduced by Douglas J. McMillan and Kathryn Smith Fladenmuller (1997); second edition, selected and introduced by Daniel Marcel La Corte and Douglas J. McMillan (2004)

Women and Monasticism in Medieval Europe: Sisters and Patrons of the Cistercian Reform, selected, translated, and with an introduction by Constance H. Berman (2002)

Medieval Notaries and Their Acts: The 1327–1328 Register of Jean Holanie, introduced, edited, and translated by Kathryn L. Reyerson and Debra A. Salata (2004)

COMMENTARY SERIES

Haimo of Auxerre, *Commentary on the Book of Jonah*, translated with an introduction and notes by Deborah Everhart (1993)

Medieval Exegesis in Translation: Commentaries on the Book of Ruth, translated with an introduction and notes by Lesley Smith (1996)

Nicholas of Lyra's Apocalypse Commentary, translated with an introduction and notes by Philip D. W. Krey (1997)

Rabbi Ezra Ben Solomon of Gerona, *Commentary on the Song of Songs and Other Kabbalistic Commentaries*, selected, translated, and annotated by Seth Brody (1999)

John Wyclif, *On the Truth of Holy Scripture*, translated with an introduction and notes by Ian Christopher Levy (2001)

Second Thessalonians: Two Early Medieval Apocalyptic Commentaries, introduced and translated by Steven R. Cartwright and Kevin L. Hughes (2001)

The Glossa Ordinaria on the Song of Songs, translated with an introduction and notes by Mary Dove (2004)

MEDIEVAL GERMAN TEXTS IN BILINGUAL EDITIONS SERIES

Sovereignty and Salvation in the Vernacular, 1050–1150, introduction, translations, and notes by James A. Schultz (2000)

Ava's New Testament Narratives: "When the Old Law Passed Away," introduction, translation, and notes by James A. Rushing, Jr. (2003)

History as Literature: German World Chronicles of the Thirteenth Century in Verse, introduction, translation, and notes by R. Graeme Dunphy (2003)

VARIA

The Study of Chivalry: Resources and Approaches, edited by Howell Chickering and Thomas H. Seiler (1988)

Studies in the Harley Manuscript: The Scribes, Contents, and Social Contexts of British Library MS Harley 2253, edited by Susanna Fein (2000)

The Liturgy of the Medieval Church, edited by Thomas J. Heffernan and E. Ann Matter (2001); second edition (2005)

TO ORDER PLEASE CONTACT:

Medieval Institute Publications
Western Michigan University
Kalamazoo, MI 49008-5432
Phone (269) 387-8755
FAX (269) 387-8750

http://www.wmich.edu/medieval/mip/index.html

Medieval Institute Publications is a program
of The Medieval Institute, College of Arts
and Sciences, Western Michigan University

Typeset in 10/13 New Baskerville
with Golden Cockerel Ornaments display
Designed by Linda K. Judy
Manufactured by Cushing-Malloy, Inc.

Medieval Institute Publications
College of Arts and Sciences
Western Michigan University
1903 W. Michigan Avenue
Kalamazoo, MI 49008-5432
http://www.wmich.edu/medieval/mip

 WESTERN MICHIGAN UNIVERSITY